NORWAY, EUROPEAN INTEGRATION AND ATLANTIC SECURITY

ᴍᴀᴀ PRIO

International Peace Research Institute, Oslo
Fuglehauggata 11, N-0260 Oslo, Norway
Telephone: (47) 22 54 77 00
Telefax: (47) 22 54 77 01
E-mail: info@prio.no

The International Peace Research Institute, Oslo (PRIO) is an independent international institute of peace and conflict research, founded in 1959, governed by an international Board of seven individuals. The results of all PRIO research are available to the public.

PRIO's publications include the bi-monthly *Journal of Peace Research* (1964–) and the quarterly *Security Dialogue* (formerly *Bulletin of Peace Proposals*) (1969–) and a series of books. Recent titles include:

John Markakis: *Resource Conflict in the Horn of Africa* (1998)

Ola Tunander, Pavel Baev & Victoria Ingrid Einagel, eds: *Geopolitics in Post-Wall Europe: Security, Territory and Identity* (1997)

Valery Tishkov: *Ethnicity, Nationalism and Conflict in and after the Soviet Union: The Mind Aflame* (1997)

Pavel K. Baev: *The Russian Army in a Time of Troubles* (1996)

Johan Galtung: *Peace by Peaceful Means: Peace and Conflict, Development and Civilization* (1996)

Jørn Gjelstad & Olav Njølstad, eds: *Nuclear Rivalry and International Order* (1996)

Kumar Rupesinghe & Khawar Mumtaz, eds: *Internal Conflicts in South Asia* (1996)

Olav Schram Stokke & Ola Tunander, eds: *The Barents Region: Cooperation in Arctic Europe* (1994)

Nils Petter Gleditsch et al.: *The Wages of Peace: Disarmament in a Small Industrialized Economy* (1994)

Robert Bathurst: *Intelligence and the Mirror: On Creating an Enemy* (1993)

NORWAY, EUROPEAN INTEGRATION AND ATLANTIC SECURITY

CLIVE ARCHER
AND
INGRID SOGNER

PRIO

International Peace Research Institute, Oslo

SAGE Publications
London • Thousand Oaks • New Delhi

SAGE Publications Ltd
6 Bonhill Street
London EC2A 4PU

SAGE Publications Inc
2455 Teller Road
Thousand Oaks, CA 91320

SAGE Publications India Pvt Ltd
32, M-Block Market
Greater Kailash – I
New Delhi 110 048

British Library Cataloguing Publication data

A catalogue record for this book is available from the British Library.

ISBN 0 7619 5967 X

Library of Congress catalog card number 98-060855

Typeset by M Rules
Printed in Great Britain by Biddles Ltd, Guildford, Surrey

Contents

This book is dedicated to the memory of
Ellmann Ellingsen

Foreword

Norway's relationship to Europe and the Atlantic region – both within and without the remit of security policy – has been dominated in the 1990s by the question of membership of the European Union (EU): preparing for it, campaigning about it, rejecting it, doing without it. Through this process, Norway has decided – by a small margin and amid heated controversy – to stand virtually alone. Most of what was left of the European Free Trade Association in 1990 had joined the EU by the time Norway decided not to in 1994, and the states of central and eastern Europe have been lining up to get in.

The immediate background to this study by Clive Archer and Ingrid Sogner is Norway's 1994 rejection of EU membership. Ever since World War II, Norway has had an uneasy relationship with the process of European integration; by contrast, it has been solidly committed to the Atlantic Alliance as the main way to provide for its security. The book examines the meaning of these contrasting perspectives on Europe and the North Atlantic. The Norwegian political elite saw the country's involvement in European integration as a means of ensuring that Norway would not become marginalised in the next century. Their case for entering the EU was based on security. This was not to do with a short-term fear of some external threat: rather, it was a matter of not wanting to be left out when decisions were made that would shape the architecture of European security for the next half-century. The majority of voters were not sympathetic to this, however, and saw no reason to restrict Norway's perceived freedom of action outside the EU.

In Part I, Archer and Sogner examine Norway's European policy from 1945 to the 1994 referendum. Norwegian governments face contrary pressures: the pressure from long-term economic and political trends in Europe is towards integration; the pressure from within Norway is pro-integration from business, but anti-integration from public opinion. Efforts to balance these contradictory pressures must find a tightly constrained zone of compromise.

In Part II, the authors focus on Norway's postwar security policy. As in most of Europe, the key choices were made in 1948 and 1949 – the period of the Marshall Plan for the postwar reconstruction of Western Europe, of the Communist takeover in Czechoslovakia, the formation of the North Atlantic Treaty Organisation, and the Berlin blockade. In security as in other policies, international requirements had to be balanced against domestic concerns. The result was NATO membership as the unquestioned cornerstone of security, but with certain constraints about what kind of undertakings and actions were possible.

As oil has provided more prosperity for Norway, so the ability to make choices has increased; Norway can now stand alone without facing serious short-term costs. As a result, domestic pressure means more in Norway than in some countries, because the option of an independent policy is neither impossible nor impracticable. However, it is rare that domestic pressure has pushed Norway in a new direction. Thus, Norway has not really had a domestically driven foreign policy: it has had a domestically restrained policy. In international relations, this balance of pressures has led Norway to support the rule of law and to take intergovernmental institutions seriously. This could be regarded as a classic pattern for a small state, especially one on the periphery of a major geopolitical region. Yet the range and intensity of Norway's activities abroad – in development aid, participation in United Nations peace-keeping, and in the 1990s in active diplomacy to mitigate and resolve armed conflicts – is greater than that which might normally be expected of a European small state. Norwegian policies have a wider impact than any observer would have thought even remotely conceivable when viewing the European scene fifty years ago.

With this book, Clive Archer and Ingrid Sogner contribute to our understanding of these policies, of the contradictory pressures that shape them, of the compromises they express. Professor Archer has visited PRIO many times during the course of the book's preparation, and Ingrid Sogner has been a PRIO researcher for two periods. I am happy that we have been able to contribute to this important study in this way.

Dan Smith
Director, PRIO
Oslo
March 1998

Preface

This is a study of Norway's involvement in both European integration and Atlantic security. These two aspects of Norway's external policies have overlapped during the postwar years, in particular since the end of the Cold War. However, while the story of Norway's involvement in Atlantic security – in the form of NATO membership – has been one of cautious commitment, the country's engagement in the process of European integration – as typified by the European Communities and European Union – has been at arms' length. In particular, the Norwegian electorate has been sharply divided on the issue. This book aims at giving an insight into the seeming paradox of security commitment and integration reluctance.

The book is the result of a study supported by the Economic and Social Research Council of the United Kingdom (grant R000233844) which allowed research to be undertaken by the two authors. However, the work also reflects a longer involvement in the relevant issues by both authors and assistance by a number of individuals and organizations. The institutions that provided particular help were, in Norway, the Norwegian Atlantic Committee (DNAK), the Institute for Defence Studies (IFS), the Norwegian Institute of International Affairs (NUPI), and the International Peace Research Institute, Oslo (PRIO) and the Ministries of Defence and of Foreign Affairs. Within the United Kingdom, particular assistance was given by the University of Aberdeen and the Manchester Metropolitan University, and the Leverhulme Trust. A number of individuals contributed in one way or another to the study, and it is hoped that the impersonal nature of an alphabetical list will not detract too much from our sincere thanks: Alyson Bailes, Mats Berdal, Bernt Bull, Kjell Colding, the late Ellmann Ellingsen, Nils Petter Gleditsch, Eirik Glenne, David Greenwood, Sture Hovdal, Aneurin Hughes, John Hughes, Ola Listhaug, Janne Haaland Matlary, Eamonn Noonan, David Ratford, Olav Riste, Per Sjaastad, Martin Sæter, Rolf Tamnes, Ola Tunander and Hilde Henriksen Waage. Of course, their help in no way commits them to the findings of this book. We also wish to express our heartfelt appreciation of the support and tolerance of our spouses, Liz Archer and Eamonn Noonan.

This work has been a joint effort, but there has also been a division of labour. The original research concept was that of Clive Archer, who was responsible for directing the ESRC project. He wrote Chapters 10 to 13, the introductory and concluding chapters (Chapters 1 and 14) and part of Chapter 9, and had overall responsibility for the final text. Ingrid Sogner wrote Chapters 2 to 8 and part of Chapter 9. Both of us are grateful to PRIO – especially to Dan Smith and Ole Berthelsen – for the involvement in bringing this work to publication.

Clive Archer
Ingrid Sogner

1

Introduction

1.1   The Problem Stated

On 28 November 1994, a majority of those voting in the Norwegian referendum on EU membership rejected the government's proposal that Norway should join the EU and, implicitly, the terms negotiated for membership. This was not the first time that the Norwegian electorate had distanced itself from the European integration process associated with the Community concept; in September 1972, membership of the EU's forerunner, the European Communities, was also turned down in a hard-fought referendum.

The following chapters will seek to explain the uneasy relationship between Norway and European integration. After some years of mutual lack of interest, a flirtation began leading to a promise of marriage. Wedding plans were halted at the last moment. There was always another party to the relationship – the United States – that seemed able to provide security, but was threatening to move out. In the end, the prospect of a long-term commitment to the European partner and loss of freedom just proved too much. However, the cost of continuing to 'live together' under the terms of the European Economic Agreement (EEA) may yet prove to be as high as that of marriage.

What has been the nature of Norway's relationship with European integration and why has it been so precarious? Has Norwegian association with Europe been determined more by external factors or by domestic considerations? Has Norwegian dependence on the United States for its security been replaced to any great extent by a Europeanisation of that security? Has the country's search for security within NATO demonstrated something about its preferences concerning European integration?

This book will examine these questions. It is essentially about two paths to the vote of 28 November 1994, and its consequences. One approach to that vote concerned Norway's response to the development of the wider European integration process with specific reference to the Community process; the other was about the place of Norway in the security of Europe. While these aspects are dealt with separately, they are two sides of the same coin, the crown or *krone* representing Norwegian sovereignty. One side shows the reluctance of Norwegians to be embroiled in continental plans for a more united Europe, the other reflects a cautious willingness to be committed to an Atlantic Pact that is seen to enhance the security of the country. In the immediate postwar period the elements of reserve and commitment seemed to coexist without much embarrassment in Norway's trade and defence policies respectively. By 1994, both in Europe and in Norway, commercial and security policies had become intertwined, not least in the policies and institutions of the European Union. It was thus less easy to keep apart the response to these two elements, a fact recognised by the Labour government when it applied for membership of the EU. Yet the Norwegian electorate made a distinction: by a large majority it wanted its security provided in the context of NATO; and by a plurality it did not want a whole raft of policies decided in the framework of EU membership.

What were the consequences for Norway of the 28 November vote? The immediate problems were fairly well known, but the long-term reverberations are less easy to analyse. Could Norway's security position be affected? Will Norway be allowed another try at betrothal?

To analyse the postwar approach of Norway to the European integration process, and to see it in the light of the country's Atlantic commitments, require an understanding of the wider foreign policy context within which Norway has functioned since the Second World War.

1.2   The Approach to the Subject

In May 1945 Norway was a small, weak country that had just emerged from five years of grinding occupation and repression. The northern part of its territory was still occupied by one of the liberating powers, the Soviet Union, and the help of the United Kingdom was needed to re-establish some of the basic aspects of government and the economy. Nevertheless, a widely-based coalition took power and Norway was a founder member of the United Nations, with its foreign minister, Trygve Lie, becoming the UN's first Secretary-General. The main foreign policy concerns of the new government were to re-establish full sovereignty over its territory – especially North Norway and the archipelago of Svalbard – and to obtain the right conditions and assistance for the rebuilding of the economy. In that context, the Norwegian merchant marine, which had played a useful role on the allied side during the Second World War, was of importance (Thowsen, 1995). If Norway could also contribute to the maintenance of a peaceful world based on the premises of the UN Charter, then that was a welcome addition.

Fifty years on, Norway had one of the highest per capita incomes in the world, was a major oil producer and exporter, had a strong currency and was able to turn down membership of the main European cooperative arrangement. Norway's foreign policy profile by 1995 was complicated and prolific for a state of some four million people. It was tied into a series of institutions within Europe and was linked in its security policy with the USA through NATO, as well as by a number of bilateral deals. A cooperative relationship had been established with Russia through the Barents Euro-Arctic Council, again complemented by bilateral agreements. Norwegian troops were serving under the UN flag across the world, and Norwegian diplomacy had made significant contributions to ending conflicts in the Middle East, Southern Africa and Central America.

This brief and crude comparison highlights a number of points that should be made before embarking on an analysis of Norway's relationship with European integration. In the postwar period, it is a truism to say that Norway has changed, the world has altered and the interaction between Norway and its international environment is also different. But how can that interaction be understood? A useful framework is provided by Russett and Starr, who recommend a concern with both 'the possibilities and constraints that face decision-makers (*opportunity*) and with the choices that they make in light of these possibilities and constraints (*willingness*)' (Russett & Starr, 1992, p. 21, italics in original).

Opportunity requires an environment that allows interactions between states; states 'that possess adequate resources to be capable of certain kinds of actions', and decision-makers aware both of that range of actions and the extent of capabilities available (ibid., p. 22).

In May 1945 interaction between many states was physically difficult because of the immediate effects of a devastating world war, and a number of states – including Germany, Austria and the Baltic republics – had lost their ability to interact in the world system. Norway had very limited resources for international interaction, both in terms of its diplomatic corps and the means available – including economic strength and armed forces – to implement policy. The Norwegian decision-makers, especially after the war period in exile, were well aware of the limitations resulting from the international environment and the shattered state of their country. Their foreign policy 'menu' was a short one.

Fifty years later, interaction between states was permitted as never before. Over 180 sovereign states existed and there was a panoply of institutions and organisations through which their representatives could meet, with many of these available to a country such as Norway. Diplomacy, 'back channels' and non-governmental organisations thrived. By 1995 Norway had developed a strong and practised foreign service, its other ministries were also engaged in external policy and it had the economic resources in terms of trade and economic resources, as well as a small but effective armed force, to underline this capability. Its decision-makers faced a wide range of interactions but had more resources than most small powers to 'play the game'. These decision-makers were experienced and well-educated and had the services of an active bureaucracy to explain the options to them.

The *willingness* of decision-makers to adopt one option rather than another is based 'on perceptions of the global scene and of domestic political conditions'; it is therefore dependent on '*choice* and *perception*' (Russett & Starr, 1992, p. 23, italics in original). In 1945, the perception of the Norwegian decision-makers of the international scene was one coloured by their wartime experience. The independence of their country had been lost some 35 years after it had been achieved in 1905 and, after five years of struggle, had been regained. However, it had been the collective effort of the United Kingdom, the United States, the Soviet Union and other allies that had allowed the king and government of Norway to return to their country. Members of that government were not likely to forget either the '9 April 1940' – when Norway was invaded – nor the '7 June 1945', when King Haakon of Norway returned home. Their perception of domestic political conditions was again influenced by the wartime experience when people from all the non-collaborator parties had worked together. Furthermore, ministers were part of a grand coalition government containing Communists, Conservatives, Liberals, Agrarians and the Labour Party. The choices made were thus in line with the general wish to restore Norwegian sovereignty over its lands, re-animate its economy and to cooperate with the former allies in establishing order in Europe.

By 1995, the perception of the international scene by Norwegian decision-makers was one whereby they were still trying to understand the post-Cold War world. They saw an international scene where there seemed to be more scope for action by a small, rich state such as Norway, but they also feared marginalisation, especially in Europe. They saw a world of uncertainties that threatened new dangers but allowed opportunities. The domestic political conditions were those of consensus on security policy, but with public opinion again split on EU membership. The membership issue was seen to be divisive, though relations with the EU short of accession seemed to create little public interest.

The simple comparison indicates something of the change not just in the global context for Norwegian decision-makers between 1945 and 1995 and in Norway's own condition, but also in the inter-relationship of Norway and its environment. The following chapters will indicate the international conditions within which Norway was operating as well as the main domestic constraints. It will indicate the perceptions of those in government of their situation, and will outline the decisions they took. What will be seen is that the mix between internal and external factors – both in the opportunities available to Norway and the willingness of decision-makers to avail themselves of the options – varied over time, with internal constraints coming to the fore on a few key issues in security and European policies.

The question of the dominant forces in Norwegian external policy-making has been discussed by a number of writers. Their contributions will be examined to see how they may aid an understanding of Norway's postwar security and European policies; but first some more general studies on small states will be discussed.

A review of the literature on small states considers that many writers have an implicit perception 'that small states are merely diminutive versions of the great powers with the same interests and goals, only with fewer resources for achieving the desired ends' (Papadakis & Starr, 1987, p. 423). By this reckoning, Norway would clearly have been in the 'small state' class in 1945 but its accumulation of resources by 1995 would have made that status more ambiguous, especially in particular issue areas. As the relevant factor in judging small states seems to be that of availability of resources (ibid., p. 424), then Norway's extension of its offshore domain (see section 9.5) in 1977 and its exploitation of petroleum resources would have increased its capability to act. This would mean that Norway would be less 'slow to perceive various opportunities and constraints' (Reid, 1974, p. 46), no longer so obviously 'having less margin for error than the more powerful states' (Barston, 1973, p. 19). However, the dependence on petroleum could still leave Norway 'vulnerable to fluctuations in the world economy and open to domination by [its] trading partners' (Papadakis & Starr, 1987, p. 425).

Internally, a small state may benefit from its size facilitating 'administrative coordination and integration and promote the responsiveness of public servants' (Rapoport, 1971, p. 148). In examining the content of small state foreign policies, another literature review claims that they are expected to exhibit a 'low level of participation in world affairs'; 'high levels of activity in intergovernmental organizations'; 'high levels of support for international legal norms'; 'avoidance of the use of force as a technique of statecraft'; 'avoidance of behaviour which tends to alienate the more powerful states in the system'; and 'a narrow functional and geographic range of concern in foreign policy activity' (East, 1975, p. 160). However, a closer examination of the empirical literature shows that when such states have much at stake and a limited ability to gather information and initiate policy responses, then 'they must engage in high risk, active and conflictual behaviour' (Papadakis & Starr, 1987, p. 430; East, 1975). It should also be noted that most of the work cited analysed the position of the small state in the context of the Cold War and a divided world.

The implicit message of the work on small states is that they have a shorter 'menu for choice' than middle-range or large powers, and that their foreign policy is thus more subject to the international environment, leaving their decision-makers less choice than their counterparts in large states. These decision-makers have to resort to a number of tactics, such as concentrating their effort, or have to await an increase in resources before having the luxury of choice.

Has this been the case in Norway? The title of an article on Norwegian foreign policy – 'Norway: Domestically Driven Foreign Policy' – would suggest not. The proposition is that, while a compromise over security policy has softened the tension between 'external pressures and internally generated aspirations', when the *Storting* (parliament) or the electorate decide policy (as in the 1972 referendum), 'foreign policy may become the nonlogical outcome of complex, underlying lines of domestic conflict' (Knudsen, 1990, p. 101). Is this observation supported elsewhere?

Studies of Norwegian foreign policy have been grouped into various schools which in many ways reflect developments in Norway since the Second World War (Tamnes, 1986a; Knutsen, 1995, pp. 21–2, 26–31).

Jens Arup Seip (1963) looked at national decision-making in Norway after the war, claiming it was controlled by the Labour Party's leadership. He stressed the power of the party, and that the government had become its executive arm, with the *Storting* as merely a means for registration. His analysis pointed to an intersection between politicians and bureaucrats within the Labour Party, with the Party as the source to power. His thesis concerned the 'battle for power' (*maktspill*) with the stress on the role of individuals, the rise of the bureaucracy at the expense of the Storting, and the Labour Party as a homogenous elite. One work that places great emphasis on the machinations within the Labour Party as the main explanatory factor for what he calls the 'semialignment' of the country's security policy is that of Nils Ørvik (1986, pp. 235–7).

Seip's notion of Norway as a 'one-party state' may have been justified during the immediate postwar years. Even then, it does not cover the attention the Labour Party government clearly paid to both the centre-right parties and the business community in a number of issues, especially that of the Scandinavian customs union negotiations. By the early 1960s, Seip's stress on the *Storting*'s weak position no longer reflected the situation in Norway, especially after the minority Labour government fell from power in a parliamentary vote of no-confidence. Talk of an homogenous elite does not fit the facts well: there were factions within the Labour Party in the leadership, as well as in the lower ranks. Ironically, Gro Harlem Brundtland, during the 1981 to 1996 period while she was Labour Party leader or prime minister, had to face a number of disruptive foreign policy issues but successfully managed to control the element of disagreement within the party.

The approach taken by Gudmund Hernes (1975) dealt with foreign policy questions, stressing the importance of the many actors outside the traditional political arena, such as the interest groups. His ideas were based on Stein Rokkan's insistence (1970) that votes count, but resources decide. Whereas Seip stressed the symbiotic relationship between party and bureaucracy, Hernes emphasised the connection between organisations and bureaucracy, and the link between the public and the private sphere. There is more emphasis on the ministries to the detriment of the Storting and the political parties. This model may also reflect the situation in Norway from the mid-1960s until the early 1980s when there were coalition or minority governments and a growing civil service. Furthermore, it was a period when Norway was feeling the effects of interdependence and when corporate and group interests were more dominant in foreign policy issues (Knutsen, 1995, p. 27). Tamnes (1986a) has criticised the Hernes school for its emphasis on fragmentation and segmentation, which he considers cannot give a full understanding of defence policy with its basis in international cooperation.

The above two approaches – those of Seip and Hernes – may help in understanding the willingness side of Norwegian foreign policy decision-making equation, particularly in the period from 1945 to about 1980, insofar as they address the perception and choice of the decision-makers. The third group referred to by Tamnes was concerned more with the opportunities available to the decision-makers.

Magne Skodvin (1971) stressed the international framework for Norway's foreign and security policy, and the connection between Norway as an actor and the external international environment. Norway was seen as a small state, the basis for whose choices were decided by others. The stress was on the perception of rational actors, and the work was based on the 'realist' view of international relations that stresses power, especially military strength and the industrial-economic potential, and national interests. Those who have followed Skodvin, such as Udgaard (1973), Lundestad (1980) and Riste (1985a), have also placed the emphasis on the international context within which Norwegian policy was made. However, all three were writing about the security aspects of Norwegian policy during periods of war or Cold War, though Riste's work has covered a longer historical period.

More recent work from this school has also stressed the international constraints on Norwegian policy. Tamnes's own work on the United States and Norway (1991) places the emphasis on geopolitics and, to a lesser extent, ideology as the shaping factors of the strategic relationship between the two states (p.19), though a thorough account is given of domestic Norwegian factors that affected the implementation of particular policies (for example, pp. 160–5, 265–9, 289–93). Berdal's work on Norway in US strategy in the 1950s takes a broadly geopolitical approach – the emphasis is anyhow on US policy – though Norwegian domestic considerations are mentioned in, for example, the creation of the base policy (1996, p. 8; see also Chapter 9 below).

The case for a heavy emphasis on the environmental factors seems strong, in particular for Norway's security and commercial policies in the two decades after 1945. Norway was highly dependent on its foreign trade, especially that in raw materials, which made it dependent on the trading policies of its major partners. Its geostrategic position on the front-line between the Soviet Union and the Atlantic powers seemed to suggest that its security would be dependent on the calculations of the larger powers. However, even those writers who placed an emphasis on strategic factors sometimes referred to domestic debates.

In reality, even geostrategic factors change: what was important in the era of the bomber has a different weight in the missile age. What was strategically vital at the height of the Cold War may lose importance after the ending of that confrontation. Furthermore, those factors have to be perceived by the decision-makers before they can affect policy. That perception may be clouded by historical experience and by culture. Even then, choices have to be made, bringing in the nature of the decision-making process and the range of options available. To say that the great distance from Norway to the power centres of Europe has somewhat disposed Norwegians to think along different geopolitical lines than other European nations (Knutsen, 1995, p. 23) may contain a kernel of truth but is a wide generalisation and misses out some causal links.

Likewise an emphasis on political culture as an explanatory factor for policy, particularly when examining the perceptions of politicians, holds dangers. Intuitively, it seems reasonable that Norwegian moralism and the isolated nature of the coastline settlements has had an effect on its governments' approach to foreign policy. However, the difficulty lies in catching the nature of a political culture and in tracing possible causal links with foreign policy decisions. The advantages in examining the two referenda are that each provided one definite decision on an important policy issue and both allowed open discussions of contrasting cultural beliefs.

One of the conditions for an 'opportunity' to be available to a state is that it has resources adequate 'to be capable of certain kinds of action' (Russett & Starr, 1992, p. 22). This is not just an objective evaluation of such resources available, as the decision-makers have to be aware of the capabilities open to them (ibid.). Also in talking about 'willingness', a perception of the objective factors is all-important. In understanding Norway's response to European integration and to its security dilemma, consideration will be given not just to the position ascribed Norway by economists, strategists or the decision-makers of other countries, but to the perception of Norway's own situation as expressed by the Norwegian decision-makers.

It is the general contention of this book that, while the opportunities open to Norway in its European and security policies may have been limited, they have expanded over time both with changes in Norway's international environment and with the increase in the resources Norway has at its disposal. Secondly, within the perceived set of opportunities, there was still room for a meaningful choice by decision-makers, even at the height of the Cold War. The exercise of choice one way or the other depends on a number of factors. First, the decision-makers must be identified: are they civil servants, party leaders in government (or opposition), parliamentary institutions or the wider public? Next, the decision-makers, whether overtly or implicitly, make a calculation of the costs and benefits of various actions. This may include external factors – those from outside the country – such as the demands of foreign governments or the loss of a market or the promise of assistance. Especially in a democracy, it also involves an estimation of domestic factors such as the response of particular groups, the economic effect on regions or the electoral consequences.

This raises the question of how internal needs may be balanced against external requirements. Rosenau dealt with this issue by suggesting four 'modes of adaptation'. When decision-makers are responsive both to external and internal factors they have a preservative orientation; when the external is given preference, they are acquiescent; preference for internal needs gives them an intransigent orientation; and when they are not responsive at all (except to their own values), they are promotive (Rosenau, 1970, p. 5; see also Mouritzen, 1996, p. 4). This book will catalogue the movement between the first three orientations (the fourth being very scarce) by Norwegian decision-makers.

1.3 An Outline of the Book

The three parts of this book are divided by reference to the two elements of security policy and European policy.

Part I covers Norwegian European policy from 1945 to 1994. The whole period is divided into five chapters covering distinct stages in Norway's relations with the process of European integration.

This process was not a simple one. It had a number of strands. Until 1989, it was one that primarily involved the countries of Western Europe. In the security field much of the integration took place within the context of the North Atlantic Treaty Organisation (NATO), though there were a number of efforts conducted at the West European level.[1] Human Rights and cooperation on other policies, such as education and social policy, were undertaken within the Council of Europe; economic coordination was a task of the Organisation for European Economic Cooperation (OEEC) and its successor, the Organisation for Economic Cooperation and Development (OECD); and a pan-European perspective on human rights and security was undertaken by the Organization for Security and Cooperation in Europe (OSCE, formerly the CSCE). Regional groupings such as the Nordic Council and Benelux achieved substantial integration between their members, and functional institutions such as the European Danube Commission dealt with limited issues.[2] For most of the period, the main institutions associated with integration in the trade and economic field – and later in other policy areas – have been those of the European Communities, the European Coal and Steel Community from 1951, the European Economic Community (EEC) and Euratom from 1957, the European Communities (EC) from 1967, and the European Union from 1993. A side-show – but one in which Norway has participated – has been the European Free Trade Association (EFTA), existing since 1960, and the European Economic Area (EEA), established between the EU and most EFTA members and which came into force from 1 January 1994. From 1989 many of these institutions opened up membership – or association – to Central and East European states.

The years after the War until the first British application to the EEC in 1961 are covered in Chapter 2. During this time, Norway's relationship with the European integration process (outside of security) was mainly concerned with trade and economic matters. Norway manoeuvred between the Nordic, wider West European, continental West European and 'Outer Seven'(later EFTA) options. The chapter shows the official Norwegian attitude towards the proposals on offer, and examines the extent to which Norway was acquiescent towards what was on offer internationally and the extent to which it showed any intransigence, especially based on a response to domestic opinion.

Chapter 3 tells of an option placed on Norway's 'menu' by the country's lodestone on commercial matters, the United Kingdom. When the United Kingdom applied for EEC membership in 1961, it could be safely predicted that Norway would follow suit. However, the chapter also examines the fissures opened up within Norway from 1961 to 1972 by this, and subsequent, applications. The reasons for the rejection of EC membership in September 1972 – a supreme example of intransigence – are examined. Was the case for membership lost during the campaign, or were the chances of it ever being accepted low from the beginning?

Chapter 4 looks at the period from the late 1970s to the early 1990s, during which time Norway was trying to adapt to the new European situation, that of a wider and deeper EC. Why was there a period of 'denial' for almost 15 years after 1972, whereby the EC was seemingly ignored by Norway? Did the EC have nothing to offer, or were domestic considerations paramount in ministers' minds? What inspired the gradual opening by EFTA towards the relaunched EC of the mid-1980s? How far was it the activity of the EC itself and to what extent was it a factor of the Norwegian political system?

From 1989 to 1994 the European Communities adopted an ambitious programme that involved the creation of the Single European Market (SEM), the SEM's extension to the EFTA states, plans for Economic and Monetary Union (EMU) and the negotiations for the Treaty of Maastricht and the European Union. The EC also became a major centre of attraction for the Central and East European states liberated from Soviet hegemony and Communist rule. However, the European dream soured. Ratification of the Maastricht Treaty ran into trouble and popular opposition; the Exchange Rate

Mechanism came under threat, placing a question mark by EMU. The Central and East Europe countries found that EU sympathy did not translate easily into trade opportunities.

The Norwegian response, especially to the idea of the European Economic Agreement, is related in Chapter 4. At a time when was on offer as a new type of relationship between the EC and EFTA, what was Norway's attitude? In particular, the domestic debate is examined, as it proved to be a forerunner to the later EU battle. What then of the application for EC (later EU) membership? Why did the government apply when it did? Was it 'bounced' by the Swedish government and did the timing of events have a significant effect on its strategy?

The negotiations between Norway and the European Union are outlined in Chapter 5. The subjects salient for Norway are given particular emphasis as well as the overall settlement. However, the political background is also covered, especially the 1993 general election and the domestic effect of the negotiations. To what extent did these affect the chances of Norway becoming an EU member?

The decision whether or not to join the EU was fought out during the referendum campaign. Chapter 6 describes the lead-up to the vote and the result. What were the issues stressed by the two sides? How did the political parties and interest groups contribute to the campaign and how did external factors – especially the results of the referendums in Finland and Sweden – influence the Norwegian vote? To what extent was the 1994 outcome a reflection of that in 1972?

Part II deals with Norway's security policy set in its Atlantic perspective. The years from 1945 to 1948 led into the Cold War, those from 1986 to 1989 saw a thawing of its intensity, and from 1989 the old battle-lines dissolved. There were distinct phases within the 1948 to 1986 period during which relations between East and West were either more cooperative or more conflictual.

The first chapter in this section (Chapter 7) covers the four years after the Second World War when Norway moved from being an unaligned state trying to build bridges between the victorious powers to being a signatory of the North Atlantic Treaty. After the War, Norway found itself in a changing and deteriorating security environment in which one of its liberators, the Soviet Union, was increasingly being perceived by the Western states as a threat, and this view was one that most Norwegians came to share, with a majority willing to join a Western power bloc (Holst, 1967b, p. 235). However, the security choice available in 1948–9 was by no means a short-list of one. In theory there were four clear alternatives: join a Western bloc, join a Scandinavian grouping, remain neutral, or join the Soviet bloc. In reality the last choice was never discussed (outside the small Norwegian Communist Party). What factors determined the final decision to sign the North Atlantic Treaty in 1949? Was it a foregone conclusion for a country that had always depended on its Atlantic colleagues for security, or was there a complex equation between pressure from the Western allies, Swedish intransigence over the nature of any Scandinavian defence agreement and the preferences of the Labour Party leadership? To what extent was the evolution of Norway's decision not to have bases on its territory a response to external considerations, or was it more a reflection of domestic fears? This period was vital for Norway as it tied it into the Cold War confrontation in Europe and institutionalised its Atlantic orientation in security matters. It saw the rejection of a regional European (Scandinavian) response to the northern countries' defence dilemmas.

Chapter 8 examines Norway security policy in the period of the height of the Cold War, from 1949 to 1962. During this time Norway developed the security profile that it has maintained since. In a Cold War environment where its decision-makers and a majority of its population considered there to be an enduring threat – however indeterminate – from the Soviet Union, the Atlantic Alliance was seen as Norway's insurance policy. However, as time went by it was clear that this insurance had its price. The discussions with allies are examined to see how often Norway showed responsiveness, and how often intransigence especially when in response to domestic considerations. What does the extent of Norway's commitment to NATO indicate about that country's view of West European considerations? Was it ever seen as an opportunity to encourage a West European defence effort in which Norway could also participate?

The period from 1963 to 1989, covered in Chapter 9, can be typified as being two periods of détente with the New Cold War in between. Norway found that it had a freer hand during the two periods of détente, but when relations between the two superpowers froze in the late 1970s, and the Norwegian Sea became an area of strategic interest, there seemed to be less room for manoeuvre. How did Norway respond to these changes? Did it swim with the strategic flow, or were further adjustments required to Alliance policies in Northern Europe to suit the region's needs and Norwegian political preferences? To what extent did changing US interest in Norway during this period offer the opportunity to encourage increased European interest in the country's security?

The background to Chapters 10, 11 and 12 is that of a world after 1989 where a New World Order was promised but did not arrive. The Cold War was over and it seemed as though the West had won. The Soviet bloc crumbled, as did the Soviet Union. The new strategic situation, especially as it touched Northern Europe and Norway, is outlined in Chapter 10. Was Norway affected differently from Central Europe? How did developments in the US and in Europe affect Norway's relations with them? How did Norwegian domestic opinion respond to these changes? What then was that response, especially when the security issue began to fuse with the question of EU membership? How might the policy response be typified and why was such an explicit link made between security and European policy by the government? That question is picked up in Chapter 11, which examines the role of the security policy element in the 1994 referendum campaign. The issue is traced in the government's approach and in the response of its opponents and the electorate.

Part III examines Norway's position after the referendum. Chapter 12 continues the security theme. After the November 1994 result, how did the government respond to the rejection of EU membership which was meant to be an important element in the development of its security policy? How did Norway adapt internationally? The chapter also projects Norway's security dilemma forward, asking how its decision-makers may respond to a given set of scenarios or 'opportunities'. Could changes in the international environment encourage a future Norwegian application for EU membership based on security considerations?

Chapter 13 addresses the referendum result in political and commercial terms. It examines the domestic political consequences of the battle. It also looks at the steps taken by the government to mend relations with the EU. How was their negotiating position affected by being outside an expanded EU? What was the country's response to the issues coming before the Intergovernmental Conference of EU member states? What longer-term options are there for Norway in its relations with the EU? What are the arguments for the status quo? Under what conditions might Norway consider joining the EU?

Could there be a third referendum on Norwegian membership? If so, the Norwegian electorate will be able, once again, to make its choice about the form of the country's relationship with the European integration process.

Chapter 14 offers the conclusions of this study. In particular, responses are given to the questions raised in this chapter in sections 1.1, 1.2 and in this book outline. It seeks to understand the nature of Norway's relationship with European integration and the role played by the country's security link with the Atlantic powers. In particular the domestic elements that shaped the preference structure of the people and politicians of Norway on these issues are examined. Norway may be a small power that has little influence on its international environment, but this does not mean it has no choice in its external policies. Neither does it mean that the most important of those decisions are going to be taken without reference to the feelings of the Norwegian people.

Notes

1   For example the Treaty of Dunkirk 1947; the Treaty of Brussels, 1948; the attempts to create a European Defence Community from 1950 to 1954 and the subsequent establishment of the West European Union; and the security aspects of European Political Cooperation and the EU's Common Foreign and Security Policy.

2   For an account of the European integration process and the various organizations, see Archer, 1994c.

PART I

NORWEGIAN EUROPEAN POLICY

2

Rebuilding: 1945–1961

2.1 Introduction

In the fifteen years following the Second World War, the Norwegian economy and Norwegian trade policy had to adapt to rapidly changing economic and political circumstances. The period saw not only the political division of Europe into two hostile blocs, but the creation of two trade groups within Western Europe. For the West generally, the period was one of substantial economic growth underpinned by the Bretton Woods institutions created in the immediate postwar period. This was mirrored by a rise in world trade and a gradual liberalisation of the regulations governing that trade.

Efforts were made throughout the 1950s to liberalise West European trade but it soon became apparent that the approach taken by the six states belonging to the European Coal and Steel Community – the Six – was different from that taken by Britain and the Scandinavian states. Broadly, the Six wanted a customs union with strong institutions and including agriculture, while the United Kingdom preferred a free trade area, excluding agriculture, and with intergovernmental institutions (Camps, 1964). In this they were supported by the Scandinavians, though Denmark wished to include agriculture and Norway fish in any trade agreement. After the Six signed the Treaty of Rome in March 1957, discussions on a wider European free trade area were clearly in difficulties. The Six had not wanted to make any commitments before their agreement was signed (Hansen, 1990, p. 70; Camps, 1964, pp. 110–111). In February 1957 the British tried in vain for an agreement in principle on the wider free trade area but the Six, realising the frailty of the French government and fearful that elections would bring a change of government in Germany, pushed ahead with the Treaty of Rome (Griffiths, 1991b, p. 17).

As a fallback position after the failure to achieve a West European-wide free trade area, the United Kingdom turned to the other European states that had supported its position. They proposed a smaller free trade area among themselves, partly because of its economic benefits and partly to strengthen their hand in any negotiations with the EEC (Archer, 1994c, p.169). The negotiations for a European Free Trade Area (EFTA) were more straightforward than the wider free trade deliberations. Indeed, it may seem remarkable that EFTA was created with such ease. Talks began in June 1959, and the Stockholm Convention was concluded on 20 November and formally signed in January 1960.

The Norwegian economy developed apace during this period. After the Second World War Norway emerged with a shattered economy. However, there was broad political agreement across the political parties about economic targets such as full employment, economic growth and greater economic equality. This agreement was formalised through the so-called 'Joint Programme' hammered out by representatives of the different parties during the concluding months of the war. All the political parties, from the Communists on the left to the Conservatives and Agrarians on the right, agreed on the necessity of control and planning during the immediate reconstruction period. Planning was considered as necessary for the reduction of inflationary pressures, for the central allocation of import licences and for the conclusion of foreign trade agreements, as well as for the maintenance of price and wage controls and the rationing of consumer goods (Bergh, 1987a; Bergh, 1987b). The priority of rebuilding Norway's export industries was achieved with exports reaching their pre-war level by 1950 (Bjerve, 1965). Throughout the 1950s Norway kept a tight control on capital while being prepared to enter agreements on trade liberalisation. Even during the 1960s, the Norwegian government kept a tight rein on demand and investment. At the same time, the government entered into deals with sectors of the economy – such as agriculture and shipping – that were far from liberalising, representing the form of corporatism for which the Nordic states became famous (Steen, 1989). The protection of the interests of these sectors of the economy was something that the Norwegian government quickly understood through its close contacts not just with the Labour movement but also with the leaders of the other economic interest groups.

The fifteen years between 1945 and 1961 saw a striking stability in Norwegian politics as the Labour Party was in power throughout. The postwar all-party coalition was quickly replaced by a Labour government and the Labour Party held a parliamentary majority until September 1961 but after then relied on the support of the Socialist Peoples Party.[1] During this time, the Labour Party can be said to have exercised a hegemony over Norwegian politics. This does not mean that only the interests and views of the party were taken into account in government decision-making. Far from it. A consensus was obtained with other parties on broad outline of economic and foreign policies, and a network of relations with industry, commerce and agriculture was established. The system seemed to be a classical mixture of numerical democracy and corporate pluralism (Rokkan, 1966).

2.2   Adjusting to the Outside World: Plans for Scandinavian Cooperation

On hearing the United States' offer of economic aid to Europe in the form of Marshall Aid in 1947, the Norwegian government at first considered rejecting it. This was based on a realisation that an acceptance meant alignment with one of the great powers. Norway would thus have had to abandon its cherished bridge-building policy. The decision was also based on an evaluation of the economic situation as Norway's financial position at that time was considered satisfactory (Pharo, 1976, pp. 128–130). The idea of a coordinated European economic policy was also rejected by Norwegian policy-makers, who were deeply sceptical of the continental European countries' economic policies, and had no immediate intention of easing their thoroughly controlled economic policy. The government disliked the American economic system and mistrusted its push for a reconstruction plan for Europe (Pharo, 1976, pp. 149–153).

This was the context for a proposal in July 1947 by Norway's Foreign Minister, Halvard Lange, for closer Scandinavian economic cooperation.[2] Lange's initiative in July seems to have been a spontaneous idea, without much preparation from the Norwegian side. The three Scandinavian countries' foreign ministers then set up a committee of experts to examine the question by looking at the possibilities of mutual economic support and at long-term economic cooperation involving the possible elimination of mutual customs barriers (Stortingsmelding, 1954; Jensen, 1989, p. 63). The Scandinavian countries had relatively low tariffs, with Norway's as the highest of the three, but all had a well-developed system of quota restrictions through which trade was controlled.

The idea of a Scandinavian customs union was by no means new. It was raised by Swedish representatives at a Nordic Social Democratic party congress immediately at the end of the war[3] (Eriksen, 1987, p. 252). At that time, however, Norwegian politicians rejected the thought. Even when the Swedish Minister of Trade Gunnar Myrdal, inspired by the fear of increased autarky after the war, argued in favour of the idea, the subject was not seriously discussed.[4]

On the surface, Lange's proposal seemed a positive response to the American call for closer European integration. However, he argued that closer Scandinavian cooperation would demonstrate that Scandinavia did not need American aid, but could stand together against any infringement of their national sovereignty by the US (Jensen, 1989, p. 63). The Norwegian suggestion was a way of showing independence, rather than a proposal in which cooperation was seen as being desirable in itself (Sogner, 1993, p. 10).

A consideration of simple economic realities reinforces this interpretation. Immediately after the war, Norway was relatively less developed than Denmark and Sweden. The foundations of both the Norwegian and the Swedish economies were iron ore, wood products and cheap electricity, and fish in the Norwegian case, but Swedish industry was more diversified. The two economies were in competition with each other in both their domestic and export markets. Norwegian manufacturing industry feared Swedish competition; Swedish industry was more advanced than Norwegian before the war, and was less affected by depletion and destruction. Denmark, on the other hand, had a strong and mainly export-oriented agricultural sector, and it could have easily challenged Norwegian agriculture if restrictions on intra-Scandinavian trade had been abandoned. It was, however, clear from the start of the Scandinavian talks that agriculture would not be included.

Though the Norwegian initiative to widen Scandinavian cooperation may have had other motives, it soon acquired a life of its own for Norwegian policy-makers. Soon after the August 1947 decision to proceed with an investigation, Norwegian planners realised that Norway stood to gain from an extension of the division of labour between the Scandinavian countries within a planned context, and opposed a customs union (Sogner, 1992, pp. 28–29). However, the investigations concerning closer Scandinavian cooperation, including a customs union, began in February 1948 using the institution of the 'Joint Nordic Committee for Economic Cooperation' [Det felles nordiske utvalg for økonomisk samarbeid].[5] This removed the issue from the political agenda until 1949–50.

Even with the Labour Party firmly in the saddle in Oslo, the Cabinet – for domestic political reasons – wished to stress that negotiations with the Scandinavian neighbours did not imply the establishment of a customs union. Norway's economic position, less developed than Sweden and Denmark, and with higher tariff barriers, made the idea of a customs union highly controversial, even within the governing party. This was stressed by Lange both in the press and in the state of the nation debate [trontaledebatten] in the Storting in February 1948 (Utenriksdepartementets arkiv, 1948; Verdens Gang, 1948). The government also stressed that the customs union was only a minor element of Scandinavian cooperation (Brofoss, 1948, Box 150). Nor was it clear what kind of cooperation the Swedes and Danes had in mind. The Labour government also had to consider the views of the opposition, which was highly sceptical about Scandinavian cooperation. All the centre-right parties – the Conservatives, the Liberals, the Agrarian Party, the Christian Democrats – showed considerable distrust of the other two countries, particularly as both were run by Social Democrats. They were concerned that Norway should not again be dominated by its neighbours, as it had been in the period from the fourteenth century until 1905. The term 'union' did not ring well in Norwegian ears.

The call for closer European cooperation was equally unattractive. In the autumn of 1948 France proposed a Council of Europe, and after hard negotiations the United Kingdom and France reached a compromise over the Council in January 1949 (Røhne, 1989, pp. 14–15). Norway constantly supported the British intergovernmental attitude in the negotiations and in the early meetings in the Council. Its relationship to the United Kingdom was of great importance after 1945. Behind its bridge-building facade, Norway was closely linked to the UK ideologically, economically and militarily (Archer, 1989; Eriksen and Skodvin, 1981; Riste, 1982; Riste, 1984).

Closeness to Britain was an impediment to the success of the Scandinavian talks. In the autumn of 1948 the Norwegian government turned to Britain, suggesting that the two countries coordinate their long-term programmes. The proposal was enthusiastically received on the British side. The British Labour Party harboured strong illusions about Scandinavia in general (Milward, 1984, p. 316). Britain was Norway's most important trading partner[6] (Bergh, 1987a, p. 293; Hanisch and Lange, 1986;). Britain like Norway disliked the economic policies of the continental countries, and the two had similar attitudes to economic planning. Both supported high employment and a high investment level, and general views on the ends and means of economic policy were broadly similar (Bergh, 1987a; Milward, 1984; Pharo, 1986; Pharo, 1988a; Pharo, 1988b). The Norwegian proposal was also aimed at finding financial support for its investment programme, but Britain saw no advantages in such a proposal. A 'British-Norwegian Economic Committee' was formed. Although the committee never attained great prominence, it met regularly to discuss trade policy matters of mutual interest and both governments paid close attention to the connection thus established.

In November 1949 Britain proposed extending Anglo-Scandinavian cooperation to the Scandinavian foreign ministers. The Norwegian government's response was positive, while the Danes and the Swedes were more reluctant (Milward, 1984, pp. 316–319; Sogner, 1992). Closer links to the Sterling Area were put forward as a possibility, and the four countries agreed to investigate the idea at Cabinet level. Though the British initiative must be seen as a tactical move vis-à-vis the United States, and as a response to the so-called Fritalux project, the actual proposal was not as far fetched as it may seem[7] (Griffiths and Lynch, 1984; Milward, 1984, p. 306). The Scandinavian countries had formed part of the Sterling Area during the 1930s, and held large quantities of sterling. This time the outcome was more modest. In January 1950, the Anglo-Scandinavian project resulted in the creation of a cooperation committee, Uniscan, which as a useful forum for informal discussions on trade political topics concerning the four countries.

Security issues held centre stage in Norwegian foreign policy until 1949 (see Chapter 7). The breakdown of negotiations for a Scandinavian defence union, coupled with Norway's formal turn to the West by becoming one of the signatories of the Atlantic Treaty in Washington in April 1949, created a climate of caution in foreign policy. The failure to build a Scandinavian defence union left the Norwegian government with the task of bridging the gap among the Scandinavian countries, and economic issues seemed a promising instrument for this purpose.

Within the 'Joint Nordic Committee for Economic Cooperation', it quickly became clear that the Scandinavian countries had clashing interests. The Danes, and specifically their chief negotiator, Bramsnæs, pushed for the establishment of a Scandinavian customs union. The Norwegians, on the other hand, regarded a customs union as at best a long-term target. This clash delayed its final report. When the report was delivered in January 1950, it revealed that the Norwegian representatives were staunch opponents of the customs union. This information was met with sharp reactions by the Swedes and Danes, who blamed Norway for not taking Scandinavian cooperation seriously (UD, doss. 44 3/4, Vol. 5. Various documents). Shaken by this response and by the failure of the Scandinavian defence union, the Norwegian Foreign Ministry initiated a new Scandinavian cooperation proposal in March 1950, this time for a Scandinavian free trade area.

In November 1950 the 'Joint Committee' received a new mandate to investigate the problems involved in abolishing tariffs in certain sectors, and to identify sectors where cooperation could be of common benefit. This mandate was drafted by the Norwegian Foreign Ministry and was in line with Norwegian thinking. It soon transpired that the Danes and Swedes had somewhat lost interest. The committee had the same members as before and the same problems persisted. In contrast to the preceding period, however, the Norwegians took the initiative, while the Danes and Swedes adopted a waiting attitude (UD, doss. 44 3/4 Vol. 6. Note to the Foreign Minister by O. Sollie, 29 September 1950).

However, the Nordic game had not been played to the end. In late summer 1951, the former Danish Prime Minister Hans Hedtoft proposed a Nordic inter-parliamentarian council. The idea provoked debate, especially in Norway, and eventually resulted in the Nordic Council, which held its first meeting in February 1953. Opposition to the Nordic Council in Norway came from the same quarters which had opposed economic cooperation – within the non-socialist parties – and it was rooted in a fear of ceding elements of national sovereignty (Narum, 1972).

The report the 'Joint Committee' delivered in March 1954 contained two conclusions, one by the Norwegian members, and one by the Danes and the Swedes. The Norwegian experts, with few exceptions, opposed a 'common Scandinavian market'.[8] Reflecting its relative strong position, positive signals came from the Norwegian fish processing industry, which considered a larger market an advantage. This met Danish and Swedish opposition. Norway was not alone in supporting its own sectoral interests; all three nations tended to consider the question mainly in a short-term perspective. The readiness to compromise was not strong during this period; Scandinavian sectoral cooperation seemed a dead issue.

In the spring of 1954, however, the Norwegian government launched yet another Scandinavian initiative. The Minister of Trade, Erik Brofoss, was its driving force and Norway's economic position was the reason. Faced with a huge trade deficit and a general lack of investment capital, Brofoss saw Scandinavian cooperation – involving Swedish investment as well as increased capital flows from Britain – as the remedy. The strategy was not entirely new, but it was discussed at Cabinet level, with a view to moulding cooperation in accordance with perceived Norwegian interests.

The new offensive primarily aimed at promoting joint Scandinavian projects. This had two reasons: capital was scarce, and it was feared that the European Payments Union

(EPU) would be wound up.[9] Norwegian policy-makers still opposed a Scandinavian customs union, and supported a Scandinavian division of labour. In earlier talks this Norwegian preference generally gave way to Danish and Swedish interests and to pressure for a customs union. In the spring of 1954 Brofoss modified his line of argument. A progressively stronger Germany was generally considered a threat by Norwegian business, which had started to give support to the Norwegian government's proposals. This new approach was considered so important that the Norwegian government once more softened its negative attitude towards a customs union. At the August 1954 meeting of the Nordic Council, it again accepted a customs union in principle, despite the fact that the Labour government still preferred cooperation on specific projects (Sogner, 1992, pp. 319–321).

Negotiations proceeded at Cabinet level, with the setting up of a new cooperation committee including a 'Cooperation Minister' from each of the three Scandinavian countries. The 'Nordic Economic Cooperation Committee' ['Det nordiske samarbeidsutvalg'] immediately set to work on two issues. First, it was to elaborate a framework for a Scandinavian common market, with a common tariff and the elimination of internal restrictions. Secondly, it was to define precisely the rules for cooperation within certain sectors. The two tasks were closely entwined. Cooperation on production within one field would also affect tariffs and trade restrictions. In addition to investigating commodities relatively unhampered by restrictions, as the Joint Committee had done between 1950 and 1954, the new committee was allowed to investigate the iron and steel industry, the electro-metallurgic, chemical metal, and semi-manufactured metal industries, areas which embraced 70–75% of intra-Scandinavian trade in all. All these commodities were of particular interest to Norway (Stråth, 1978, p. 127).

Apart from the resolution calling for a customs union, Norway felt it had a relatively good deal (Sogner, 1992, pp. 319–323). The most ambitious new element was a projected Scandinavian iron and steel combine. The merging of the Swedish and the Norwegian steel industries would make the region self-sufficient and thus independent of the continental steel trusts. This brainchild of Brofoss implied a wide-ranging division of labour, including specialisation between iron and steel companies. As such it represented a clear attempt at cartel-building on a Scandinavian basis. The proposal met with strong opposition among the Swedish iron and steel industry, which feared that the Scandinavian governments were trying to control the process of production. The Swedish government, on the other hand, viewed the project favourably, as did the Danish government (Stråth, 1978, p. 128).

The 'Cooperation Committee' delivered a preliminary report in December 1955 on areas covering eight fields different sectors which represented 45% of intra-Scandinavian trade. The report met opposition from the non-socialist parties of Norway, while Danish, Swedish, and Norwegian government representatives were all very positive. Much of the opposition reflected the fear that Norwegian business would suffer in a too small Scandinavian market. This had been the view of the Norwegian Federation of Industries ever since the idea of a closer Scandinavian cooperation was launched. It preferred wider liberalisation, whether at European, North Atlantic or global level (UD, doss. 44 3/4, Vol. 4a; UD, doss. 44 3/4, Vol. 19; EB, Box 151). The 'Cooperation Committee', however, continued its work.

2.3   Manoeuvring Between Plans: Scandinavia, Wider Free Trade, EFTA

Norway had participated actively in both GATT and the OEEC from the outset. The two organisations were both based on cooperation at intergovernmental level, and this suited Norway much better than concepts of supranational integration. The Norwegian government viewed economic planning as an exclusively national affair and approved international liberalisation only as long as its pace was not forced.

The great variations in the European countries' tariff levels were considered a problem, both at Scandinavian and European level. Within Scandinavia, increases in 1952 in the already high Norwegian tariffs further reduced Norwegian industry's taste for Scandinavian cooperation. They had the opposite effect on Danish and Swedish industry. At the European level, the OEEC's plan for quota reductions, which Norway had somewhat reluctantly accepted, was considered unfair by low tariff countries. These included the Benelux countries and Switzerland, as well as the Scandinavian countries. High tariffs in many ways neutralised the effect of quota elimination. The 'Low Tariff Club' pressed the OEEC to shift its focus from import restrictions to tariffs, and in 1956 it introduced an automatic tariff reduction plan (Asbeek-Brusse, 1991, p. 200f, p. 204, pp. 214–229; Laursen, p. 4). This came at the same time – May 1956 – as the six countries, Belgium, France, Italy, Luxembourg, Netherlands and West Germany, reached an agreement to create a customs union.[10]

The agreement on a customs union between the Six and the automatic tariff reduction plan triggered a British proposal in July for an industrial free trade area covering the OEEC countries. The proposal was meant to derail the tariff reduction plan, and to undermine the plans for the EEC (Griffiths, 1991a, pp. 21–22). At first, Norway showed little interest in the British suggestion, but it soon adopted a favourable attitude. The government felt that it could not categorically reject an initiative coming from its most important trading partner and political supporter, the United Kingdom (Hansen, 1990).

The British proposal and the negotiations for a wider free trade area had no immediate influence on the Scandinavian negotiations. In the medium term, however, it acted as a brake on these talks, and ultimately contributed to their failure. The Norwegian government continued to give priority to the Scandinavian talks for a year after the British proposal. In August 1956 the Nordic Economic Cooperation Committee emphasised that the Scandinavian countries had to cooperate in the negotiations on the wider free trade area. The concept of Scandinavian cooperation within the larger European framework seemed natural, and there seemed to be no reason to interrupt the Scandinavian discussions (UD, doss. 44 3/4, Vol. 15a; UD, doss. 44 3/4, Vol. 15b).

Norway and its Scandinavian neighbours participated actively in discussions on a wider European free trade area. Norway had a representative in the OEEC's working party no. 17, constituted to investigate this proposal, from the beginning. The three Scandinavian delegations tried to set up a common front in these talks, reflecting their existing practice in general OEEC matters, but their different interests made this difficult. In line with this ambition, Norway supported the Danish push for the inclusion of agricultural products in trade liberalisation (Riksarkivet, 11 December 1956). This aspiration was firmly rejected by the United Kingdom, which in turn became isolated on the issue; the Six supported it, though they did not press the point (Hansen, 1990, p. 74).

As long as the Nordic Economic Cooperation Committee continued its deliberations, Norway did not need to choose between the two cooperation plans. Yet by the summer of 1957 the European and Scandinavian plans could not really be evaluated separately. The Scandinavian talks had to take account of the European plans which were dealing with substantially the same issues. In effect, Norwegian policy-makers started to give preference to the wider European free trade area.

The Cooperation Committee presented its report to the Scandinavian governments in October 1957. By this time, a new round of talks had started within the OEEC, and the Scandinavians decided to extend their investigations to the remaining 20% of intra-Scandinavian trade. The two set of negotiations would thus cover the same ground, including fish and agricultural products. A resolution of the Scandinavian negotiations was thus officially postponed, and the Norwegian government made no further move for over a year.

The inclusion of agriculture and fisheries brought dormant conflicts, hitherto carefully avoided, to the forefront. The Cooperation Committee's work was further complicated by the fact that these sectors were under consideration in the European negotiations, and especially by the 1 January 1959 deadline for the establishment of a Scandinavian Common Market. The Cooperation Committee completed an additional report in September 1958, in which the possibilities within Scandinavia were considered on the assumption that an OEEC-based European Free Trade Area would be set up. The Scandinavian proposal contained some reservations. In the industrial sector these were not of any importance, but in the areas of agriculture and fisheries no agreement was reached. The Scandinavian governments were still not ready to make definite decisions.

Negotiations on a wider European free trade area reached a deadlock in November 1958, and the Nordic Council decided to resume the Scandinavian talks. The three governments had not entirely discarded the Scandinavian alternative. The Danes, however, wanted to wait, still hoping for a wider European free trade area including agricultural products. Denmark was reluctant to bind itself to Scandinavian cooperation, as long as the fate of the European plans was unclear (UD, doss. 44 3/4, Vol. 21). Shortly after the breakdown, the OEEC delegations of Britain, Switzerland, Austria and the Scandinavian countries met. The Other Six, as they were called, being the countries that had been most in agreement with each other during the wider free trade area negotiations, decided to approach the EEC as a group (Camps, 1964, pp. 210–211; Griffiths, 1992, pp. 35–36; Hansen, 1990, p. 88 and p. 92). Their ambition was to attain the same degree of free trade for the whole of the OEEC area as the EEC countries were to have internally. They hoped to prevent trade discrimination after 1 January 1959, the date of the EEC's first tariff reductions and quota increases. Contacts between 'the Seven', as they became with the inclusion of Portugal, was thus established.

In the spring of 1958 the industrial federations of the Other Six actively tried to encourage their respective governments to take some form of collective action. Their main aim was to strengthen the negotiating position of their governments vis-à-vis the Six, but the idea of establishing a free trade area among themselves was also discussed. This possibility was further examined during the autumn as the odds lengthened against an OEEC-based arrangement (Camps, 1964, pp. 212–213). At the end of January 1959 it was clear that the wider European free trade area was dead unless the Six embraced the idea. Actual negotiations for a smaller free trade area, however, did not start until July 1959, although preliminary investigations were initiated as from February 1959.

The Scandinavian alternative was not abandoned until July 1959, when the three governments turned their full attention to the European negotiations on the smaller

European free trade area. By this stage, they had found a solution in the agricultural sector, but still had problems on fisheries. A Scandinavian solution had influential supporters in Norway, such as Erik Brofoss, even after EFTA became the most attractive alternative. None of the Scandinavian governments dared to press for a Scandinavian solution within EFTA because of British opposition, but they continued to emphasise the importance of Scandinavian cooperation after EFTA was set up. None wished to be the first to declare the patient dead.

At the time the Scandinavian negotiations were abandoned and EFTA was agreed upon, the decisive questions in Norwegian politics concerned domestic economic policy. The European and Scandinavian questions occupied the government and the Labour Party, and to some extent the opposition parties, but were not matters of broad public concern. The only recognisable pressure groups were the big organisations such as – first and foremost – the Federation of Industries, but also the Shipowners' Association, the Export Council, the Bankers' Association, the Employers' Organisation, the Central Federation of Agricultural Cooperatives, and the Federation of Trade Unions (LO). In spite of the rapid internationalisation of the economy, Norwegian policy-makers still wanted extensive controls. The Norwegian government saw the EFTA agreement as the best deal they could get, and was for the time being satisfied with it.

2.4   Conclusions

The introduction of the Marshall Plan and the American demand for closer European cooperation triggered the investigations of a Scandinavian customs union. However, this examination was conducted in order to contain American pressure, and Norway had a firm belief in its own economic strength. The aim in economic cooperation during the early part of this period was to secure Norwegian and Scandinavian autonomy, rather than cooperation in a broader context. This contrasted starkly with Norwegian intentions in the security field , which were aimed at ensuring American and British involvement in Norway's defence (see Chapter 7).

The Scandinavian governments also had ideals and long-term economic goals. During the autumn of 1947, even before the Scandinavian investigations got under way, the Norwegian government saw positive advantages in Scandinavian cooperation on a broader basis. It was at the time aware of a currency shortage, but many in government also saw long-term advantages in specialisation, division of labour and larger scale production. These goals were at this point only vaguely formulated. Indeed, 1954 stands out in the Scandinavian negotiations as the year in which economic cooperation again became a live issue in the press and the *Storting*, and clashes of interest within Norway reached a new level. In the course of five months, the Labour government abandoned the negative stance expressed from January to the end of March 1954, and at a meeting of the Nordic Council in August 1954 it supported a resolution favouring a customs union. At the same time, the centre-right parties engaged in active opposition. In contrast, a broad spectrum of political parties very quickly accepted that the Scandinavian context was not the best for defence cooperation (see Chapter 7).

The Norwegian attitude towards Scandinavian cooperation seems at first glance to have been rather ambiguous. All the initiatives to investigate economic cooperation came from Norway, while at the same time it adopted the most negative attitude towards such cooperation. However, behind this apparent contradiction there was a comprehensive Norwegian view, one which had a much broader perspective than the Danish and Swedish plans. This attitude developed from 1947, when the idea of closer Scandinavian cooperation was first introduced, and culminated in 1954 with the efforts of Erik Brofoss to achieve it in the iron and steel sector. Irrespective of the increasing Norwegian interest in Scandinavian cooperation, Norway was never interested in a Scandinavian customs union. Norwegian policy in this question was quite clear, but it tended to become fudged when confronted with pressure from Denmark and Sweden and with other external demands. The Norwegian government hoped for broader Scandinavian cooperation, without a customs union, and it therefore took a pragmatic attitude for tactical reasons. In the end, it only accepted the customs union as one element of cooperation, both in 1948 and in 1954. The fight over this issue, however, meant the project had to be given up.

Incompatible ideas and divergent interests among the three countries led to the failure of the Scandinavian plans. Internal Norwegian opposition also played its part. On the other hand, the Scandinavian investigations and, more clearly, the OEEC Free Trade negotiations, cleared the ground for the establishment of EFTA. In the course of two years of EFTA cooperation, intra-Scandinavian economic cooperation in many fields reached the levels the negotiators had sought during the preceding years. In 1963 Sweden overtook Britain as Norway's most important trading partner.

Norway's attitude to the efforts to create closer cooperation on the Continent was somewhat distant. Political circles in Norway, as in Britain, showed a general scepticism towards the Continental countries, and strongly opposed any kind of supranationality. Cooperation on an intergovernmental level, on the other hand, was a different matter. When Britain advanced the idea of a wider free trade area, in July 1956, Norwegian policy-makers were interested. From then until July 1959 Norway tried to manoeuvre between the Scandinavian alternative and the two different European alternatives. Until the summer of 1957, the Scandinavian negotiations had priority over the wider free trade area, but from the beginning the European alternative had impinged on the Scandinavian plans. It became more important, although no political decision was made to that effect; thus Norway's destiny within the European system was manifested during 1957 without Norway's specific approval. After the failure of the hopes of a wider free trade area, there was no question but that Norway would follow the EFTA countries into a smaller free trade area. The Scandinavian project was throughout a kind of back-up project to be developed in case the European alternative failed.

If the preferences of the Norwegian authorities for cooperation in the four circles of global, wider Western, narrower West European or Nordic contexts in the two functional areas of security and European policies are expressed in table form (Table 2.1), then – to paraphrase an earlier statement – 'Norwegian membership of NATO and Norwegian participation in European integration are not exactly two sides of the same coin' (after Brundtland, 1968, p. 171). Indeed, the comparison of the two policy areas made in 1968 by Brundtland can be refined by dividing the periods into three and by changing his broad categories of Atlantic, European and Nordic into the more meaningful ones of Global (A – through the UN); wider Western (B – through OEEC and NATO); narrower West European (C – through either the Communities' institutions or EFTA or Uniscan; or Nordic (D – including arrangements limited to two or three of the Nordic states).

Table 2.1 demonstrates how the economic policy preference of Norway's decision-makers widened out geographically from a preference for solutions closer to home after 1945 to an acceptance of the West European-wide solution by the mid-1950s – very much following Britain's line – to the Hobson's choice of EFTA once a wider Free Trade Area had been struck off the agenda. In contrast, the preference for security through the global institutions of the United Nations in 1945 narrowed down to the attempt to achieve a Scandinavian Defence Union in 1948 and an acceptance of a subscription to the Atlantic Alliance in 1949. It will be seen in Part II that the factors determining security policy – and the mix between external and internal determinants – were different from those shaping the choices in economic policy from 1945 to 1961. Nevertheless both had one common, important element – a willingness to use the United Kingdom as a lodestone.

Table 2.1   *Norway's Preferences in Economic and Security Policies, 1945–61*

	A	B	C	D
Economic policy				
1945–54	4	3	2	1
1955–9	4	1	3	2
1960–61	4	2	1	3
Security policy				
1945–7	1	2	4	3
1948	3	2	4	1
1949–61	2=	1	4	2=

Notes

1   Einar Gerhardsen was Prime Minister for most of this period, except between November 1951 and January 1955 when Oscar Torp held this office. The non-socialist parties in power in 1963 were the Conservative Party (Høyre), the Liberal Party (Venstre), the Agrarians (Bondepartiet, later the Centre Party, Senterpartiet) and the Christian Democrats (Kristelig Folkeparti).

2   This Norwegian suggestion formally included all the Nordic countries, and thereby justifies the term 'Nordic', which includes Denmark, Finland, Iceland, Norway and Sweden. From early on, however, it soon became clear that Finland and Iceland would not be included, and that an extension of the economic cooperation would only cover the three Scandinavian countries Denmark, Norway and Sweden. In spite of this fact, the actors of this period used the terms 'Norden' and 'Nordic', as reflected in the names of the committees established. However, for the sake of clarity and simplicity the more correct terms 'Scandinavia' and 'Scandinavian' will be preferred throughout in this work.

3   The idea of a Scandinavian customs union can, however, be traced even further back in time, as the Norwegian businessman and writer Joakim Ihlen, 1957, has done. He traces the first suggestion back to 1846, and the influence being the German *Zollverein*. The 'Norden' associations – non-governmental Nordic organisations – have also worked for closer Nordic cooperation since 1919.

4   Gunnar Myrdal was a very influential economist whose book *Varning för fredssoptimism*, Stockholm 1944, had had a strong influence on the Norwegian postwar Social Democratic government.

5   The 'Joint Committee' was headed by the Danish National Bank governor C. V. Bramsnæs, and held its first meeting in April 1948. Its mandate was to investigate the possibilities of establishing a common tariff as a precondition for a customs union; of reducing the tariffs and limiting the quantitative trade restrictions between the Scandinavian countries; of expanding the distribution of labour and the specialisation between the countries; and of extending the already existing trade political cooperation.

6   In the period 1946–50, 20% of Norwegian commodity imports came from the UK, which in turn received between 15 and 19% of Norwegian commodity exports.

7   The Fritalux project between France, Italy and the Benelux countries was initiated to free capital flows and exchange rates, and was very much welcomed in the United States.

8   In this report, as elsewhere at that time, there was a confusion of concepts. In the report 'a common Scandinavian market' was used as the collective term for what the committee had investigated, which was, according to its mandate, a 'partial' or 'limited free trade area', and not something synonymous to what was defined as a 'common market' according to GATT's definitions.

9   The multilateral system of the European Payments Union made the European member countries' currencies convertible within the EPU, and at the same time protected them against the dollar. The EPU had constituted the basis for Norway's investment policy after the conclusion of the Marshall Plan. In 1953–54, however, the question of making the British pound fully convertible was seriously discussed. This would have meant the end of the EPU. Because the EPU system had functioned very well for Norway, with its large foreign trade sector and balance of payments problems, talk of making the pound fully convertible represented a threat for Norway.

10   When the European Coal and Steel Community (ECSC) was established in 1951, it was meant to be the first of several organisations integrating economic sectors. However, the six member states showed little inclination to rush matters, and many of the sectoral plans suggested after 1951 came to nothing before this agreement was reached in 1956.

3

Applying and After: 1961–1977

3.1 The Background

During these fifteen years, Norway had to conduct its European policy against the background of a rapidly changing diplomatic environment. Not only did the nature of the EEC alter, so did the attitude of the United Kingdom to the Community venture. Economic changes were affecting Norway, and the country experienced political change and turbulence, of which the decision to apply for EEC membership was one element.

After just over a year of cooperation within EFTA, Britain formally decided to apply for membership of the EEC. This came as a surprise and disappointment to Norwegian policy-makers. In July 1961 Britain announced its intention of applying for full membership, and the formal application was submitted on 9 August. Denmark and Ireland submitted their membership applications immediately after this. For Norway, however, it took nearly a year to get the application ready for submission (Lie, 1975, pp. 223–239; Frydenlund, 1966, pp. 81–84; Allen, 1979, pp. 45–51).

In January 1963 French President de Gaulle put a halt to the British accession negotiations by declaring that Britain was not ready for membership. Negotiations had by then lasted for eighteen months and had made much headway, according to the Commission, the British, and five of the six EEC members[1] (Camps, 1964, p. 493). Although the French veto may have been possible to foresee, it came as a surprise in the light of the progress made in the talks. After a short period in which Denmark considered continuing its negotiations, talks with the other applicants ceased – the first round was over.

From 1965 the Labour government in Britain expressed concern over the widening gap between EFTA and the EEC. In 1966 a new bid for membership became firm policy, and in May 1967 a second British application was submitted, but it soon met the same fate as the first.

President de Gaulle's resignation in April 1969 and the Hague Summit the following December brought a change of climate to the European scene. Without the French veto, the membership applications of Denmark, Norway, Ireland and the United Kingdom were reactivated. Sweden also seemed to be considering an application for full membership (Lie, 1975, pp. 376–377). Talks progressed speedily, with the British case being settled within a year. Negotiations began in June 1970, and all applicants were ready to sign the Treaty of Brussels in January 1972.

Within Norway, the 1960s was a period of economic and social change. During the decade the share of the population living in communities of under 200 people had fallen from 42% in 1960 to 33% in 1970, and there had been a movement both from the north of the country to the south and to the big cities generally (Central Bureau of Statistics, 1995, p.49). The Norwegian economy was still based on the export of primary and semi-processed materials, which were the country's main earners, and a sheltered agriculture and home industry, which provided much of the employment, especially in the rural areas. During the 1960s, the share of machines and manufactured goods in Norway's exports doubled from an eighth to a quarter, while forestry and fisheries' share had fallen. However, 78% of Norway's exports still went to the markets represented by the EC and EFTA (Stortingsmelding 50, 1971–72, pp. 3 & 11). Both agriculture and fisheries had shrunk in size and economic importance in the previous twenty years (ibid., pp. 62, 92–3), but they were still powerful factors in Norwegian life. Both relied on prices and subsidies set by the government; the fishermen had weighty producers' organizations and, like the farmers, dealt directly with the government in a client status. The farming areas were over-represented in parliament[2] and there was cross-party support for the notion that there should be equality between the average agricultural and industrial wage (Stortingsmelding 92, 1969–70, p.39).

Politically the 1961 election represented a setback for Labour. They lost their overall majority and had to rely on the support of the left-wing Socialist People's Party. For a brief period in 1963, the Labour Party was thrown out of office after a parliamentary vote of no confidence and an interim administration led by the Conservative, John Lynge, took office for a month. After the 1965 election the four non-socialist parties – the Conservatives, the Centre Party, the Christian Democrats and the Liberals – took power again and remained in office after the 1969 election, though with a two-seat majority (Valen & Rokkan, 1970, pp. 287–300). However, these parties represented quite different interests, from the more cosmopolitan big business supporters of the Conservatives to the farming vote of the Centre Party. In short, the 1960s was one of political upsets for Norway.

3.2   Norway's Response to the First EEC Applications

For Norway, the question of EEC membership had been a non-issue before Britain decided to join. Norwegian politicians had adjusted to continuing internationalisation and to Norway's increased political and economic dependency on Europe, but they were not prepared for the British move.[3] Hitherto, European cooperation had been viewed as secondary to the Atlantic Alliance. As late as 1960, Foreign Minister Lange said that Norway was prepared to make a greater commitment to Atlantic than to European cooperation (Frydenlund, p. 81). The British application showed, however, that Norway had been left behind. Norwegian politicians had underrated the strength of European cooperation.

The British application was quickly followed by those of Denmark and Ireland, and in December 1961 the neutral EFTA countries applied for association agreements. The situation forced a Norwegian response. The Norwegian government had known about the British intentions since early May, and had in the beginning of June decided to investigate further the consequences of Norwegian membership. For the government and many leading figures within the Labour Party it was clear that Norway could not stay aloof from an organised economic cooperation which included not only the EEC countries, but also the UK and the other EFTA countries. However, there was great resistance towards closer affiliation with the EEC, in the party, in the *Storting* and among public opinion. This opposition proved so strong that a quick reaction such as in Denmark was ruled out (Lie, 1975, pp. 223–239; Ørvik, 1972, p. 10). In order to find a compromise, the Labour Party leadership took the long consultative way round.

It took nearly a year of investigations, discussions and disagreements before on 28 April 1962, the *Storting*, decided to negotiate for membership of the EEC. In October 1961 the government put forward a report to the *Storting* [Stortingsmelding] which did not include any conclusion as to the kind of relationship with the EEC wished by the government (Stortingsmelding 15, 1961–62). An additional report was postponed for three months to await the treatment of the question inside the Labour Party's organisational structure. As it turned out that an overwhelming majority of the regional divisions wanted negotiations for full membership, the party was finally ready to act. When the government's report was delivered to the *Storting* in March 1962, however, the minister of prices and wages, Gunnar Bøe, surprisingly dissented (Stortingsmelding 67, 1961–62, pp. 14–15). This came as a shock, as he previously had not opposed the report. Besides, the issue had been discussed over a long period, and had received support in all divisions of the party.

Clearly the Labour Party had difficulty with the EEC issue. However, the party also had serious problems generally when it lost its parliamentary majority in the election of September 1961. The strength of the opposition to EEC membership within the party surprised the leadership. By November 1961 this opposition had grown to notable proportions, and for a while it seemed doubtful whether the government and the leadership could proceed with their plans. For the majority within the Labour leadership, the significance of Britain, the fear of becoming locked out of European markets, and the question of access to capital were decisive arguments in favour of seeking membership of the EEC. Foreign Minister Halvard Lange, Trade Minister Arne Skaug, and Party Secretary Haakon Lie were among the most influential figures in favour of membership. They were responsible for bringing about a change of mood after eight months of intense discussions and disputes within the party (Bergh, 1987a, pp. 496–503; Lie, 1975, pp. 214–239). Norwegian membership was made dependent on British entry, and on adequate safeguards for the primary sectors. There was also to be a consultative referendum after the completion of the negotiations and before the *Storting*'s final vote (Stortingsmelding 67, 1961–62; Allen, 1979, p. 46).[4]

On 12 April 1962 the Foreign and Constitutional Affairs Committee submitted three different reports. The majority of the 19 members recommended full EEC membership, 4 wanted associate membership, while two Labour Party members (Trond Hegna and Johs. Olsen) preferred an economic agreement with the Six, with an associate membership as an alternative (Innst.S.165, 1961–62). In a heated debate in the *Storting* on 28 April 1962, profound differences of opinion on Norway's relationship with the EEC clearly emerged. After three days of debate, however, the government's proposal that Norway should apply for full membership was passed by 113 votes to 37 (*Stortingsforhandlinger*, 1961–62, pp. 3009–3010). In favour were all 29 Conservative Party members, 12 of the 14 Liberals, 8 of the 15 Christian Democrats, 1 from the Centre Party's 16 members, and 63 of 74 Labour Party members. Both representatives of the Socialist People's Party voted against. The Committee's minority proposal was defeated by 112 votes to 38. A Socialist People's Party proposal for a mere trade agreement got two votes; the Socialist People's Party deputies were the only ones formally to reject any form of association with the EEC (*Stortingsforhandlinger*, 1961–62, vol. 7b).

Joining the EEC implied a constitutional amendment for Norway. Paragraph 93 of the Constitution, concerning the *Storting*'s right to delegate authority from Norwegian state officials to international organisations, was redrafted. The proposed amendment introduced an entirely new principle into Norwegian constitutional law: the possibility of relinquishing domestic judicial authority to extra-Norwegian bodies. While humanitarian or international law decisions in international organisations depended on national legislative measures for their implementation, the new Paragraph 93 allowed the possibility of international organisations passing decisions with direct applicability in Norway, without the participation of national authorities (Ramberg, 1972, pp. 49–50).

Proposals for amending Paragraph 93 had been under consideration since January 1953. The first proposal was unanimously rejected in October 1956. By the time the proposal was unanimously rejected a second time in September 1960, arguments had changed to a much more positive attitude. All parties in the *Storting*, except the Communists, then managed to agree on a reformulation which was adopted in March 1962. The issue provoked one of the most heated *Storting* debates since the war. The amendment was adopted on 8 March 1962, a month before the vote on the membership application, by 115 to 35 votes (*Stortingsforhandlinger*, 1961–62, p. 2384). The Socialist People's Party and some Labour Party members voted against, together with the entire Centre Party and parts of the Liberals and the Christian Democrats. The voting pattern was the same that emerged a month later in the vote on the EEC membership application. The two affirmative votes meant that Norway could now constitutionally enter the EEC, and the government submitted its application in May 1962.

De Gaulle's 'non' to Britain also ruled out the European alternative for Norway for the foreseeable future. Norwegian politicians took the French veto calmly. Opponents of membership were obviously satisfied, but even those in favour of membership seemed relieved. Norway was not to be troubled by the turmoil which a national decision was expected to generate, as could be seen in the parliamentary debates.

EFTA had proved a success for Norway and the other Scandinavian countries. It solved the trade problems they had tried unsuccessfully to overcome by creating a Scandinavian customs union. Within EFTA the Scandinavian countries reduced their tariff barriers; and by the end of 1966, three years before schedule, intra-Scandinavian customs on industrial products were virtually gone. While trade in general increased, intra-Scandinavian trade, which was most important for Norway, expanded even more. As mentioned earlier, by 1963 Sweden had taken over from Britain as Norway's most important trading partner. Norway was flourishing outside the EEC.

3.3   The Second EEC Applications, the French 'Non' and the Failure of Nordek

With de Gaulle's veto in January 1963, the EEC question disappeared from the Norwegian political agenda as quickly as it had arisen. It did not reappear until Britain decided to reapply in 1967. Denmark's renewed application followed within twenty-four hours of Britain's, and the Norwegian application came two months later. Even Sweden declared a willingness to negotiate, though without specifying which form of association it might prefer (af Malmborg, 1992, pp. 478–480).

The situation in 1967 differed from 1961–62. Domestic political circumstances in Norway had changed, as had the merged European Communities (so named after July 1967). Norway was by then governed by a non-socialist coalition which was divided over the issue of EC membership. Five out of the fifteen ministers had expressed their preference for an association agreement in 1962. Nevertheless, there seemed to be a clear majority for membership within the government (Allen 1979, p. 51). In the *Storting* the majority was larger, but here too the dividing line cut across the party lines. After intense internal discussions, especially within the Centre and Christian Democratic parties, the government unanimously decided to recommend to the *Storting* that Norway apply for negotiations for full EC membership. Like its Labour predecessor, the government made entry conditional on British membership and on satisfactory safeguards for the primary sectors. It also promised a consultative referendum before the *Storting* made its final decision (Stortingsmelding 86, 1966–67, pp. 99–100).

For sceptical Norwegian politicians the EC's institution must have seemed less threatening than four years earlier. The intergovernmentalist approach of France under de Gaulle had had its effect on the EC, and the applications by the United Kingdom also indicated that the EC might develop less along Community-based lines than before.

Unanimity within the Norwegian government reflected the special conditions of the time, rather than a change of heart by opponents of membership. It seemed clear that France was still reluctant to admit Britain, so the prospect of Norwegian membership seemed very hypothetical (Allen, 1979, p. 52; Lyng, 1976, pp. 213 and 233). The issue for those who earlier opposed membership was therefore not membership itself, but whether they were prepared to break up the coalition. They were not. The text of the government recommendation spoke of a Norwegian application 'as the best means of clarifying the basis for Norway's relations with the EC', not a commitment to joining the EC (Stortingsmelding 86, 1966–67, p. 99). However, the application as submitted went further than the government's recommendation, stating that Norway's objective was membership and expressing the hope that any difficulties raised by Norway's special needs could be overcome during the negotiations (Stortingsmelding 92, 1969–70, p. 29). It was basically the Foreign Ministry, headed by the adherent John Lyng, that formulated the final application.

On 13 July 1967 the *Storting* voted 136 to 13 in favour of a new application for EC membership. Four Centre Party and three Christian Democrat representatives were joined by four Labour Party members and the two from the Socialist People's Party in opposition (Stortingstidende, 1966–67, pp. 4557–4558). Though the result was decisive, doubts persisted among the smaller parties that had backed the government.

Key economic organisations were far more consistent in their positive response to EC membership than in 1962. The Federation of Trade Unions (LO) and the Federation of Industries were clear in their approval. The agricultural organisations, which in 1962 had been somewhat lukewarm, were by 1967 generally positive towards the government's course of action (Vefald, 1972, p. 209). According to the polls, there was majority public support for membership in 1967, though there was no public debate of any significance as compared with 1962 (Høivik, Hellevik and Gleditsch, 1971, pp. 243–244).

After Norway, Denmark and Ireland once more had followed Britain and applied for membership in the EC, France vetoed British membership in December 1967. Negotiations had not even reached the preliminary stage. However, the applications remained in Brussels, though talks seemed unlikely in the then foreseeable future. Given this impasse, the idea of closer Nordic cooperation was revived.

In February 1968 the new centre-right government in Denmark proposed that the Nordic countries examine the possibilities of extending their economic cooperation (Dale, 1979; Leonardsen, 1984). The proposal was not presented as a substitute for the EC; the Danish argument was rather that it would strengthen the Nordic countries economically while they waited for a suitable agreement with the EC. Closer Nordic cooperation might also improve their eventual bargaining position in Brussels. In the recently completed Kennedy Round of GATT discussions, the Nordic countries had negotiated as a unit. The Danish proposal envisaged Nordic cooperation based on a customs union, freer agricultural trade, and joint institutions to coordinate economic policy. Finnish participation was considered politically possible since all the countries were outside the EC.

The four non-socialist parties had been sceptical about Nordic cooperation throughout the 1950s, and they were still so in a coalition government. However, after some amendments to the Danish proposal, Norway agreed to enter negotiations for a Nordic Economic Union (Nordek). Among the political opponents of the EC, opinions about Nordek were divided. The Centre Party, contrary to its position in the 1950s, was positive towards closer Nordic cooperation, provided it did not contain a common agricultural policy. The Socialist People's Party, hitherto the most Nordic oriented party, voted against Nordek at its annual conference in May 1969. The argument was that Nordek was created on capitalistic principles and would function as a bridge to the EC (Bjørklund, 1981, pp. 104–105).

Negotiations on Nordek were concluded in February 1970, exactly two years after the proposal was first put forward. There were serious differences between the Nordic countries: for example, the delicate Finnish foreign political position, the Swedish enthusiasm for a common external tariff, and the Danish insistence on the creation of a common market for agriculture as well as for industrial goods. Nevertheless, a far-reaching treaty was drafted and was ready for signing in February 1970 (Vaughan, 1979, pp. 180–185). The institutional framework was still essentially intergovernmental. There would be nothing like the EC Commission, and decisions would only be by unanimous agreement in the Nordic Council of Ministers. The treaty was designed to be as flexible as possible, very much with the uncertainty about the wider European situation in mind. Some specific commitments were made, for instance on the customs union's tariff levels and transitional periods, and on the financial transfers to ease structural adaptations and stabilise primary sector products. A limited increase in agricultural trade was envisaged, to satisfy the Danes. In general, however, the treaty was essentially a framework which could later be elaborated.

In the meantime the situation inside the EC had changed, and the December 1969 Hague Summit opened the way for British, Danish, Norwegian and perhaps even Swedish membership. The final phase of the Nordek negotiations thereby coincided with preparations by three Nordic states to resume negotiations with the EC. Foreign policy reasons then caused Finland to back out of a possible a customs union with three countries which might enter the EC, and in April 1970 they indefinitely postponed the signing of the treaty (Archer, 1971, pp. 108–116). The other Nordic countries did not try to persuade Finland to revoke its decision; all three were by then preoccupied with preparations for forthcoming negotiations in Brussels.

3.4   EC Membership Negotiations and the Treaties of Accession

Before Norway began its negotiations with the EC, the *Storting* had to reaffirm the 1967 application. Entry was again made conditional on obtaining terms which would 'protect special Norwegian interests in a satisfactory manner', particularly in relation to agriculture (Stortingsmelding 92, 1969–70, p. 56). The majority in the *Storting* this time was 132 to 17, only four less than in 1967 (Lie, 1975, p. 381).

Negotiations between the EC and the four prospective members started on 30 June 1970. The success of the British application was fundamental to the other three applicants, and little was done with the Norwegian case before that of the United Kingdom was effectively concluded in June 1971. In applying, Norway had to formally accept the EC's conditions for negotiations. This meant that Norway had to abide by , at least in principle, all decisions taken on the basis of EC's treaties (the *acquis communautaire*). The EC invited Norway to participate in foreign ministers' meetings even before the outcome of the negotiations was known, an offer accepted by Norway, although its attitude to EC political cooperation was cautious. The Norwegian foreign minister made two reservations concerning the *acquis*. Norway wanted permanent special arrangements for agriculture, and required further negotiations on any EC decision on fisheries policy which did not satisfy Norwegian requirements (Allen, 1979, p. 96).

Agriculture was a central issue when the Norwegian negotiations opened in June 1971. The two sides were far apart. Norway's demands were the same as in 1967; it sought to maintain a national agricultural policy within the EC, without adapting to the common agricultural policy. The agricultural organisations opposed any change in the existing pattern and level of production: this meant no weakening of import controls, no regional arrangements confined to disadvantaged areas, no change in the powers of the producer organisations, and no change in the system of price subsidies. The EC showed some willingness to meet Norway's demands, but it would not concede permanent exceptions from the common agricultural policy. After three months of negotiations, the EC acknowledged the prospect of large income losses for Norwegian farmers as a result of membership, and promised to maintain living standards. By December 1971 a compromise was agreed, accommodating some of the Norwegian demands. The EC acknowledged the objective of preventing a fall in producers' living standards, and that Norway's natural conditions made transitional measures inadequate. While it excluded the use of price subsidies in principle, it regarded them as a possibility in the important milk sector and recognised the need for transport subsidies. However, the exceptions granted were not described as permanent, and Norway was otherwise to apply the common agricultural policy (Stortingsmelding 50, 1971–72, pp. 82–87).

On the day membership negotiations opened in June 1970, the EC concluded a new fisheries agreement providing for non-discriminatory access to member states' fishing limits. This was totally unacceptable to Norwegian fishermen. Norway had not even accepted the London Convention of 1964, which laid down a twelve-mile national limit, and a recognition of other signatories' traditional rights in the outer six miles. Norwegian fishermen demanded the permanent retention of an exclusive twelve-mile fishing limit around the coast. They also wanted the extensive rights of the Norwegian producers' organisations to continue, including compulsory membership, sales rights to the entire catch, and price and regulating rights. Norway's demands were not supported by the other applicants, but the government was prepared to fight for them.

While Denmark accepted the new EC fisheries policy, Britain and Ireland did not. Ireland was prepared to wait and see what emerged, while Britain wanted a modified version of the London Convention. The agreement signed between the Six and the other three applicants in December 1971 was ultimately based on the British proposal. The common fisheries policy of 1970 was preserved, but members would maintain the six-mile limit set by the London Convention during a ten year transitional period. The applicant countries and France were to keep the outer six-mile zone in specific areas, where the population was dependent on fishing. After ten years the question would be reconsidered (Allen, 1979, pp. 97, 120–126).

Though the EC was willing to make concession to Norway's special needs and interests, and to treat Norway as the special case it claimed to be, it was not prepared to give a legal guarantee that an exclusive twelve-mile zone would continue after the transition period. Neither did it recognise Norway's interests as vital. It also proposed to divide the Norwegian coast in two, whereby the twelve-mile exclusive fishing right zone would not apply south of Egersund (Stortingsmelding 50, 1971–72, p. 97).

The Norwegian government accepted this compromise, in spite of heavy opposition back home. In a declaration formulated as an interpretation of the agreement, the government stated that it considered the EC's assurances that special account would be taken of Norwegian coastal fisheries, as a real guarantee (Stortingsmelding 50, 1971–72, Appendix 1, p. 25). This was not received with enthusiasm in Norway; anti-marketeers considered it a capitulation, and all the various fisheries organisations were in uproar. On 17 January 1972, two days after the signing of the EC–Norwegian fisheries protocol, the fishermen's national organisation unanimously rejected it. Two days later, fisheries minister Knut Hoem resigned because of the lack of an EC guarantee for the period after 1982. There was also some dissatisfaction with the agreed provisions on capital movements and business establishment. However, all four treaties of accession were signed in Brussels on 22 January 1972.

3.5   The Norwegian Debate and Referendum

Britain, Denmark and Ireland became members of the EC on 1 January 1973, almost a year after the treaties of accession were signed. By then, however, Norwegian membership had been rejected in a politically divisive referendum in September 1972, following a heated and emotional campaign.

As in 1967, opposition in the *Storting* to EC membership was less numerous in 1969 than in 1962. Grassroots opposition, however, had grown steadily from 1961 through 1967. In 1961 the issue brought out deep sentiments, particularly among opponents of membership. In 1967, neither opponents nor proponents were particularly active. Security issues, ranging from Norway's future relations with NATO to the Vietnam war, seemed more emotive and got more attention (Lie, 1975, pp. 333, 363–372). From then onwards, the EC again became a prominent issue (Bjørklund, 1981, pp. 18–19). Nordek did not mobilise EC opposition, but the Hague Summit and the renewed British application did (Bjørklund, 1981, pp. 105–106). With the reactivating of the Norwegian EC application, opposition re-emerged, and the 'People's Movement against Norwegian membership of the Common Market' was established in August 1970. The People's Movement included veterans from the battles fought in 1962 and 1967, as well as observers from each of the political parties' youth organisations. These had all, except for the Young Conservatives, declared themselves opposed to EC membership (Bjørklund, 1981, pp. 108, 116).

The People's Movement's task was to work against Norwegian membership of the EC, and to supply information to the population. The Movement wanted to be as broad as possible, and therefore sought to avoid too close links with the agricultural organisations. However, it was largely financed by these organisations, and its public face was Arne Haugestad, who had been their information campaigner. It proved a success, drawing its membership from all parties and all sections of society. Local teams were set up all over the country, but the most outspoken were in the larger towns and cities. The arguments against membership concerned the economic consequences as well as Norwegian sovereignty. In their counter-report to the government's White Paper on Norwegian membership [Stortingsmelding nr. 50 (1971–72) Om Norges tilslutning til De Europeiske Fellesskap], they criticised the Treaty of Rome for its free-market attitudes, warned that Norwegian membership would take away politicians' control over the economy, and which would lead to social injustice (Folkebevegelsen, 1972, pp. 7–17, 31–46, 188–204).

Although the Movement was able to put forward sophisticated arguments, and had many academics in its ranks, it often preferred terse and easy to understand messages: all Norwegian fish would be taken by foreign trawlers; agriculture would be finished; small industries would be ruined and bought up by foreign capital; the north would be depopulated; the country would be invaded by foreign workers, catholic ideas, rabies, continental drinking habits; and foreigners would buy up mountain huts, lakes and forests (Allen, 1979, pp. 106–107). The Movement had an advantage over the proponents of membership in that they had started their campaign once Norway's application had been announced, while the pro-marketeers had to await the outcome of the negotiations, adopting a 'wait and see' attitude.

The centre-right coalition government had been in difficulties from the time the Norwegian application was reactivated until it resigned in March 1971. It still included anti-marketeers, but they did not provoke an open confrontation because they wanted the coalition to continue. Since the Norwegian application depended on the success of the British negotiations, the opposition did not need to press its point before these were finalised. Though the four applicants' negotiations were remarkably smooth, it proved a long time for Norwegian pro-marketeers to hold back.

In the *Storting* vote in June 1970, the Conservatives and some members of the Liberal and Christian Democrats wanted to hold the coalition together and to get Norway into the EC, while seven representatives from the Centre Party and three from the Christian Democrats voted against the renewal of the 1967 application. The rest of the Centre Party did not want to join the EC either, but hoped to achieve this end without destroying the coalition. The remaining Christian Democrats and Liberal Party members, however, were mainly concerned with resolving the serious splits within their own parties, and did not participate with any vigour in the debate (Stortingsforhandlinger, 1970).

The government's dilemma came to an end on 2 March 1971, when it resigned. The middle parties were then free to oppose EC membership. For most pro-marketeers, including the Conservatives, the installation of a Labour minority government – also committed to finalise the negotiations – was a step forward as the coalition government had included elements opposed to membership. The Labour Party still had its controversies over the question, but was in general more united than the coalition government (Pharo, 1991, p. 31; Bergh, 1987a, pp. 496–503; Lie, 1975, pp. 214–239).

The new Labour government conducted and finalised the EC negotiations, which had scarcely begun by March 1971. As a minority government, it was dependent on support from the non-socialist parties in the *Storting*, but it was relatively secure in that there was little prospect of the non-socialist parties working together before the EC question was settled. The resignation in January 1972 of the fisheries minister was an ill omen both for the future for the government and the referendum result, but the conclusion of the negotiations in January 1972 seemed to boost the EC proponents, who could finally start their campaign. The Labour Party abandoned its 'wait and see' policy, and the 'Yes to the EC' campaign was initiated in March. The People's Movement's strategy in response was to hold out until the referendum in September. In August the government announced that it would resign in the event of a No-majority. Some days before the referendum, the energy director of the EEC Commission, Ferdinand Spaak, held a speech in London where he outlined the Commission's ideas for a common energy policy. This implied that Norway's oil would become a 'Community resource' once Norway had joined the EC (*Dagbladet*, 22 September, 1972). This leaked statement may have cost the pro-EC campaign dearly.

The people's verdict fell on 25 September 1972: 53.5% voted against EC membership, and 46.5% for (Central Bureau of Statistics, 1972, p. 30). Within the *Storting* the opposition to EC membership had grown from 17 in March 1970 to 40 in September 1972 (Bjørklund, 1981, p. 306). However, in the year up to the referendum, the Yes-side had gained in the polls, increasing from September 1971 to September 1972 by 12.4%. Half of this increase came from the 'uncertain' group, and the other half came from opponents (Bjørklund, 1981, pp. 333). In a September 1971 poll, 49% were opposed to membership, 27% were uncertain, and 24% were in favour. Only 79.2% of the electorate voted in the referendum, or 6–7% fewer than was usual at ordinary elections; and contrary to what election experts had foreseen (Bjørklund, 1981, pp. 171, 360). A most likely explanation of this increased abstention was that a number of Labour voters were torn between their desire to keep their party in power and their wish to stay out of the EC. They resolved their dilemma by staying at home. A week later, on the 2 October, the Danish referendum brought the opposite result, with 63.4% voting in favour of EC membership and 36.6% against, and with an extraordinary turnout of 90.4% (Martens, 1979).

3.6   The Aftermath

The referendum result meant the end of the Labour government. A new centrist minority government, consisting of the newly split Liberal Party, the Christian Democrats and the Centre Party, took over on 12 October 1972. This government had such a narrow base that it could not have functioned under normal circumstances; it was installed solely to deal with negotiations for a free trade agreement with the EC. Norway signed such an agreement in April 1973, and this came into effect the following July. The individual agreements between EFTA countries and the EC secured free trade between EFTA and the two former EFTA countries, Britain and Denmark, and set up a schedule for the elimination of the tariff barriers between each EFTA country and the EC. Agricultural products and fish were not included in these agreements.

Politically, the debate leading up to the referendum and the referendum itself created new features in the landscape. It brought old latent political cleavages both between and within parties into the open (Aardal and Valen, 1989, p. 19; Allen, 1979, pp. 159–160, 191–194; Bjørklund & Nilson, 1981, pp. 31–32; Øidne, 1958, pp. 97–114; Rokkan, 1967, pp. 367–444; Rokkan, 1970; Rokkan and Valen, 1964; Valen, 1973, pp. 214–215; Valen and Rokkan, 1974). For Norway's oldest party, the Liberal Party, it meant an irreparable split and a decline into insignificance. Already in November 1972 the majority of the party's representatives in the *Storting*, including the chairman Helge Seip, had broken away and formed the New People's Party. The split came after an attempt to prevent the party entering into government with the anti-EC Centre Party and the Christian Democrats, following the referendum. The pro-EC Conservatives had also refused to join the anti-EC government.

The Labour Party itself lost members of the 'Labour Movement's Information Committee against Norwegian Membership of the EEC' [Arbeiderbevegelsens Informasjonskomité] to the new Socialist Electoral Alliance [Sosialistisk Valgallianse], a left-wing group also consisting of members of the Socialist People's Party and the Communist Party. These were forces the Labour leadership had successfully marginalised since 1946, but which then damaged the party's electoral chances well into the 1970s. Many of the non-voters in the referendum were loyal party supporters who got caught in the middle, including traditional Labour voters who opposed membership (Valen, 1973, p. 221; *Arbeiderbladet*, 6 August 1994, pp. 8–9). As an answer to the disastrous effect the referendum had on Labour Party support, the party radicalised its programme for the 1973 election (Nyhamar, 1990, p. 207), but still it lost 250 000 voters.

The EC battle created, in other words, a confusing disorder in Norwegian politics. While the battle ended after the referendum, many of its divisions continued. Although the establishment of Anders Lange's anti-tax party [ALP] and the Workers' Communist Party – marxist-leninists [AKP-ml] came in the wake of the referendum, it is more unclear whether they were directly related to the actual conflict. The indirect connection, however, was that the conflict had changed the general political situation. New conflicts had surfaced, and the trust in the established leadership was reduced. The situation was favourable to those who wanted to advance new alternatives (Grønmo, 1975, pp. 119–153). It therefore seems unlikely that they would have seen the light of day without the upheavals caused by the referendum.

Socially, the referendum divided the country between town and countryside, and between north and south-east. These two historic divisions – an urban-rural axis and a centre-periphery axis – had not been evident in then recent elections (Heradstveit, 1975, pp. 7–19). Support for membership increased with urbanisation and in densely populated communities, while it decreased in smaller and sparsely populated communities and in those dependent on the primary sector. The East Central part of Norway was the only region with a majority for membership, whereas in the North 71.5% voted against (Central Bureau of Statistics, 1972, pp. 38–39, 41). The agricultural and the fisheries sectors proved their political strength, and demonstrated that the regions – together with allies in the towns – could turn down membership. The left-right division was also present in the referendum result, with Conservatives most strongly in favour of membership. A third area of divisiveness was between the elite and the grassroots (Gleditsch, 1972, pp. 795–804; Hellevik and Gleditsch, 1973, p. 229). This was a little more disputable, but was more obvious in relationship to the Labour Party and the trade unions. The referendum demonstrated a gap between voters – 53.5% against membership – and their representatives in the *Storting*, of whom a little over 40 out of 150 were against membership in September 1972 (Bjørklund, 1981, pp. 305–306). On the leadership level the radicals constituted the core of the opposition in urban areas (Valen, 1973, pp. 218–219).

Despite its poor showing, the Labour Party formed a government in October 1973, relying on the Socialist Electoral Alliance's 16 seats in the *Storting*. The two socialist parties had a majority of only one seat over the six non-socialist parties. Though fragile, the Labour government was relatively secure; and time was not yet ripe for a non-social-ist coalition including the Conservative Party, while a centrist coalition was still no alternative. Under these conditions no one was eager to discuss the EC question. The government's priority was to make the difficult political system work, and to implement the free trade agreement. The Labour Party also aimed to win back its lost supporters, especially among voters linked to the primary sector.

In 1973 the government was confronted with a number of tasks in relation to the enlarged EC. First, it was necessary to secure Norway's economic interests. The starting point was the free trade agreement, which worked satisfactorily and was important to the country's economic well-being. Because Norway did not join the EC in 1973, it was able to formulate its fisheries and oil policies independent of the complicated cooperation mechanisms of the Community. Seen in isolation, this was advantageous (Frydenlund, 1982, p. 79). The government was also eager to rebut speculation both in Norway and abroad that the country's foreign political stance had changed in the direction of greater political isolation. Lastly, it was important to build bridges over the divisions caused by the EC battle. The government sought to achieve this through an active European policy, towards both the EC and towards the rest of Europe.

In the first years after the referendum it was difficult for the Labour government to practice 'an active European policy'. Many were suspicious about what was seen as an attempt to bring Norway into the EC through the back door. General interest in the EC waned (Frydenlund, 1982, p.80). Nor was the EC, adjusting to enlargement, particularly interested in Norway.

After the conclusion of the free trade agreement with the EC, the Norwegian economy prospered. For a year and a half after the Norwegian referendum, the Western industrial economies generally did well; they were then hit by recession. In Norway, however, growth continued, with low employment and rising living standards. A major cause of this was the Norwegian supply of oil, foreign demand for which grew steadily. With the price of oil rising, foreign capital kept flowing into the country and investment levels stayed high (Hanisch and Nerheim, 1992, p. 406).

Integration with the EC continued after 1972 as what was originally meant as a trade agreement became much more extensive. This was done without protest from the No-side in the Labour Party with even the staunch membership opponent Hallvard Bakke having no difficulties in continuing this policy line while he was trade minister.[5] The EC debate did however influence Norwegian oil policy. A White Paper from the Ministry of Finance followed the EC debate (Stortingsmelding 25, 1973–1974) and had a 'red-green' profile, emphasising the importance of national (i.e. state) control of oil resources. This formed the basis of Norwegian oil policy in the following years (Hanisch and Nerheim, 1992, p.412).

In the September 1977 general election it was clear that the EC question was no longer part of day-to-day politics. The two parties which had tried to get Norway into the EC regained their former support and strength. Labour won over 42% of the vote, taking 76 seats in the Storting, an increase of 15 from 1973. The Conservatives took 42 seats, a gain of 12. The Socialist Left Party retained only 2 of their 16 seats. The Liberals held on to their 2 seats, despite losing votes. and the Centre Party held only 12 of their 21 seats. Neither the New People's Party nor Anders Lange's Party won seats (Central Bureau of Statistics, 1977). The result enabled the Labour Party to stay in office, dependent on support from the Socialist Left and the Liberals. This situation made it unlikely that the question of the EC membership would be raised in the short term. The Labour Party was dependent on two anti-EC parties, the Socialist Left and the Liberals, and the Conservative Party depended on close cooperation with the Christian Democrats and the Centre Party (Allen, 1979, p. 205). The pro-EC Conservatives wisely backed away from the issue. While the immediate impact of the referendum battle on the political parties had been overcome, the longer term effect endured and was still keenly felt into the 1990s.

Buoyed by high expectations of income from oil, the government introduced a counter-cyclical policy from 1975 to the end of the 1970s, with the unanimous approval of the *Storting* (Hanisch and Nerheim, 1992, pp. 442–445). The general recession and the exploitation of oil radically restructured Norway's industry. Traditional industries and shipping declined, while oil and oil-related industry expanded rapidly. Industry, research and training changed course. Norway was quickly transformed into an oil economy, heavily dependent on oil revenues (Hanisch and Nerheim, 1992, p. 467). Oil also made Norway a more interesting proposition for the EC.

3.7   Conclusions

The 1972 referendum result represented a response by the Norwegian electorate to their perception of events around them. It was not just an answer to the question on the ballot paper, but more a statement concerning the sort of society desired. By 1972 Norway had become one of the richer countries in Europe, mainly through utilisation of its raw materials – even in the pre-oil period – for export. However, it had managed to protect a way of life for the rural communities. Even if they were in decline, small settlements still made up a third of the population, and small industry provided employment out of proportion to its contribution to the Gross Domestic Product. Government in Oslo may not always be trusted but the various economic groups – especially the farmers, the forestry industry, the fishermen and the small communities – had privileged access to the ministries and members of parliament. In other words, Norway worked as a political and economic entity for these groups. Those in jobs that were possibly threatened by remaining outside the high tariffs imposed by the EC on Norwegian manufacturing exports, represented a small group, as only about 7% of the country's exports to the EC fell into this category (Stortingsmelding 50, 1971–72, pp. 65 –71). The argument by Otto Brox that sizeable groups of Norwegians felt their material and economic conditions threatened by EC membership seems plausible (1972, p.772). Workers saw their class interests under threat by a grouping that they saw as having less advanced social welfare and work conditions than in Norway, and the countryside voted for its own cultural maintenance (ibid., p.782).

It was therefore not unreasonable to expect a large section of the Norwegian population not to be well-disposed to the EC in 1972. The campaign seemed to have confirmed that position, with the No side playing exactly on the sensitive points mentioned. Against this, the political and economic establishment advised a Yes vote, and the key state in these matters – the United Kingdom – was also joining the Communities. That, together with the government making the vote a matter of confidence, led to 46.5% of those voting agreeing to membership. The No vote was there to be mobilised, and it was.

The European question from 1970 to 1972 created extensive debate in the public, as well as in the *Storting*, and it had both short-term and long-term effects on political life in Norway. A relative short-term effect was the distrust of the Labour Party leadership by its adherents, shown by the disastrous 1973 election for the party. By the 1977 election, however, Labour was back. A more stable change after 1972 was the extension of the party system and change of the party structure. The division of the Liberal Party, caused by the referendum, left an empty space which the Conservative Party partly filled. This was especially true for the Liberal Party's old core areas in Southern and Western Norway (Bjørklund & Nilson, 1981, p. 104). The 1977 election was also a victory for the Conservative Party. Long term, the electorate became more unstable from the 1970s. Political waves and currents turned quickly and changed the party political climate (Bjørklund & Nilson, 1981, p. 125), with a conservative wave breaking in Norway by the end of the 1970s.

The turbulence described above in Norway's European integration policy contrasts with the relative stability achieved by this time in its security policy (see Chapter 9). By the time of the 1972 referendum, Norway had institutionalised the US commitment to the country's defence within a NATO context and common structure. Nothing within either the moribund WEU nor within the EC itself suggested a strong necessity for Norway to support the creation of a West European defence entity. As with integration policy, the tendency was still to follow the United Kingdom's lead. This external impetus to integration policy came to a halt with the September 1972 referendum but was not matched by any disengagement in the defence field. If anything, that result encouraged Norwegian governments to be more determined in their Atlantic commitments for fear that rejection of the EC could suggest isolation in the security sphere.

Notes

1   The five were the then EC members apart from France.

2   The Centre Party – as the Agrarians had become in 1959 – had a close clientele relationship with the farmers' organizations. The electoral system also gave the rural areas more seats than if weighted only by population size.

3   In addition to its membership in EFTA, Norway had participated actively in GATT and in the OEEC, which after 1961 was reorganised and renamed to OECD. All these organisations had successfully been liberalising European trade for over a decade.

4   All referenda in Norway are consultative, as opposed to Denmark for example. Before the referendum in 1972 there had been four referenda in Norway, two in connection with the break up of the union with Sweden in 1905, and two in connection with the alcohol policy after the First World War – one resulting in a ban in 1919, and one removing the ban in 1926.

5   Interview with Bernt Bull, 21.12.94. Hallvard Bakke was trade minister from January 1976 to October 1979.

4

Finding a Formula 1977–1993

4.1 Background

After the 1972 referendum Norway remained in a reduced EFTA. It signed a free trade agreement with the EC, and developed cooperation in various areas. The 1973 general election brought the Labour Party back to power as a fragile minority government, and all talk of a Norwegian EC membership ceased. For fifteen years the European Community almost disappeared from the political agenda; the non-existence of the issue was an unspoken agreement between all the political parties. Even the governing Labour Party had to approach the issue cautiously, and it concentrated primarily on concluding the European Economic Area (EEA) agreement. The EC question was not officially opened to debate until late 1991, after the Labour government agreed to the terms of the EEA Treaty. During this period the framework for Norway's relations with European integration was one whereby that process followed an uncertain road but then accelerated towards the end of the 1980s.

At a Summit in Luxembourg in April 1984, the EFTA governments and EC representatives launched the idea of the 'European Economic Space' (Agence international d'information pour la presse, 9–10 April 1984) which would extend the range of cooperation between the two blocs. The President of the EC Commission, Jacques Delors followed up the increased EC goodwill towards EFTA by advancing two options for future EC-EFTA relations: a continuation of the bilateral model, with a free trade area as an ultimate aim, or a new, more structured relationship with common decision-making and administrative institutions. He favoured the latter (Official Journal of the EC, 1988–9, p. 75).

Between the 1984 Summit and Delors's January 1989 speech two events particularly affected the EFTA countries. First, in June 1985 EC leaders at the Milan Council agreed on the White Paper on the single European market, which led to the Single European Act of 1986. Secondly, by 1989 the EC had grown to twelve members as Spain and Portugal joined on 1 January 1986 (Greece had joined in January 1981). The potential market represented by the EC was thus still larger and more attractive for the EFTA countries. The EC, in other words, was both deepening and widening, and this made it more disadvantageous economically to remain outside (Archer and Butler, 1996, p. 163).

Norway had one economic advantage that other European states outside the EC lacked – its offshore oil and gas. In 1969 a large oil find had been made at the Ekofisk field in the Norwegian sector and this was followed by other discoveries. Official policy was that this bounty would be exploited at a moderate pace and the importance for Norwegian society in the long-run was recognised (Stortingsmelding 25, 1973–74). In the end, the market tended to dictate the terms of exploitation of these resources. Norway benefited from the upturn of oil prices in 1973–4 and 1979–81, but then suffered when the world oil price collapsed in 1985–6. Nevertheless, the gradual infusion of petroleum money into the Norwegian economy during the 1970s helped that country at a time when most of the EC states were suffering from increased oil prices.

This did not mean that the Norwegian economy was in good shape. The government allowed a combination of high wage settlements and generous support for industry and agriculture. This increased inflation to a postwar record in Norway of 14% in 1977 (Moses & Tranøy, 1995, p. 113). Meanwhile Norway had slipped into the EC-based currency agreement – 'the snake' – in 1972 and stayed there until the end of 1978. The aim was to obtain some stability after the end of the Bretton Woods system between 1971 to 1973. However, this did not stop Norwegian governments from devaluing the krone four times, partly to ease the unemployment situation within the country (ibid., p. 115). From the start of the 1980s the government pumped money into the economy, first at a time of depression and later when there was an economic upswing. Credit was easy and the banks were deregulated. Private consumption rose and Norway entered its brief 'Yuppie' period. This fell apart with the steep fall in oil prices from 1985 to 1986 and the subsequent decline in government revenues. The krone was devalued by 10% in May 1986 and the government set a new course of having a fixed exchange rate and stable prices (ibid., pp. 114–6).

The period from the late 1970s to the end of the 1980s was one of political weakness and change in Norway. The Labour government from 1973 to 1981 rested on the support of the Socialist Electoral Alliance (later Socialist Left Party) with its belief in public spending. The Conservatives took over government in 1981, first as a minority administration and then in coalition with the Christian Democrats and the Centre Party. The three parties sometimes seemed to have little in common except being in the same government. A minority Labour administration was returned in 1986 after the collapse of the centre-right government, and it found it could bolster its majority from the centre as well as from the left, thus giving it more room for manoeuvre on difficult policy matters. However, it lost power in 1990 to a centre-right coalition that was so precarious that it fell within a year.

The 1992 decision to apply for EC membership was the result of a process involving both internal discussion and a response to external events. The eventful period between the end of 1989 and November 1992 cast the whole EC issue in a different light. The simultaneous collapse of the Soviet Union and negotiations at Maastricht at the end of 1991 reshaped the political geography of Europe, with the EC/EU emerging as the most dominant feature in the landscape.

4.2   Knut Frydenlund's European Dream

At the end of the 1970s, the political aspects of the EC resurfaced in Norwegian policy debates. The 1972–73 EC–EFTA free trade agreements on industrial products were basically fulfilled in 1977, and in May 1977 EFTA leaders decided that they wanted closer cooperation with the EC. This resulted in multilateral negotiations on technical problems in connection with the free trade area, including among other things rules of origin and administrative trade barriers. For the first time, the EC treated EFTA as an independent cooperation partner. However, these multilateral negotiations were limited in scope, and all other aspects of cooperation were dealt with bilaterally. When the international economic climate again deteriorated at the end of the 1970s, both multilateral and bilateral negotiations broke down, though the planned reduction of tariffs continued.

When the Labour Foreign Minister, Knut Frydenlund, in his statement to the *Storting* February 1979 discussed Norway's relationship to the EC, it was the first time since the referendum this was dealt with extensively (Frydenlund, 1982, p. 82; Stortingstidende, 1978–79, pp. 2172–74). It became the subject of a thorough debate, and set out the basis for any future relationship. The main conclusion, that Norway should extend its cooperation with the EC, was approved by the *Storting*. Discussions with the EC led to regular, more formal, contacts between Norwegian authorities and the EC Commission (Frydenlund, 1982, p. 82).

Prime Minister Odvar Nordli's visit to Brussels in November 1980 added a political element to Norway's relationship to the EC, which had hitherto been lacking. It was decided that a Norwegian delegation and the Commission should meet annually at the political level. These high-level meetings were to outline the nature of the future relationship between the EC and Norway, and to discuss political and economic issues going beyond the free trade area. Norway also established closer contacts with European Political Cooperation (EPC) after November 1980. In contrast to before, the Norwegian side now stressed the foreign and security policies of the EC. Foreign Minister Knut Frydenlund underlined the role of the EC in the changing relations between East and West. Martin Sæter claims that Norway was trying to demonstrate an orientation towards the EC in foreign policy, and that the change of emphasis was surprisingly uncontroversial in Norwegian politics (Sæter, 1985, p. 176; Frydenlund, 1982, pp. 78–84). This reorientation did not, however, diminish Norway's strong Atlantic links and its trust in NATO (see Chapter 9).

Foreign Minister Frydenlund's active European initiative aimed at a closer working relationship with the EPC and was followed up internally in the Labour Party. A working group set up by the Labour Party's international committee, and chaired by Bernt Bull, worked for two years and delivered a report – *Norge i Europa. Program 85* – in 1984. Its recommendations were not very radical when it came to Norway's political integration with the EC. In line with official Norwegian policy it suggested an extension of Norway's cooperation with the EPC, and that Norway should work towards greater cooperation between the EC and EFTA. It did, however, go further when came to security. Here it stressed the importance of Norway participating, together with the rest of the Western European NATO countries, in the reshaping of the Western European Union (WEU). The press interpreted this as support for Norwegian membership of the WEU, which brought strong negative reactions from the Labour Youth wing (AUF), among others.

The relationship between the EC and EFTA was monitored by Norway from 1977, with some adjustments such as the Frydenlund initiative. In the summer of 1983, a Conservative Party committee led by Thor Knudsen, President of the Upper Chamber of the *Storting*, concluded that Norway should become a member of the EC (Norge og Europa, 1983). However, as the Conservative Party was in government with the Centre Party and the Christian Democrats – staunch opponents of the EC – their report was quickly buried. The question of EC membership was still judged controversial and divisive. Thus nothing was done politically to change the relationship between the EC and EFTA until the 1984 Luxembourg meeting.

4.3   Europe Relaunched, 1984–89: EFTA's New Approach

In January 1984 the EC and EFTA established a free trade area for industrial products; for some sensitive products, fulfilling the earlier agreements had taken until then. In 1980 Norway signed a fisheries agreement with the EC. Imports from the EC had steadily been around 45% of Norway's total imports since the start of the trade agreement. The share of Norway's exports going to the EC had increased, from around 47% in 1973 to 70% in 1983. This huge increase was mainly due to Norway's new exports, oil and gas (Sæter, 1985, p. 177).

The Declaration of the EC and EFTA states in April 1984 did not initially attract much public attention in Norway. The Norwegian government began to concentrate on European questions again the following year, only after the EC had decided on the creation of the internal market and the Single European Act (Stortingstidende, 1985–86, pp. 1269–1276; Sæter and Knudsen, 1991, p. 182).

The issue was still very sensitive in Norway, and little action was taken before the Single European Act in 1986. By then the Labour Party was back in office, and its official policy was that Norway needed to reconsider its relationship with the EC, because of the changes within the organisation itself. The government stressed that any decision would not be rushed. Speaking to the *Storting* in June 1986, Foreign Minister Knut Frydenlund, the architect of this active European policy, made it quite clear that the question of EC membership was not on the agenda for that *Storting*, which meant until September 1989 (Stortingstidende., 1985–86, p. 3063). External events might suggest a re-evaluation; Norwegian politics suggested a cautious process.

4.4   Norwegian Activity

In May 1987 the Foreign Ministry presented a report to the *Storting* entitled 'Norway, the EC and European cooperation'. The report analysed the different dimensions of European integration, as well as the government's chosen policy. Though it did not consider Norwegian EC membership, it did recommend closer cooperation with the EC within the existing framework, with special emphasis on the development of the EC–EFTA link. Of special interest to Norway were the internal market, cooperation on technology and research, and political cooperation (EPC). Practical consultations between Norway and the EC were to be developed, and the report proposed several areas for consultative committees (Stortingsmelding 61, 1986–87, p. 6). The *Storting* Committee on Foreign and Constitutional Affairs gave its comments on the report in May 1988 (Innst. S. 244, 1987–88), and a *Storting* debate took place in June. This ended in full support for the general lines of government policy, with little adverse comment (Stortingstidende, 1987–88, pp. 3880–3923). The Centre Party spoke out against the adjustments already made by Norway to the EC, while the Conservative Party signalled its wish for Norwegian membership of the EC. In autumn 1988 the Conservative Party was already determined to work towards membership, but the Labour Party still rejected any debate on the issue.

Following Delors's January 1989 address, the EFTA countries started to work more closely together, and they stepped up their contacts with the EC. On a Norwegian initiative, an EFTA Summit was held in Oslo in March 1989, and this confirmed EFTA's support for the formalisation of the European Economic Space (EFTA Bulletin, 1989). Point 11 of the Summit declaration stated that EFTA did not want to rule out any alternatives in its dialogue with the EC – a reflection of Austria's existing application for full membership. EFTA countries were prepared to negotiate in many areas, including:

- the fullest possible realisation of 'the four freedoms' (free movement of goods, services, capital and people) with the aim of creating a dynamic and homogenous European Economic Space;
- cooperation beyond the internal market, including such issues as the environment, education and social affairs;
- a more structured community with common decision-making and administrative institutions, with the aim of greater efficiency (St. meld. 61, 1986–1987, pp. 4–7).

Meeting in Brussels some days after the Oslo summit, EC and EFTA foreign ministers supported the notion of further cooperation and spawned a host of committees. A common steering group at official level, the High-Level Steering Group (HLSG) was set up and it established five working groups, all of which delivered their conclusions in October 1989. By November, the EC Council of Ministers decided to start negotiations on the basis of these investigations. In December, EC and EFTA leaders agreed to work towards a European Economic Area (as it was now called) as from 1 January 1993 – parallel to the creation of the Single European Market. This arrangement was intended to secure the EFTA countries' participation in the internal market and strengthen cooperation between all countries concerned.

4.5   The Incompatible Centre-Right Government

The Labour government found it difficult to win support for this policy. The Conservative Party tried to open a debate on Norwegian EC membership by announcing an active EC policy and rejecting the government's EFTA line a few days after the Storting endorsed the government's general European policy in June 1988. This effort was not successful, but it challenged the Centre Party which immediately made it clear that it would not enter a membership-seeking government (*Dagbladet*, 21 September 1989). Conservative EC policy became less outspoken during the spring of 1989, for two reasons. In the first place, the EC itself – in the form of Commission President, Jacques Delors – clearly supported the EC–EFTA cooperation line; secondly, there were indications that the September 1989 general election might bring the Conservatives back to power.

The election did indeed lead to a change of government. A centre-right coalition, consisting of the Conservative Party, the Centre Party and the Christian Democrats took office in October 1989. This heralded a change of attitude towards the idea of broadening of EC–EFTA relations, but not in the direction expected of a centre–right government led by the pro-EC Conservative, Jan P. Syse. The two coalition partners were less than enthusiastic about closer relations with the EC. The Centre Party was arguably even more anti-EC by 1989 than in 1972, and the Christian Democrats were hesitant. The government quickly arrived at a restrictive attitude towards the EC issue.

In its inaugural statement, the Lysebu declaration, the new government ruled out both a customs union and the free movement of persons between EFTA and the EC

(Regjeringens informasjonsutvalg for Europasaker, 1990, Annex 16). Being in office meant that all the three parties had to soften their attitudes. The Centre Party and the Christian Democrats had accused the Labour government of keeping negotiations between the EC and EFTA secret. Yet the coalition government took over the Labour Party's European policy. The new government's approach was based on the European Report issued by the Labour government in May 1987 (Sæter and Knudsen, 1991, p. 182). Criticism of the Labour Party ceased, and the three governing parties actively cooperated.

The customs union and the free movement of persons were the most controversial issues for the government. However, a month after the Lysebu declaration, Kaci Kullmann Five, the Conservative trade minister, softened the government's categorical rejection of a customs union option. In her statement to the Storting, she referred to the results of the EC–EFTA Working Group I – on the free movement of goods – which had been functioning since the Oslo Summit of March 1989. The working group found that joint EC–EFTA targets could be reached through either a fundamentally enhanced free trade area or a customs union. The trade minister stated her government's preference for the former. She also stressed the need for continued limitation of labour movement within a European Economic Area (Stortingstidende., 1989–90, pp. 565–570). This statement signalled that the Centre Party had changed its attitude since the Lysebu agreement. Hitherto it had firmly rejected a customs union, but by November 1989 it accepted an investigation of both alternatives.

This about-turn did not go unremarked in the Storting debate of 1 December 1989 (Stortingstidende, 1989–90, pp. 1075–1153.). The debate included the trade minister's statement and the Standing Committee on Finance's recently published proposal on Norway's adjustment to the EC's internal market. The majority in the Finance Committee – the Labour Party, the Progress Party and the northern-based Aune list – agreed to keep open the customs union option. Committee members from the coalition parties reaffirmed the government's support for the trade minister's statement, while Socialist Left Party members were alone in opposing a customs union. The Centre Party's about-turn was vigorously challenged in the debate, especially by the Socialist Left Party. In response Johan J. Jakobsen, the Centre Party's leader, stated that the party had not changed its policy since its March 1989 annual conference (Stortingstidende, 1989–90, p. 1130). The question of a customs union was later dropped from the EEA negotiations, and the centre–right government went along with the timetable already adopted for EEA dealings with the EC.

The Lysebu declaration represented a compromise between three very different parties with varying election promises. The government sought to show its willingness to keep these many promises, however incompatible they were. The incentive of coming into government was decisive for all three parties in arriving at this compromise. The question of Norway's relation to the EC remained extremely sensitive; the Conservatives, the strongest proponents of membership, entered government with the staunchest anti-EC parties, the Centre Party and the Christian Democrats.

Both Labour and the Conservatives had for some time been interested in closer cooperation with the EC, and the Labour Party had begun to study the issue in detail. Because of the negative experience from 1972, the Labour Party was reluctant to initiate a public debate. Mrs Brundtland and the then party secretary Thorbjørn Jagland had already agreed in 1988 to take out the vital sentence which had been in the Labour Party's programme since 1973 about respecting the referendum result, and change it to a sentence saying that Norway's relationship with the EU should be based on Norway's interests (Jagland, 1994, p. 8). After the 1989 general election, Labour showed some willingness to raise the question (*Dagens Næringsliv*, 7 October 1989). Yet public attention in the spring of 1990 was focused on the great changes in Eastern Europe, and not on the start of the EEA negotiations. The EFTA countries were taken up with preparing their own negotiating positions.

Within a year, the centre–right government ran into difficulties. Prompted by the Centre Party, in September 1990 it proposed an exemption from EC regulations for Norwegian laws which favoured Norwegian business over foreign investment. The Commission responded negatively, but the Centre Party would not compromise. This and a number of issues divided the government parties. The government submitted its resignation on 29 October 1990, ending a phase of fragile cooperation. A minority Labour Party under Gro Harlem Brundtland immediately took office, relying on Centre Party support on most social and economic issues. A year of conflict and compromise was over, and the Centre Party could finally throw itself into the EC battle.

4.6   The EEA Negotiations and Internal Politics

The EEA negotiations had started on 20 June 1990 after a year of preparation. The hope of reaching an agreement by the end of the year was soon abandoned, as was the next target of the following summer. But, in the end, the Labour government congratulated itself on having successfully concluded the European Economic Area agreement by 21 October 1991.

After the Labour Party returned to power in November 1990 it made great efforts to conclude the negotiations with the Commission. However, more time was needed than anticipated. Initially the negotiations were to be concluded at the EC Summit in Luxembourg on 18 June 1991, and after this meeting, trade minister Eldrid Nordbø informed the Storting that a political decision had been reached (Stortingstidende, 1991a, pp. 4482–6). However, in August the government had to call an extraordinary Storting session to explain that an agreement had not been reached in spite of earlier declarations (UD-informasjon, 20 August 1991; 21 August 1991). This was an obvious embarrassment for the Labour government, and the Centre Party knew how to make the most of it.

During the spring of 1991, while the Labour Party went ahead with the settling of the EEA agreement, the Centre Party stepped up its campaign as the main opponent of the government line. Anne Enger Lahnstein had been the new party leader since March 1991. She showed bulldog persistence in the battle against the EEA. The Centre Party's national leadership conference at the end of June unanimously decided to oppose the EEA agreement. This Norwegian battle over Europe thus reached a peak in the summer of 1991. The Centre Party's activism coincided with the government's mistake of presenting the EEA result prematurely. There was more to come.

After the centre–right coalition government split over the EEA issue and resigned in October 1990, it was somewhat easier for the new Labour government to have a distinct and positive EEA policy. The question of EC membership, or any steps beyond the EEA, however, were still avoided. The Centre Party, on the other hand, forcefully discussed the issue, and did its best to put the EEA agreement in a bad light. This strategy seemed successful. The Labour leadership were reluctant to see the whole European issue brought up during the September 1991 local elections, but the Centre Party, the Socialist Left and anti-EC elements in the Labour Party pushed the issue on the agenda (*Dagbladet*, 4 September 1991). The local election results showed startling support for the Centre Party. The party gained 90,000 new votes, giving them 12% of the vote. This came as a surprise, and it signalled that the electorate perhaps had become more preoccupied with the EC question. Part of the Centre Party's strategy was to force the new Labour government to admit that it intended to apply for full EC membership. The government repeatedly denied this was so.

The Conservative Party also tried to pressure the Labour government, in this case to encourage an application for full membership. The pressure became more outspoken after Sweden decided to apply, in the summer of 1991 (UD-informasjon, 13 June 1991). In the state of nation debate [*trontaledebatten*] in the Storting in October 1991, the Centre Party, the Socialist Left Party, the Christian Democrats and the Progress Party all proposed that the EEA agreement be put to a referendum. This was voted down by Labour and the Conservatives (Stortingstidende, 1991b).

4.7   The European Economic Area Agreement

The European Economic Area agreement was finally concluded on 21 October 1991, to take effect from 1 January 1993. It was by far the most extensive economic agreement Norway had signed, surpassing even the EC membership agreement of 1972. The EEA process stipulated adaptation by the EFTA countries to the EC's internal market. It had an increasing speed and scope of process, and it established common institutions for the implementation and monitoring of the agreement. It also meant that Paragraph 93 of the Constitution was used for the first time, as will be outlined below.

A precondition for the accession to EEA agreement was a fulfilment of the basic EC principles of European identity, democratic reliability and respect for human rights. The EFTA countries also had to agree to the *acquis communautaire* (the body of primary and secondary legislation making up the Communities' framework) and to show an openness towards the Treaty's future political objectives (the *finalité politique*). The EEA negotiations focused on adjustment by the EFTA countries to the EC's internal market and its four freedoms of movement of goods, services, capital and labour. This entailed open competition for public procurement, the harmonisation of product standards, the free movement of capital, open competition in services and the free movement of persons. The option of a customs union was put aside when the negotiations began, in favour of discussions of this enhanced free trade area. Because the EEA did not include the elimination of border controls as planned by the EC countries, the harmonisation of sales tax and other indirect taxes, and of agricultural standards, was not necessary for EFTA. Adjustment to the EC's Common Agricultural Policy was not required since the EEA agreement did not include adherence to the common agricultural or fisheries policies.

The EEA agreement did include limited free trade in fish and agricultural products. This was part of a package linking agriculture and fisheries to the establishment of a regional fund for the development of poorer regions within the EC; EFTA countries were to contribute financially to this fund. Over five years, 500 million ECU in grants and 1.5 billion ECU in low-interest loans were to be disbursed. A separate bilateral fisheries agreement between Norway and the EC followed the EC principle of allowing access to the EC market in exchange for access to Norwegian resources (Innst. S. nr. 15, 1992–93). This accorded with an EC principle which was highly unpopular in Norway. The EC's quota of arctic cod within the Norwegian economic zone north of 62 degrees latitude was to increase gradually from 2.14% to 2.90% of the largest catch allowed. The EC would also receive an extra quota of 7,250 tonnes of cod in 1994, increasing to 11,000 tonnes in 1997. These increases would be reciprocated with quotas of other species of fish for Norwegian fishermen in the EC's fisheries zone (Regjeringens informasjonsutvalg for Europasaker, 1994, pp. 16–17).

The EFTA countries had to adapt to EC legislation in competition law – a main pillar of the internal market. In exchange, the EC agreed not to apply anti-dumping measures against EFTA exports (Regjeringens informasjonsutvalg for Europasaker, 1994, pp. 12–13). Some adjustments would also be made to a number of flanking policies: research and development, information services, education, training and youth, environment, social policy, consumer protection, small and medium sized enterprises, tourism and the audio visual sector.

The question of common institutions was one of the most difficult issues of the EEA negotiations. The EC's rules and regulations for the internal market were the point of departure, and the EFTA countries were expected to adapt to them. One implied consequence was the establishment of an EEA Council to set guidelines, give political impetus to the implementation of the agreement, assess its development and decide on amendments. The Council would consist of one member from each EFTA government and each EC government, together with representatives of the EC Commission. Decisions in the Council, which would meet twice a year, were to be taken by agreement between EC on the one hand and the EFTA states on the other. An EEA Joint Committee would also be established, with the responsibility of ensuring the agreement. Any party could raise any matter causing difficulty. The Joint Committee would comprise representatives of the EFTA and EC states and the EC Commission; the decision procedure would be the same as in the EEA Council.

The EEA agreement also stipulated an EFTA Surveillance Authority (ESA), which was to ensure compliance with the agreement's obligations by EFTA states.[1] Together with the EC Commission, it was also to ensure a uniform surveillance policy and to receive complaints about the application of the agreement. An EFTA Court was to take actions concerning surveillance regarding EFTA states, to hear appeals about competition initiated by the EFTA Surveillance Authority, and to act in disputes between two or more EFTA states. An EEA Joint Parliamentary Committee was also established, made up by an equal number of members of the European Parliament and members of the EFTA states' parliaments. EC decision-making would be affected by the EEA, in that the EEA agreement provided that the EC Commission should informally seek expert advice from within the EFTA states in preparing new legislation in fields governed by the agreement. Copies of EC Commission proposals were to be transmitted to EFTA governments as well as to the EC Council (Archer, 1994c, pp. 180–5).

The main parallel between the EEA agreement and EC membership was the adaptation to the internal market and to EC competition policy. The difference was in the maintenance of frontier controls, making it unnecessary to harmonise VAT and indirect taxation. The EEA did not imply a customs union with a common trade policy towards third countries. Important fields of EC cooperation were not covered by the EEA, including the Common Agricultural Policy (CAP), the budget, regional policy, foreign policy, monetary policy and aspects of the European Union, such as a Common Foreign and Security Policy.

The *Storting* voted on the EEA agreement on 16 October 1992 (Stortingstidende, 1992–93, pp. 179–341). Because of uncertainty about whether the agreement implied renunciation of sovereignty, the government decided to invoke paragraph 93 of the Constitution. This paragraph stipulates that a three-quarter majority of the *Storting* is needed to delegate sovereignty to an international organisation. The *Storting* debate was based on a resolution from the foreign policy committee, in which the majority, made up of the Labour, Conservative, and Christian Democrat members, endorsed the agreement. An earlier proposal from the Centre, Socialist Left, Progressive and Christian Democratic parties to postpone the debate until after a referendum was voted down. So was a suggestion from the Centre and Socialist Left parties to wait until the government investigated the consequences for Norwegian oil policy, 'social dumping' and controls on foreign ownership of Norwegian business[2] (Stortingstidende, 1992–93, p. 179).

In the *Storting* debate, Kaci Kullmann Five, leader of the Conservative Party, praised the conclusion of the EEA agreement, and lauded Gro Harlem Brundtland for taking the initiative in 1989. She stressed her party's preference for full membership of the EC, and characterised the EEA as a step along the way. Fridtjof Frank Gundersen of the Progress Party spoke in favour of both the EEA agreement and full EC membership. Paul Chaffey of the Socialist Left Party opposed both the agreement and EC membership, and complained that the majority in the foreign policy committee was undermining Norway's existing free trade agreement with the EC. He argued that the EEA agreement involved 'dramatic changes' for Norwegian society. A majority of Christian Democrat members of the *Storting* was in favour of the agreement. One of these, Kåre Gjønnes, stated that the EEA agreement made for predictability and market access, and attacked the Centre Party and the Socialist Left for ignoring this. Both Gjønnes and most of his colleagues restricted their support to the EEA agreement; they strongly opposed EC membership.

Anne Enger Lahnstein interpreted the EEA agreement as an attempt to create a large market based on the four freedoms, in order to increase economic growth relative to the United States and Japan. Lahnstein argued that to say yes to the EEA was to accept what the people had rejected in 1972. The EEA was not about market access, which was ensured by the existing free trade agreements, and which could be further developed. These agreements could also be supplemented with bilateral arrangements. Lahnstein felt that Norway would not have enough of a say within the EEA, and that power would be transferred from democratically elected organs in Norway to the EEA system in Brussels and Geneva, the EFTA headquarters.

Gro Harlem Brundtland stressed that the EEA agreement was forward-looking. It served as an independent alternative which would secure Norway's interests when the internal market came into force from 1993. For the government full employment and the EEA agreement were targets which served the same purpose: to secure the basis for the development of the welfare society. It was important to have rules and regulations protecting Norwegian trade, but the world had changed. In that respect she described the EEA agreement as the free trade agreement of the 1990s. Yet it was also a new kind of economic cooperation agreement. Unlike the other speakers, Brundtland was reluctant to discuss the EC, but she was happy to refer to the Nordic context. The EEA agreement succeeded where Nordek had failed 20 years previously: it created a Nordic home market.

At the same time Nordic countries gained a common European framework for economic cooperation. Brundtland also said that it was important that the Nordic countries could and would influence Europe, and cited the text of the agreement as an example of the Nordic countries' ability to have a say: it specified that 19 European states were to work for 'sustainable growth and responsible exploitation of resources, a high protection level in health, security and environment, and to fight for full employment, a better standard of living and better work-conditions' (Stortingstidende, 1992–93, p. 215).

The *Storting* ratified the EEA agreement by 130 votes to 35 (Stortingstidende, 1992–93, p. 341). Labour, the Conservatives and the Progress Party voted in favour, and together with the majority of the Christian Democrats the necessary three-quarters majority was secured.

4.8 Brundtland's Plan and the EC Membership Application

The government's refusal to open a public EC debate – in good Labour Party tradition – lasted until late 1991, when it had agreed to the terms of the EEA Treaty. Central figures within the Norwegian Labour Party – headed by Gro Harlem Brundtland – originally hoped to ease Norway into the EC through the EEA. The broad aspiration was that – originally – the EEA agreement could be completed by early 1991, giving Norway and other EFTA countries almost two years to prepare themselves to become part of the Single European Market from 1 January 1993. This would have meant that the core aspect of the European Communities – the four freedoms of movement of goods, services, capital and labour – would become an integral part of Norwegian economic life over a period of some years. Once the European Union was created – originally it was hoped that this would also be on 1 January 1993 – and the EEA was running, then the EFTA states could consider full membership, say from 1996. This would have given almost five years to 'socialise' Norwegian public opinion to accept first the Single European Market, then the European Union. The 'apprenticeship' in the EEA would show the Norwegian electorate that the EC was not as alien as they feared but would also strengthen the argument that, having accepted the Single Market, Norway would be better placed as a full EU member, and as part of the EC, Common Foreign and Security Policy, and Justice and Home Affairs decision-making.

These hopes had to be abandoned when the Swedish Social Democratic government suddenly decided to apply for membership and submitted an application in July 1991, to be followed by a Finnish application. The Norwegian government continued to pursue the EEA negotiations, still believing that the EEA would help the cause of eventual EC membership. However, the situation was changed radically by Norway's neutral Nordic neighbours seeking EC membership, and, later, by the problems in ratifying the Treaty of Maastricht and the EEA treaty. At the end of 1991 the government established a state secretary's[3] committee and a research group for Nordic and European questions, charged with investigating alternative attachments to institutionalised European cooperation and their consequences for Norway. By April 1992 Mrs Brundtland was able to announce to the Labour Party's Hordaland meeting that it had been decided to submit a membership application to the EC, with the changes in Europe and the Swedish and Finnish applications being cited as reasons (*Aftenposten*, 9 April 1992, pp. 6 & 7). First the wider Labour Party needed to be squared. The government revised its original plan for a long lead-in to membership, and submitted an application for full EC membership in November 1992.

In November 1992 the Labour Party conference voted by 182 to 106 in favour of applying to the European Community for membership negotiations. For personal reasons, Gro Harlem Brundtland stepped down as party leader in early November 1992, but remained as prime minister. The former party secretary, Thorbjørn Jagland, took over as party leader. Shortly before, in September 1992, Brundtland had reshuffled her cabinet and appointed two ministers who had been sceptical about the EC: Jan Henry T. Olsen as fisheries minister and Grete Knudsen as minister of social affairs. The party conference vote was very much a personal triumph for Brundtland, who worked hard to get the proposal through after the government's plans had to be revised. The conference resolution also promised that Norway's negotiating stance would emphasise Norwegian control over its own natural resources, and satisfactory arrangements for primary industries and rural districts (*Aftenposten*, 9 November 1992, pp. 2 &14). Despite these manoeuvres, a sizeable minority of those attending the conference – some 37% – voted against the resolution on the EC. This scarcely boded well.

This Party decision was quickly followed by a *Storting* vote on submitting a membership application to the EC; 104 voted in favour, 55 against. The opposition included 15 Labour representatives, 12 from the Christian Democrats, all of the Centre Party (11) and all of the Socialist Left Party (17). The remainder supported the application. By comparison the decision to apply for membership in 1967 had been passed by 136 votes to 13. In 1967, however, Norwegian membership had seemed highly hypothetical because of France's reluctance to allow Britain join, and Norwegian membership was made conditional on British membership. The 1967 resolution also included the qualification that Norway would apply for membership negotiations 'as the best means of clarifying the basis for Norway's relations with the EEC' (see Chapter 3).

4.9   The Nordic and European Dimensions

Five EFTA members applied for EC membership even before the EEA agreement came into operation: Austria, Sweden, Finland, Switzerland and Norway. These were popular applicants from the EC's point of view, given their economic success, political stability, social and environmental standards and prospective contribution to the Community's weight in trade negotiations.[4]

The revived EEA issue and the discussion about membership of the EC led to a reconsideration of Nordic cooperation. On a Norwegian initiative, the Nordic countries decided in 1991 to work towards closer cooperation. There was hope that the relationship to the EC could give Nordic cooperation a 'clearer definition of priorities and greater concentration' (Secretariat of the Presidium, 1991, p. 6). The Swedish EC membership application in the summer of 1991 was an important factor which underlined the need for an agenda for the future of Nordic cooperation. At the same time, however, it put immediate pressure on the rest of the Nordic countries to follow suit in the march to Brussels.

In spite of efforts to keep a common Nordic front in the EEA negotiations, Nordic differences over questions of vital interest were revealed. Agriculture and fisheries were the obvious ones, but there were also disparities in the structure and strength of industry and competitiveness. Although agriculture was not covered, the negotiations on trade with agricultural products revealed enough differences to make the point about the lack of a common Nordic position. In the fisheries negotiations, Iceland and Norway became isolated and had to conduct negotiations on their own. An additional point was that Denmark was now on the other side of the negotiating table (Værnø, 1993, p. 108).

International questions, especially the concern for the Baltic states, were very much common Nordic issues that were deliberately pursued, but each country had to plough its own furrow on a number of trade matters.

The Maastricht European Council on 10 December 1991 paved the way for a European Union. The signing of the Treaty on European Union on 7 February 1992 considerably expanded the competencies of the European Communities (Treaty on European Union, 1992, Title I, Common Provisions, Article A). The Treaty foresaw a single market, a single currency, a Common Foreign and Security Policy (CFSP), common Union citizenship, cooperation in justice and home affairs, and the strengthening of economic and social cohesion. The new EC context also changed the criteria for prospective new members. The central article was Article 237 of the Treaty of Rome, as amended by the Single European Act (SEA), and by Article O of the Maastricht Treaty; which stated that 'any European state may apply to become a member of the union'; but that ratification by the European Parliament was required for enlargement.

The Maastricht process slowed in 1992–93. Ratification by the member countries proved more difficult than expected. Denmark rejected the Treaty in a referendum in June 1992, and voted on a somewhat exclusively altered version a year later. In France, the referendum brought a 'petit oui', a wafer-thin majority. The United Kingdom also had problems with its ratification. International economic recession, the collapse of the Exchange Rate Mechanism (ERM) and of plans for European Monetary Union (EMU), and the EU's failure to pacify Yugoslavia, all helped take the shine off European integration for the Nordic peoples. The EEA then ran into problems. The European Court of Justice's opinion about the legal institutions of the EEA led to changes being made; then, at the end of 1992, the Swiss population refused to ratify the agreement. This meant that the entry into force of the agreement was delayed a year, until 1 January 1994.

4.10 Conclusions

The EC's 1985 White Paper on completing the internal market as foreseen by the Treaty of Rome also had implications for the EFTA countries; it meant that closer cooperation between EFTA and the EC could only come about if it became more ambitious. Consequently, new institutional arrangements and adjustments by the EFTA countries to the internal market were the two central dimensions of the EEA process (Melchior, 1991, p. 14).

From the early 1980s, Norway was also beginning to examine the EC as a partner in security policy cooperation. This reflected increasing concerns in Norway about some aspects of US defence policy and the growing activities of the EC members within European Political Cooperation (EPC). The drawing together of EPC and the EC in the Single European Act gave notice to other West European states that the EC would not remain just an economic organisation but would develop a security dimension, as it did in the Maastricht Treaty.

What was agreed in the EEA negotiations was beneficial for Norway insofar as it gained access to the developing Single European Market. It also allowed the government to maintain a close political dialogue with the EC at a time when that organization was developing into the European Union. As events in Europe sped up in 1991 and early 1992, the proposed European Union started to emerge as the core area of the 'New Europe' and Sweden and Finland indicated their intention to adhere to that core. The EEA then became not just an end in itself but a potential waiting room for EU membership. For opponents of the EU, the EEA agreement bore too much of a resemblance to EU membership: national sovereignty would be undermined and Norway exposed to unacceptable transitional costs. For proponents of the EU, on the other hand, the EEA meant that Norway assumed the burden of economic adjustment and transitional costs without gaining access to the decision-making process as an equal partner, and without participation in the political aspect of EU cooperation (Melchior, 1991, p. 11). From either viewpoint, the EEA was hardly a durable solution.

The time taken to establish the EEA and the early application for full EU membership by some EFTA members changed Norway's timetable and caused difficulty for the Labour government in Norway. The notion of a decent time lapse between the EEA Agreement and the start of membership negotiations with the EC/EU was undermined, and the government was rushed into an early application. Meanwhile the ratification of the EEA Agreement was being pushed through the *Storting* with the acceptance into Norwegian law of the *acquis communautaire* associated with the agreement. Many of the arguments advanced in that parliamentary debate previewed some of the later ones in the EU debate. Furthermore, the government had announced that there would not be a formal application for full EU membership until after the EEA treaty was ratified. It is perhaps scarcely surprising that a number of politicians linked the EEA with EU membership, considering it as a sprat to catch a mackerel.

Notes

1   The EEA Agreement originally (October 1991) included an independent EEA Court and an independent Court of First Instance. These were later dropped following criticism by the EC Court of Justice.

2   'Social dumping' referred to the tendency of some firms to site factories in areas which had poor social conditions and, thus, low welfare costs.

3   The position of State Secretary in Norwegian ministries is equivalent to that of a junior minister though, unlike such ministers in the British system, they do not have parliamentary responsibilities.

4   Turkey applied in April 1987, Commission avis (report) December 1989; Austria July 1989, avis August 1991; Cyprus July 1990; Malta July 1990; Sweden June 1991, avis July 1992; Finland March 1992, avis October 1992; Switzerland May 1992, (referendum turned down EEA in Nov. 1992, membership application was not pursued); Norway December 1992, avis April 1993.

5

Negotiating for Membership: 1993–1994

5.1 Introduction

By the start of 1993, the minority Labour government in Oslo had succeeded in ratifying the European Economic Area agreement and had submitted its application for full membership of the European Union. However, the prospect of an easy ride towards full membership was not available – events in Europe and the developing domestic landscape saw to that.

As shown in Chapter 4, the process of European integration had already started to slow in 1992. The ratification process of the Maastricht Treaty had proved to be more perilous and contested than predicted. Even before it developed into the European Union in November 1993, the European Communities ran into trouble with the collapse of the Exchange Rate Mechanism and in its inability to cope with the Yugoslav crisis. The Single European Market – trailed as '1992' – was a more gradual and incomplete process than advertised. The whole ratification process dragged out through much of 1993 with a second Danish referendum, a long battle over the Treaty in the British House of Commons and a challenge in the German constitutional court by the Länder. Russia descended into social, economic and political confusion and the wars in former Yugoslavia splattered blood over the map of Europe.

Within Norway, 1993 was an election year. The centre–right parties placed themselves out of power since the 1989 election, and the minority Labour government had had some success. During 1993, unemployment peaked at 6%, a figure well below that in many other West European states. A banking crisis was adeptly handled, the growth in public consumption was slowed in order to tackle the budget deficit, inflation had been kept low, the public sector was expanded as part of an active job creation policy, paid for by an increase in Norway's offshore oil production. The krone had broken away from the European currency unit (ecu) at the end of 1992, but the government undertook a policy of a managed float, keeping the krone stable against the major European currencies (Ecomomist Intelligence Unit, 1995c, p. 9). Inflation was at 2.3% and the Gross National Product rose by 2.1% during the year (ibid, p. 13). In short, the Norwegian economy was not doing too badly and was performing better than its neighbours in Sweden and Finland. The Labour government took credit for guiding Norway through a difficult time economically and was looking forward to improving its parliamentary position in the September 1993 election.

However, they faced one major problem, that of the EU application. As the November 1992 party conference had shown, a sizeable number of supporters were already against membership, even before the referendum campaign had fully started. The EEA debate had sharpened the divisions: the Centre Party and the Socialist Left had opposed the EEA in preparation for the larger battle. The Christian Democrats and a section of the

Labour Party had indicated that they were prepared to swallow the EEA, but nothing more. Wiser from the experience of 1971–72 and wary of splitting the country once more, the Labour government proceeded cautiously in the 1993–94 membership negotiations with the EU. It took pains not to hurry Norwegian public opinion, either before, during, or after the negotiations.

5.2   The Opening of the Membership Negotiations

Negotiations on Norwegian membership of the EU opened on 5 April 1993, just over four months after the application was submitted, and two months after negotiations with Austria, Finland and Sweden began. For the EU, Norway's application raised no political problems; Norway fulfilled the three main preconditions for EU membership (European identity, democracy and respect for human rights). It was a founding member of NATO and was about to become an associate member of the WEU. Norway did not raise any major economic problems. Free trade for industrial products had already been established, and the EEA agreement meant that Norway broadly accepted the *acquis communautaire* related to the free movement of capital, labour, goods and services. A Norwegian accession was likely to strengthen the European Union in a number of policy areas, such as democratic control, currency, low inflation and environment. However, problem issues were obvious from the outset of the negotiations. These especially included regional policy, fisheries, agriculture and energy, as well as state aid and state monopolies, alcohol restrictions, social policy and trade policy (Council of Ministers, 1993, Conclusions). When applying for EU membership, Norway had to accept that transition periods would be given for sectors raising particular problems, but that there would be no permanent derogations (*Agence Europe*, 24 March 1993, p. 7; 25 March 1993, p. 5). Another potential hurdle was the precondition that accession would be to the European Union, and not to the European Communities. EU–Norwegian relations were sound economically, but Norway's protection of its own trade and industries was expected to create difficulties, especially as Norway had a strong and vocal opposition to EC membership, with historical roots.

Even during the preliminary negotiations, fish, petroleum, agriculture and regional policy (Stoltenberg, 1992, p. 11) – as well as the broader sovereignty issue – were important to key sections of Norwegian public opinion. In the case of fish and oil, the EU was adjusting its own policies in ways that could well affect Norway and its future in the EU. Early in the negotiations, the Norwegian government concentrated on these two issues, both in the talks and in the media. This may have been a tactical move in advance of the September 1993 *Storting* election, the purpose being to direct voters' attention to two relatively understandable subjects, and away from the larger, more complex and more controversial EU question.

Compared with the pre-1972 negotiations, Norway's position in 1993 was more specific, and yet more flexible. Norway had to accept the *acquis communautaire* in full and, in principle, all the decisions taken on the basis of the EU's (or EC's) treaties, with adjustment through transitional arrangements. However, in 1971 Norway had wanted permanent special arrangements for agriculture, and re-negotiation of those aspects of EC fisheries policy which did not satisfy Norwegian requirements (see section 3.4). By 1993 Norwegian requests were more modest.

When the formal negotiations started in September 1993, Hans van den Broek, Commissioner for External Affairs, led for the Commission. Ambassador Eivinn Berg fronted the negotiations at official level for Norway, while Ketil Børde from the Ministry of Foreign Affairs acted as coordinator for the preparations and the negotiations. Einar Bull from the Ministry of Foreign Affairs was deputy leader. Jonas Gahr Støre, special advisor on European questions in the Prime Minister's office, was the only member of the Norwegian delegation able to operate in French. In the absence of Gro Harlem Brundtland, Støre had a special role in the negotiations in keeping the Prime Minister's office informed and even had private meetings with Jacques Delors. The rest of the Norwegian delegation was made up of experts from the various ministries.[1] Six of the team had been involved in the EEA negotiations, including Berg (Economist Intelligence Unit, 1993c, p. 8).

The negotiating team from the Norwegian side was headed by the European Committee which consisted of the Prime Minister, Foreign Minister (Godal), Trade Minister (Knudsen), and Finance Minister (Johnsen) and which was joined by other ministers – especially Fisheries (Olsen), Agriculture (Øyangen) and Local Government (Berge). This group met more than once a month and oversaw strategic policy. The three ministers most involved in the detailed negotiations were the newly appointed trade minister Grete Knudsen, who led the Norwegian side, agriculture minister Gunhild Øyangen and fisheries minister, Jan Henry T. Olsen. The foreign minister, Bjørn Tore Godal, and the finance minister, Sigbjørn Johnsen, also visited Brussels during the main negotiations in March 1994. Prime Minister Brundtland did not attend the talks, but acted as mediator with both Jacques Delors, the Commission President, and Spain's Prime Minister Felipe Gonzales at critical stages. On the Commission side, Jacques Delors intervened during the final stage of the negotiations, though the EU's interlocutor was officially the President of the Council.

At the next level there was the State Secretaries' Group which did not meet so frequently and tended to consider questions of principle rather than take concrete decisions. At the civil service level there was a Coordination Committee chaired by Ambassador Berg, to which the representatives of all ministries were invited (*Stortingsmelding* 40, 1993–4, pp. 442–3). These meetings exchanged information about the negotiations and were useful in informing each ministry of the advance made in other functional areas, but did not set priorities among the issue areas. From the beginning each department mapped out its goals and priorities for the negotiations. For most of negotiations with the EC, there was little effort made to highlight departmental priorities nor to bargain between departments concerning what might sacrificed to achieve the most important priorities. Indeed, in the autumn of 1993 when Norway sent papers to form the background for the Commission's negotiating brief, it seemed to have been left up to the Commission to sort out a synthesis of the Norwegian case.

The form of the presentation of this case was determined by certain internal and external factors. Internally, both the political tradition of consensus, the precarious parliamentary position of the government and the vocal 'no' campaign's advance in the country meant that the government was going to take both a cautious and maximalist approach to the negotiations. This meant that, until forced, the negotiators were not going to emphasise one aspect of their brief to the detriment of another, which would have meant admitting defeat on a particular area and possibly losing political support as a result. Externally the main constraints were those set by the other applicants and the

EC/EU. It was agreed that membership should start from 1 January 1995; any later would impinge on the preparations for the EU review at the Inter-governmental Conference starting in 1996. Sweden's constitutional position meant that results had to be placed before its parliament previous to the summer of 1994, and, anyhow six months would be needed to secure ratification by the European Parliament and the then twelve existing member states. In order to allow for drafting corrections and translations, negotiations had to be completed by April 1994. This left 29 headings or 'chapters' to be completed with four applicant states in little over fifteen months. Though a number of these chapters had been covered in EEA negotiations, each was potentially a minefield with deals that could be reopened by any of the applicants and existing members. So while the political imperative in Norway spoke for drawn out negotiations with no deals between the chapters, the pressure from outside was for a speedier settlement of difficult issues with – if need be – horse-trading across issue areas.

In the end, the key areas that were negotiated right up to the end of the meetings with the EC were those of regional aid, agriculture and fisheries.

5.3   The 1993 General Election

Once the talks were underway, the Norwegian government had more cause to worry about domestic public opinion than about attaining a good settlement. It needed to prepare for the September 1993 general election. Gro Harlem Brundtland's minority government had been in power since October 1990. In common with most other European governments, it had been confronted with economic recession, in addition to political turmoil over the future of the European Communities. To maintain the support of the *Storting*, however, it had had to tread softly on issues such as employment (Economist Intelligence Unit, 1993a, pp. 6–7). The necessity to compromise left the government vulnerable to criticism from both left and right. The EU membership question was also fraught with electoral risks. Three to four months before the election, opinion polls suggested that support for the Labour Party was down by 10 percentage points from its 1989 vote (Aardal, 1994, p. 172).

After leaving the Conservative-led government in October 1990 and appointing Anne Enger Lahnstein as new leader in the spring of 1991, the Centre Party campaigned actively against membership. In the summer of 1993, Lahnstein published a book on the EC and the Constitution in which she stressed that the final say on membership lay with the *Storting*, as the Constitution provided only for a consultative referendum. The composition of the *Storting* was therefore crucial (Lahnstein, 1993). In the election campaign the Centre Party made the EC question their central issue, and the results seemed to vindicate their strategy.

A poll in October suggested that Norwegian opposition to EC membership rose to a record 60% after the election. It stood at 58% just ahead of the election in which the Centre Party emerged as the largest opposition party. Those in favour of membership fell to 28%, and opposition to membership within the Labour Party rose to 36% (*Financial Times*, 12 October 1993). Opposition to the EC was growing in Sweden, with an opinion poll showing 48% were against membership, with 30% in favour and 23% undecided (*Dagens Næringsliv*, 25 October 1993).

The 1993 general election turned into an EC election, against the wishes of the Labour government. Their desire to banish the EC issue from the campaign backfired on them. The anti-EC parties had started making membership an issue during the EEA negotiations and pushed the issue during the election. Almost two-thirds of the electorate named the EC question as the most important for their own voting intention (Aardal & Valen, 1995, p. 19). The Centre Party's emphasis on the EC issue brought it striking gains. It almost tripled its share of the vote, and its *Storting* representation rose from 11 to 32 seats. Contrary to earlier forecasts, the Labour Party won four seats, rising to 67. The other anti-EU party, the Socialist Left, lost four new seats, returning with 13 seats. The main losers were the Conservative Party which lost nine of its 37 seats, and the Progress Party, whose representation fell from 22 to 10 seats (Archer, 1995).

With the Centre Party's success, and in spite of the Socialist Left's performance, anti-EC parties held more than one quarter of the seats in the *Storting*. The two parties held 45 seats, more than enough to block Norwegian EC membership outright. Even if a consultative referendum voted in favour of membership, the *Storting* had more than the blocking minority of 42 votes.

Labour remained in office, again as a minority government. It was dependent on the support of at least two other parties to implement its policy. Both Labour and the Conservatives had tried to prevent the EC becoming an election issue. The Labour Party, in particular, was divided on the issue. Internal dissent in the Labour Party reappeared as the negotiations with the EC began; as in 1972, a Labour Party anti-EU group was formed, Social Democrats against the EU (SME) (*Dagbladet*, 27 October 1993.)

All opinion polls during 1993 showed a majority against joining the EU. Subsequent polls seemed to show that the attempt to exclude the EU from the election campaign was a mistake. October's polls showed over twice as many against EU membership as for. Even the region of Oslo and Akershus, formerly staunchly pro-EU, showed for the first time an equal percentage of opponents and proponents of EU membership.[2] This trend softened during the autumn, although a majority was still firmly against joining. Compared with the results from polls a year earlier the trend was clear. Polls indicated opponents of membership leading supporters by some ten points with even about half the respondents against joining (Economist Intelligence Unit, 1993a, p. 9). This increased the need for a favourable settlement of the negotiations in progress.

5.4 Summary of Negotiation Results: The Specific Areas

At the start of the membership negotiations 29 negotiation areas or chapters were identified. Many of these were already settled by the EEA agreement (Table 5.1).[3]

Chapter 1 was largely settled by the EEA agreement. In a number of areas where Norway had transition arrangements under the EEA agreement, solutions were found within EU regulations which would permit Norway maintain its standards for health, security and environment. Norway was allowed to keep its national standards in the thorny area of animal and plant health.

Chapter 2 included the securing of the rights of foreign companies to offer employees accident insurance in Norway, this being obligatory in Norway. Norwegian authorities reserved the right to restrictions should an aggressive campaign on the Norwegian market have negative consequences for the country's efforts to limit alcohol consumption. This chapter also covered regulations about the right to establish business throughout the EU area.

Table 5.1   *Areas of Negotiation*

Chapter	Title	EEA status
1	Free exchange of goods	x
2	Free exchange of services	x
3	Free movement of labour	x
4	Free movement of capital	x
5	Transport policy	x
6	Competition policy	x
7	Consumer & health policy	x
8	Research & information technology	x
9	Education	x
10	Statistics	x
11	Corporation law	x
12	Social policy	x
13	Environment	x
14	Energy	o
15	Agriculture	o
16	Fisheries	o
17	Customs union	o
18	Trade policy towards third countries	o
19	Structural funds	o
20	Regional policy	o
21	Industrial policy	o
22	Tax	o
23	Economic and monetary union	o
24	Foreign & security policy	o
25	Justice and police	o
26	Other Maastricht decisions	o
27	Finance and budget decisions	o
28	Institutions	o
29	Other questions	o

Key: x = fully, or mainly, resolved under the EEA
o = not, or partly, resolved under the EEA

In chapter 4 Norway was granted a transition period of five years in relation to its existing regulations requiring foreigners buying leisure property to seek special permission. Chapter 5, on transport policy, provided Norwegian-registered ships the right of cabotage in the EU area. In chapter 7, consumers' rights were to be covered by the EU's general product safety directive, coming into force from June 1994.

Chapter 8 was rapidly settled as Norway participated in nearly all of the EU's framework programmes for research, and there was agreement on participation in the two exceptions on nuclear physics. Chapter 9 provided that students from member countries would receive equal treatment to Norwegian students in regard to fees.

Chapters 10, 11 and 12 were basically resolved by the EEA. The shaping of welfare arrangements in EU countries remained a national responsibility. The principles of economic and social progress, full employment, improved living standards and working conditions formed the basis of the EU's social policy.

In chapter 13, Norway negotiated a special declaration on whales confirming that Norway would respect EU regulations designed to preserve or increase the whale stock. Norway believed that the matter should be dealt with in the International Whaling Commission. The declaration provided for this and affirmed that Norway would work for the adjustment of EU regulations to take account of new knowledge based on scientific material. Norway was given a transition period until 1997 to reduce SO_2 waste gases from the titanium dioxide industry. Norway accepted EU regulations on the EURATOM treaty, while the choice of energy sources remained a national affair.

5.5   The Key Negotiation Areas[4]

This section will outline the main negotiating areas not solved under the EEA agreement, demonstrating their important areas in the internal debate in Norway. In the Prime Minister's address to the *Storting* both before and after the negotiations, special attention was paid to four issues : energy, regional policy, agriculture, and fisheries (*Stortingsforhandlinger*, 1992–93a, pp. 1130–1; Brundtland, 1994c). These proved to be key issues in the negotiations.

5.5.1   Off-shore petroleum

In 1972 Norway began the process towards becoming a major oil producer, and it was already clear that oil and gas would make a major contribution to the Norwegian economy. From the late 1970s, Norwegian oil and gas exports rose steadily, strengthening both the sector's influence in the Norwegian economy and Norway's position as energy supplier to Western Europe. The value of Norwegian oil and gas production in 1993 was around one seventh of the country's GNP, while the sector made up one third of total exports. Nearly 90% of petroleum exports went to Western European countries (Stortingsmelding 40, 1993–94, p. 184).

The political principle followed in the petroleum sector had been that of Norwegian sovereignty and national rights over resources, labelled 'national guidance and control'. This involved the administration of resources, national guidance of work on the continental shelf, the right to state participation, and the state's right to impose taxation and of ownership of petroleum resources (Stortingsmelding 40,1994, p. 184). The vehicle for this policy was the state oil company, Statoil, which held a 50% share of all licences. In 1985 the state became even more closely involved through the State's Direct Economic Engagement [SDØE], establishing a direct state share in all licences (Matlary, 1993, p. 53).

In autumn 1991, the EC tabled a draft directive which proposed that EC companies could bid for off-shore resources on a non-discriminatory basis, regardless of nationality and of whether they were state-owned or private (Economist Intelligence Unit, 1993b, p. 10). With Norway in the EC, the draft directive would affect Statoil's automatic part ownership of all blocks on the Norwegian shelf, as well as its position as both operator and administrator of the SDØE in off-shore activity (*Dagens Næringsliv*, 28 September 1993). The draft directive met with scepticism in Norway, though it did confirm for the first time that off-shore resources belonged to the state in whose sector they were found; they were national, rather than EC resources (Economist Intelligence Unit, 1993b, p. 10).

The draft directive was not universally popular within the EC. At a meeting of EC energy ministers in June 1993, Denmark found itself in a minority in defending the right to favour national oil companies; other countries wanted free competition and opposed discrimination against other EC oil companies. The Commission decided to work towards an outcome by 10 December 1993 (*Dagens Næringsliv*, 27 September 1993; *Dagens Næringsliv*, 28 September, 1993).

The draft directive was heavily criticised in Norway. As Western Europe's largest oil producer and as the third biggest supplier of natural gas to the EC, Norway was prepared to be assertive in relation to the energy sector. In his report to the *Storting* in June 1993, then trade minister Bjørn Tore Godal stressed Norway's favourable position as one of the EC's main energy suppliers. He argued that the EC's general energy situation would change fundamentally with Norway as a member, through increased security and pre-dictability of supply. He portrayed Norway's membership as being of vital importance to the EU's future energy policy.[5]

In defending its oil interests, Norway stressed the principle of subsidiarity within the EU. Delegating decisions to the national level was appealing to Norway, with its long history of scepticism towards supranationality. Subsidiarity promised a response to one of the most telling anti-EC arguments in the 1972 referendum. The government also argued that it was in the EU's interest that Norway, with a successful and well-established system of controls and regulations, continued to administer resources in the Norwegian off-shore areas (Olsen, 1993). Brundtland pointed to the effect the directive could have on Norwegian opinion when she said 'the situation reminds me of 1972, when the EC formulated its fisheries policy just before the Norwegian referendum on membership. [The policy] had a considerable influence on the outcome of the vote' (*Norinform*, 18 May 1993, p. 6).

The EC move in the energy sector was a dilemma for the Norwegian government. However, some adjustments along the lines of the new EC policy had already been made. A simple technical remedy could have been to divorce the State's Direct Economic Engagement off-shore from Statoil and to allocate it to the Ministry of Industry and Energy, thus allowing Statoil to act as a normal competitive company (Harbo, 1993). It would also end Statoil's lead position in Norway's Gas Negotiating Committee (GFU), which included the private sector companies Norsk Hydro and Saga, as well as Statoil. Membership in the GFU had already been broadened in 1992, opening it to foreign companies producing gas from the shelf (*Norinform*, 31 August 1993, p. 9; Matlary, 1993, p. 59). Statoil's participation in blocks of lesser commercial interest was not always regarded positively and none of the Norwegian oil companies, including Statoil, opposed the draft directive. Harald Norvik, Statoil's managing director, said that the directive furnished an opportunity for the already competitive Norwegian companies to become even stronger (*Dagens Næringsliv*, 25 June 1993; Matlary, 1993, p. 59).

The Norwegian government trumpeted its disquiet with the draft directive partly for tactical reasons; it needed to demonstrate its defence of Norway's interests, especially in the run-up to the 1993 election. In addition, Statoil's position was important for the Norwegian government's control of the utilisation of offshore resources. The basic political point was that the Norwegian government did not want to be seen to change its off-shore policy at the behest of the EC. For one of the leading energy producers in

Europe to accept such a fait accompli could be seen as a political defeat, possibly adversely affecting the referendum result. This prospect was averted by Protocol 4 to the Norwegian agreement with the EU that reiterated Norway's position concerning sovereignty over the petroleum resources (Stortingsmelding 40, 1993–4, p. 186–7).

It should be noted that existing directives – the Utilities Directive (90/531/EEC) and the subsequent Remedies Directive – could also have affected Norway's national preference in its off-shore sector. Furthermore, the effect of these directives, opening up supply and works off-shore to EU-wide tendering, could have been extended to Norway through the EEA, a factor not readily discussed in Oslo (Thomas, 1993, pp. 20–21). In the area of goods and services for the oil sector the EEA agreement had been followed by a significant change of policy. Hitherto, paragraph 54 of the Norwegian Petroleum Act had ensured that goods and services for the oil sector were to be Norwegian, provided they were competitive in price and quality. The EC's public procurement directive, however, banned national protection, including in the energy sector. This directive formed part of the EEA agreement, and the government had to amend the Petroleum Act. The official reason for the change was that Norwegian industry had become so competitive that this stipulation was no longer necessary (Matlary, 1993, p. 58).

Norway's fight against the draft directive paid off, as important Norwegian demands were taken into account in the final text of the EC directive which was adopted by the EC energy ministers on 10 December 1993. Some Norwegian demands, such as the continued participation of Statoil in all blocks, had to be surrendered but this, as seen, was no real sacrifice. On the other hand, the continuation of Statoil in the SDØE was secured, confirming Statoil's position as an important political tool, as well as representing the state's continued direct involvement. In the membership negotiations Norway insisted on obtaining a protocol to the ultimate agreement with the EU reaffirming national control over petroleum resources.[6] The significance of this was that the protocol would form part of the EU's primary legislation, and thus accord stronger legal protection than the directive, which was liable to amendment in the future.

Securing Norwegian energy resources was important, and not only tactically. Norwegian industry's development potential and the continued subsidy of many sectors of Norwegian public life, inside or outside the EU, were at stake.

5.5.2   Regional Policy

Although their respective regional policies differed, both the EU and Norway had both attached importance to avoiding depopulation and encouraging development in rural areas (Council of Ministers, 1993, p. 16). In its second negotiation document on regional policy, put to the Commission in September 1993, Norway requested that all of the country from Trondheim up to the Russian border should qualify for EU support as an especially underdeveloped region (*Dagens Næringsliv*, 24 September 1993). The issue of subsidies for Arctic and sub-Arctic farmers and for sparsely populated regions met with sympathy from EU officials, though it was pointed out that the GDP per capita in the region was not low enough to be eligible for assistance under Objective 1 of the EU's Regional Policy (*Dagens Næringsliv*, 19 October, 1993, p. 5; *Dagens Næringsliv*, 9 February 1994, p. 13; Stortingsmelding 40, 1993–4, p. 245).

In the settlement, Norway agreed with the EU that population density would be the criterion for regional aid. The four northernmost counties – Finnmark, Troms, Nordland

and Nord-Trøndelag – were to receive about Nkr 0.5bn yearly from EU funds, and the Norwegian government would provide matching grants (Stortingsmelding 40, 1993–4, p. 244).

This deal did not satisfy the Centre Party, which was strongest in the countryside and which wished to keep national control over regional policy. The Labour Party group opposing membership (SME) also pointed out that Norwegian criteria for regional policy were quite different from those of the EU and that membership would mean cuts in agriculture and fisheries, both of which were important to regional policy (Gerhardsen et al., 1994, p. 22).

5.5.3   Agriculture

EU membership would have strongly influenced the Norwegian agricultural sector. The Norwegian case during the membership negotiations was that the climatic, topographical and demographic conditions were completely different from those in other EU countries, and the resulting disadvantages for agricultural production had to be taken into account in order to guarantee earnings similar to those of farmers elsewhere in the EU (*Agence Europe*, 5/6 April, 1993). Norway shared this problem with Finland and Sweden, and all three entered negotiations with the request that the EU acknowledge a special Arctic and sub-Arctic status for their agriculture.

Neither Finland nor Sweden wanted to push for a joint Nordic negotiating position in the two most difficult issues, Arctic agriculture and adjustment time. Norway was left to tackle these problems alone. Though Norway would have preferred permanent derogations, it was ready to accept most of the EU's agricultural policy, provided a deal could be reached that would help Norwegian agriculture in the near future. The Norwegian agricultural minister, Gunhild Øyangen, requested special arrangements to ensure that the CAP would be adopted effectively by Norway whilst maintaining the regional policy aspect of Norway's own agricultural policy. Norway's main problem was that its producer prices were twice as high as those in the Community, partly because of its commitment to an agricultural structure designed to ensure the viability of rural communities in all parts of the country (Council of Ministers, 1993, p. 16).

In 1993, 77% of Norwegian farmers' income came from state aid. EU membership thus provided a long-awaited excuse for the Norwegian government to reduce this heavy subsidy, a task already started in 1993. Since 1945 the aim of Norwegian agricultural policy had been to secure for farmers an income equivalent to that of industrial workers. The new policy – as outlined in a Proposition to the *Storting* (St. prp. 8, 1992–93), and approved by the *Storting* in February 1993 – was to bring farm earnings into line with the average income of whole population. Production goals were to be dropped, except for milk, in which Norway was still to be self-sufficient.

The government's new agricultural policy was supported in the *Storting* by the Conservatives and the Progress Party, and opposed by the Centre, Socialist Left and Christian Democrats (Innst. S nr. 92,1992–93; Economist Intelligence Unit, 1993a, p. 13). It resulted in a reduction in government subsidies for the Norwegian farmers for the first time since the 1970s (Economist Intelligence Unit, 1993b, pp. 12–13). The change of policy eased Norway towards conformity with the CAP, which itself had shifted towards an income support framework. It also placed the Labour government in opposition to the two main farmers' associations, the Farmers' Association and the Small Farmers'

Association, and other relevant associations. All these considered – as in 1972 – that it would be impossible to maintain Norwegian agriculture inside the EU, thus threatening Norway's distinctive nature. In the words of the Farmers Association, 'agriculture is part of our history and cultural heritage' (Stortingsmelding 40, 1993–4, p. 470; *Aftenposten*, 6 July 1993).

The outcome of the negotiations was that the CAP would be extended to Norway. Agricultural prices were to be adjusted to EU levels from the first day of membership. During the first five years, special measures to prevent severe market disruption were permissible, and the foodstuffs industry could be given support during the first three years for investment and product development purposes. The CAP's support policy was to be extended to the whole of North Norway and to parts of the south, and in these areas national support could be added. However, total and permanent support could not exceed the then existing level, and subsidies contrary to current CAP schemes were to be phased out over five years. Norway was also granted a seven-year period in which it could subsidise farms producing pork, poultry and eggs, which otherwise did not qualify for EU subsidies (Stortingsmelding 40, 1993–4, pp. 194–214).

In the original Norwegian position paper for the negotiations, the food processing industry was omitted through an oversight, but was included in the following paper. This sector was not immediately identified as a problem area, but it became clear that the industry would not be able to adjust to EU rules overnight. A three-year transition period was agreed.

The settlement did not appease farming representatives. The Farmers' Association claimed that membership would have a substantial effect on employment in agriculture (Stortingsmelding 40, 1993–4, p. 470). Farming organisations would also lose their special relationship with the Norwegian Ministry of Agriculture, and would have to fight many of their battles in Brussels.

5.5.4   Fisheries

Fish was mainland Norway's second most important export with 90% of the total catch exported, and 60% going to the EU. Norway supplied a quarter of the EU's fish imports (Stortingsmelding 40, 1993–94, p. 214; Næringslivets Hovedorganisasjon, 1993, p. 39). From the beginning, Norway's negotiating position was to seek adjustments to the Common Fisheries Policy, while generally accepting the framework of existing EU rules and regulations (Olsen, 1993).

In 1972, EC fisheries policy caused deep political problems for the Norwegian government. This time, the minority Labour administration displayed greater caution. It wanted the principle of 'relative stability' to remain the basic principle behind fishing quotas (Olsen, 1993; *Agence Europe*, 9 July 1993). Norway wished to keep its existing quota regime, and to maintain the strict enforcement of quotas and catching regulations. The government asserted that no new fishing rights in Norwegian waters could be granted to Communities' vessels, and requested unrestricted access to the EU for its fisheries products. Jan Henry Olsen, the fisheries minister, stated that Norway had no more fish to give away to the EU (*Financial Times*, 7 July 1993). Norway sought recognition of the dependence of its coastal settlements and fisheries resources, and asked to preserve its 12-mile exclusive fisheries zone at least until 2002. It wanted the continuance its system of direct sales associations. The Norwegian preliminary paper on fishing stated that, in light of the importance of this industry for it, Norway should play a major role in the development of the EU's new Common Fisheries Policy, which should accordingly cater for Norway's interests.

When talks on fisheries began in September 1993, the chairman, the Greek Foreign Minister, Theodoros Pangalos, suggested the subdivision and delegation of the negotiations. Out of an EC 'troika', consisting of the German, Dutch and Belgian permanent representatives, the German, Dr. Dieter von Küaw, was assigned responsibility for the fisheries negotiations. He was helped by the extensive diplomatic work which had gone on beforehand, and by the presence of Klaus Kinkel, the German Foreign Minister, at the most important discussions.[7]

Norway's fisheries delegation was high powered, featuring three times as many experts as the Commission delegation. The biggest problems proved to be access to markets, access to resources, transitional measures north of 62°N, and the problem of third party fishing.[8] The talks were difficult, but the outcome represented something of a victory for Norway though Mr Olsen had to modify his assertion that he had no fish to give away, as he proved to have a few to exchange.

From the Commission point of view, Norwegian membership meant increasing the number of fishermen and vessels in an already overcrowded fishing industry. As Norwegian membership would also increase the tonnage of the EU fishing fleet by 17%, strengthening the EU's weight globally (Council of Ministers, 1993, p. 17), the Commission was also willing to compromise. Initially, it rejected Norway's request to 'retain sole control over resources north of 62° latitude', including the sensitive Russian–Norwegian 'Grey Zone' (*Norway Daily*, 11 January 1994, p. 1; Stokke and Tunander, 1994a; Churchill and Ulfstein, 1992). The Norwegian demands for market access without reciprocity were also unacceptable. Opposition to Norway's demands came mainly from France and Spain, with some support from the United Kingdom. Around this time, the French government, under pressure from their own fishermen, tried to exclude Norwegian fish imported under the EEA arrangements (*Norway Daily*, 10 February 1994, p. 1). At the end of the negotiations, Madrid demanded that an additional annual quota of 11,000 tonnes of cod from Norwegian waters should be allocated to the southern EU members, with 7,000 tonnes of this going to Spain (*Norway Now*, April 1994, p. 9).

The agreement affirmed that a future permanent system for fish quotas would be based on 'relative stability', as Norway urged. Norway also obtained duty-free access to EU markets for its seafood from the first day of membership. In a four-year transitional period, a surveillance arrangement was to be established for eight species (including salmon, herring, mackerel, and shrimp) where Norway was in competition with existing EU states, to see whether sales exceeded an agreed upper limit or created serious market disturbances. Norway was allowed to keep its 12 nautical mile exclusive coastal fishing zone, with the interests of coastal communities to be taken into account when the continuation of the zone was discussed at the end of 2002. In return, the EU was allowed to fish an extra 2,000 tonnes of cod in Norwegian waters, on top of the 11,000 tonnes provided under the EEA agreement (St. prp. nr. 100, 1991–92, Protokoll 9, Artikkel 2). Laws requiring Norwegian citizenship for the ownership of Norwegian-registered fishing vessels were to be dropped after a three and a half year transitional period, at which point EU citizens would be able to purchase Norwegian boats. The right of management of fish resources in Norwegian waters south of 62 degrees latitude was to be handed over to the

EU from the first day of membership, and in the waters north of 62 degrees, management was to be transferred no later than 1 July 1998. From that date too, the EU would take responsibility for annual negotiations with Russia on the management of the 'Grey Zone' in the Barents Sea. EU market regulations would replace Norwegian ones on the sale of fish, and membership of the wholesaler's co-operative would no longer be compulsory (Stortingsmelding 40, 1993–4, pp. 226–235). In effect, Norway exchanged ultimate control over the regulation of its offshore fisheries – and a few extra cod – for freer access to a lucrative market.

The settlement terms were enough to allow fisheries minister Olsen to give a favourable recommendation, unlike his predecessor in 1972. He saw the agreement securing the development of the fishing industry. Olsen noted that Norwegian rights to fisheries resources were to be maintained, and Norway's relative shares of the various species would be stated in the accession. Yet the immediate response of the fishermen's organisations, unsurprisingly, was to reject the deal (*Aftenposten*, 9 March 1994, p. 6; *Aftenposten*, 16 April, p. 4; *Nordlys*, 15 April 1994). The Norwegian Fishermen's Association [Norges Fiskarlag], the Troms Fishermen's Association, and the Norwegian Coastal Fishermen's Association all complained about the loss of sovereignty over Norway's fish, and were especially irritated by the additional concessions to Spain (Stortingsmelding 40, 1993–94, pp. 449–50). The 2,000 tonnes of additional fish which Mr 'No-Fish' Olsen had conceded provoked anger. The Norwegian Raw Fish Association was sceptical about the wholesalers' cooperative becoming subject to the EU's market regulations (*Aftenposten*, 17 March 1994, p. 3). However, the opening up of the EU seafood market was an enticing prospect for the fisheries industry as a whole, as the Fisheries Industry's National Association pointed out (*Aftenposten*, 16 March 1994, p. 7).

Ivan Kristoffersen, who as a former state secretary in the ministry of fisheries and editor of the Labour Party Tromsø-based newspaper *Nordlys* was an influential figure in the fisheries community, strongly opposed the agreement in his newspaper and elsewhere. His main objection was the loss of control over fisheries resources (*Nordlys*, 22 July 1994; *Dagbladet*, 23 July 1994). For Kristoffersen, Norway would lose the most important legal protection its coast had ever had, namely the control over the sea and shelf within the 200 nautical miles economic zone. In his interpretation, the EU agreement did not imply any particular obligation of control, neither regarding total quotas nor regarding its own catch capacity. He also asked how the Norwegian coastguard could exercise control, when the catch was to be administered by the EU Commission and Norway together, and he criticised the concession of Norway's right to negotiate with Russia (*Dagbladet*, 23 July 1994).

The fish breeding industry, on the other hand, was in favour of Norwegian EU membership. The sector was responsible for 30–40% of the income from Norwegian fish exports. The main markets were Sweden and the EU; the EU had imported 78% of Norwegian production in 1993. At the same time, sales to America had fallen drastically following the introduction of new trade barriers. Leif Inge Karlsen, director of the fish breeding company, Hydrotech, believed that 10,000–15,000 new jobs could be created in fish processing if Norway joined the EU. If Norway did not join, it would face demands for quotas and be partly excluded from the EU market (*Aftenposten*, 24 October 1994, p. 23). This had been the case hitherto, and Norway had hoped that the EEA agreement would have solved this dilemma; but the EEA contained few definite assurances.

Norwegian conditions were among the best for the breeding of fish, and production prices were already lower than, for example, Scotland. It was therefore important to secure this industry's promising future.

5.5.5   Sovereignty

A major issue in the 1972 campaign was Norway's ability to rule itself. The question was again taken up by anti-membership campaigners, who portrayed Brussels as remote and interfering; it was also claimed to have a different agenda than was appropriate for Norway (Gerhardsen et al., 1994, p. 3). The Prime Minister, Gro Harlem Brundtland, sought to tackle this issue by describing EU membership as bringing 'additional democracy'. Membership would provide Norway with a degree of national sovereignty far beyond that which it could obtain alone. She also suggested that 'if Norway wants to leave the EU after first having entered into it, the issue will be decided by a majority in the Storting' (*Norway Daily*, 10 January, 1994, p. 1). How this might be achieved in practice was not explained.

In the wake of the discussion about Qualified Majority Voting (QMV) in the EU's Council of Ministers, Mrs Brundtland also pointed out that the 25 million Nordic citizens would have a larger weighted vote in the Council – if the three Nordic applicants joined Denmark – than that of Germany with its 80 million citizens. However, this argument scarcely counter-acted the main thrust of the opponents' case on sovereignty, which was that membership of the EU would diminish Norway's ability to take decisions in a wide range of policy areas.[9]

5.6   Conclusions

The success of the Norwegian membership negotiations can be measured according to several criteria. Judged against what was expected by the government, the outcome was quite reasonable. There were some gaps in the fisheries settlement but the whole package probably represented as near as possible to a good deal. According to the opponents, the agreements both confirmed their worst fears and failed to ameliorate their causes for complaint. Control over fisheries was to be given away; agriculture and the regions undermined; and even Norway's offshore oil and gas subject to EU regulations. From a political perspective there was no group that could be 'swung' by a satisfactory deal in Brussels, though there were a number – from *nynorsk* users to occupants of Svalbard and the Sami people – that would have complained had their interests not been addressed.

Though the outcome of the negotiations depended mainly on the match between Norwegian and EU requirements, the result in particular areas also depended the dynamics of the negotiations. In the main issues, Norway was able to obtain a good settlement in that of offshore petroleum as EU policy was still being formulated, Norway had the most to offer and Norway was supported within the EU by Denmark. On regional policy, the Norwegian case was advanced together with those of Sweden and Finland, the particular problems of the Nordic states were explained and understood, and the three were anyhow to be net contributors to the EU budget. Agriculture was more difficult, as Sweden had already reformed its policy and Finland's foreign minister was a former farmers' representative partly in place to get rural support for a deal (Arter, 1995, p. 376). After Sweden and Finland had settled with the EU on agriculture, Norway held on for another week to gain a few more concessions (Granell, 1995, p. 127). Fisheries was most difficult as the Norwegians had little in common with the Swedes and Finns and were potentially in conflict with fishing interests from not only Spain, but also the United Kingdom and Ireland. Negotiations lasted until 15 March and were complicated by Spain linking an outcome in that chapter with their acceptance of the closing of the chapter on the EMU. In the end the extra fish offered Spain and the bringing forward of their integration into the Common Fisheries Policy (Granell, 1995, p. 130), combined with heavy pressure from the German Foreign Minister, led to an agreement. Indeed, the very last minute hold-up to this settlement was occasioned by the Irish, who managed to wring a concession on mackerel fishing from Norway, a move later regretted by Mrs Brundtland (1994c, p. 7).

During the negotiations Norway's case was helped by support from particular members of the EC/EU. Britain and Denmark were two traditional allies, though on some issues – for example, fisheries and agriculture – they had interests conflicting with those of Norway. Perhaps the weightiest political support came from Germany, which was anxious to see a Northern extension to redress the balance of the southern extension of the EC in the 1980s. Another means of supporting the Norwegian case was the use of domestic opposition. Norway was playing a 'two-level game' whereby they tried to wring concessions from EU members by referring to the need for a settlement acceptable at home (Putnam, 1988). This received a positive response in most cases, but ran into difficulties when faced with a similar strategy being used by the Spanish over fisheries questions.

Negotiations with the EFTA applicants were completed in March 1994. This left less than nine months to organise referenda and to conclude ratification procedures. The European Parliament accepted the terms of the settlement with Norway by 374 to 24 votes on 4 May 1994. The Commission delegation in Oslo had sent regular briefings and reports back to Brussels. This helped the Commission form a more nuanced opinion and thereby encouraged a more forthcoming attitude in the negotiations.[10] At the same time, there was still a tendency in Brussels to talk about four applicants – and three potential new members. From the EU's point of view its task was over once negotiations were concluded.

The timetable decided at the Copenhagen European Council in June 1993 provided that the EFTA applicants would enter the EU on 1 January 1995 (*Agence Europe*, 23 June 1993). This posed problems for the Norwegian government. To safeguard its position, Foreign Minister Bjørn Tore Godal stated that 'the EU is aiming for Norwegian membership on 1 January 1995. Norway would be satisfied with accession a year later. The EU will not be mapping out the further course of its development before 1996' (Stortingsmelding 40, 1993–94, p. 1).

The government had hoped that the negotiations would take time; this would have allowed the Norwegian population to become 'acclimatised' to the EU through the implementation of the EEA. In this scenario, the electorate would come to realise that they had accepted the EU's 'Common Market' and might as well have a greater say in its workings. The government would be seen to stand up to the EU in lengthy negotiations. A longer timetable would also have given time for Sweden and Finland to conduct referenda; if Norway's Nordic neighbours joined the EU, it would be easier for the Norwegian government to persuade the electorate to vote yes.[11]

The Norwegian attempt to play the membership question long was unsuccessful. At the EU level, the slowing of the Maastricht Process in 1992–93, with the Danish referenda, the French 'petit oui' and the United Kingdom's difficulties over ratification caused problems. International economic recession and the collapse of the Exchange Rate Mechanism (ERM) – plus the failure of the EU in Yugoslavia – took the shine off European integration. Nor did the year-long delay in the entry into force of the EEA help. At the Nordic level, support for the EU in opinion polls in Sweden and Finland declined during 1993, while both countries had major difficulties with their economies (*Nordisk Kontakt*, 1992a; 1992b; 1993; *Financial Times*, 2 September 1993). At home, the length of the negotiations – and the delay in settling vital issues – gave the anti-membership campaigners the upper hand. Even though the outcome of the negotiations was about the best that could have been expected, this had little effect on the debate. In the end, the main opponents were opposed to the lifestyle represented by EU membership – something cosmopolitan, continental and unNorwegian. The details scarcely mattered.

Notes

1   These were, among others, Torben Foss from the Fisheries Ministry, Gabriella Dånmark from the Ministry of Agriculture, Erik Himle from the Ministry of Energy and Amund Utne from the Ministry of Finance. Sources: interview with Ambassador Aneurin Rhys Hughes 11 May 1994; Stortingsmelding 40, 1993–94, p. 442. Other information was received from members of the team involved in the coordination of the negotiations.

2   The poll, taken by Opinion for *Aftenposten*, 18 October 1993, showed 38% support for both the 'yes' and the 'no' side, while 24% did not know.

3   The table and subsequent section are largely based on Stortingsmelding 40, 1993–94, pp. 19–64. See also Granell, 1995.

4   An earlier version of this section can be found in Sogner & Archer, 1995

5   Trade Minister Bjørn Tore Godal became Norway's foreign minister after the death of Johan Jørgen Holst in January 1994.

6   Protocol no. 4 in the Accession Treaty, see St.meld. nr.40, 1994, p.188–9.

7   Interview with Ambassador Aneurin Rhys Hughes, Oslo, 11 May 1994. See also Granell, 1995, for an account of the negotiations.

8   Interview with Ambassador Aneurin Rhys Hughes, Oslo, 11 May 1994.

9   Under QMV in the Council, Denmark would have 3 votes, Sweden 4, Finland 3 and Norway 3, making 13 altogether. Germany has ten votes.

10   Interview with Ambassador Aneurin Rhys Hughes, 11 May 1994.

11   Sweden had to have membership accepted in two parliamentary sessions with an election in between. The September 1994 election returned the Social Democrats to power. The advisory referendum was held 13 November 1994.

6

Between the Negotiations and the Referendum

6.1 Introduction

A year and five months after Norway's Labour Party government submitted its application to the EU, and a year after the membership negotiations started, a settlement was reached in March 1994. The time was then ripe for the yes campaign to start, but it did not. The government had to wait until the Labour Party's extraordinary annual conference in mid-June, and this was followed by the traditional summer break in July. On 15 August 1994, five years after the no side started its campaign, Gro Harlem Brundtland officially opened the government's yes campaign.

6.2 The Government's Campaign

The ministers involved in the talks all praised the settlement, including fisheries minister Jan Henry T. Olsen and trade minister Grete Knudsen, who both earlier had been sceptical about membership. Gro Harlem Brundtland's statement on the outcome stressed the importance for Norway of being able to participate fully in the future development of Europe. She described the result as good: Norway could maintain its welfare system, settlement pattern, high employment and strong economic growth, without losing sovereignty. Mrs Brundtland also stressed the importance of the Nordic dimension. It was then up to the Norwegian population to make the right decision (Brundtland, 1994a).

Foreign minister Bjørn Tore Godal welcomed the settlement and considered it to be in accordance with the government's wishes (Stortingsmelding 40, 1993–94). Trade minister Knudsen said that the agreement would secure Norway a good basis for developing its welfare society, securing high employment, strengthening environmental policy and working for European security wishes (Stortingsmelding 40, 1993–94). Fisheries minister Olsen noted, as seen in Chapter 6, that the settlement maintained Norwegian rights to fisheries resources wishes (Stortingsmelding 40, 1993–94). Gunhild Øyangen, the agriculture minister, stressed the importance of the permanent arrangements for Northern agriculture, which ensured it could still play an important role in employment and settlement over the whole country. This added a new dimension to the EU's agricultural policy (Stortingsmelding 40, 1993–94).

It appeared as if the whole EU membership question with all its preparations, meetings, negotiations and press briefings finally had come to life, and that people began to believe that it would be possible to get a positive vote from the Norwegian electorate. At the onset, however, very few key figures in the government and within the different ministries believed Norway would join the European Union. Given this background, the most pressing question is: why did they do it, why did the Norwegian government start the whole membership process? It is clear, as seen already, that without the Swedish application in June 1991, the Norwegian one would not have come so soon, if at all. The government was also moved by a common socialist feeling, with Jacques Delors steering the Commission and strongly supporting the Scandinavian socialist-led countries' plans to join. After the negotiations, optimism in the 'yes' camp grew, but it was realised that a skilled degree of persuasion of the sceptical Norwegian public was needed.

The Labour Party's leadership accepted this challenge with forbearance. The strategy it laid down after the settlement was dependent on the referendum result in Sweden. Events seemed to be helping. In May the government published its report on membership (Stortingsmelding 40, 1993–94). This made public the full details of the negotiations, as well as the government's views. In early June, the Oslo Labour Party board meeting voted clearly in favour of membership, with 182 for, 62 against and two blank votes (*Arbeiderbladet*, 8 June 1994, p. 8). At Labour's extraordinary annual conference on 18 and 19 June, 197 voted yes, while 93 voted no, showing the depth of opposition within the party. Nevertheless, Labour's campaign could begin, although there was some holding back until the Trade Union Congress (LO) convention in September was over (*Aftenposten*, 20 June 1994, p. 3).

Gro Harlem Brundtland opened the government's yes campaign on 15 August 1994 in Måløy, the scene of a daring allied commando raid in December 1941. She stressed security as a key reason for EU membership (see Chapter 11). Membership would secure the defence of Norway, Norwegian welfare and Norway's environment. She also stressed the importance of entering the EU side by side with the country's Nordic neighbours. EU membership would give Norway, which shares a border with Russia, the safest basis for peace and security. Although Norway traditionally looked to NATO for its security, NATO itself was increasingly influenced by the view that Europeans should take a greater responsibility for their own security. Mrs Brundtland said she wanted Norway to be a first-rank country in European security policy, and the EU and the Western European Union would in future assume a greater role in security matters (Brundtland, 1994b).

Mrs Brundtland argued that EU membership would strengthen the basis for environmentally friendly agriculture, as the area of Nordic agriculture recognised by the Commission could receive national support at then current levels. She reiterated that Norway would retain the right to keep its 12-mile exclusive fisheries zone along its coast until 2003, when the EU Common Fisheries Policy would be reviewed. She maintained that this right could not be changed without Norway's consent. She did admit, however, that the settlement on mackerel fishing, whereby boats from certain EU states could fish parts of their quota from Norwegian stocks, was not what the government had wanted. On the other hand, she pointed out that Norway might one day wish to fish for parts of its quota in another state's waters (Brundtland, 1994b, pp. 5–7).

Gro Harlem Brundtland, Thorbjørn Jagland as party leader, and Jens Stoltenberg as deputy leader, were the main actors in the government's campaign. The Labour Party's strategy was to refute the opposition's arguments that the EU was a source of both unemployment and environmental problems. The Labour Party also focused on how Europe had changed, and on the difference between the EEA and the EU. As in 1972, the party was split internally on the question of EU membership. A June 1994 opinion poll showed that 40% of the Labour Party voters in favour, 36% opposed, and 25% undecided, which was scarcely any better than 1972 (*Aftenposten*, 9 August 1994, p. 2).

This time, the Labour Party opted to tolerate organised opposition within its ranks, to avoid a post-referendum split. In 1972 opposition within the party was not initially accepted. It was clear that this permitted difference of opinion within the party would make it more difficult to win the EU battle. On the other hand, the parties opposing membership were unanimous in their standpoint, and could follow their own timetable in the campaign. The Labour Party and the Conservative Party had to take internal divisions into consideration when preparing their campaigns. In 1972, many loyal party voters who came under pressure from both sides, solved their problem by staying at home. This was especially true of the Labour faithful (see section 3.5).

After the vote at the LO convention on 22 September it was clear that the Labour Party had yet another problem to deal with. The majority of the convention voted against the LO-leadership's proposal advising their members to vote Yes in the referendum, by 156 to 149 (*Aftenposten*, 23 September 1994, p. 32). Gro Harlem Brundtland's immediate reaction was disappointment, but she also claimed that the Labour Party always had been open to different views, and that the convention was only advisory. However, this was the government's first blow in the run-up to the referendum.

6.3   The No Movement

The most important organisation opposing Norwegian membership of the EU was 'Nei til EF' ['No to the EC'], later renamed 'Nei til EU'. This started up as the 'Information Committee on Norway and the EC' ['Opplysningsutvalget om Norge og EF'] in November 1988. In 1990 it was transformed into a political organisation which presented itself as being national in scope, cross-party and anti-racist. The organisation grew quickly. In May 1991 it had 50,000 members, two years later this had risen to 130,000, making it Norway's largest political organisation. By the autumn of 1994 the number of members reached its peak at 140,000. In contrast to 'Folkebevegelsen mot EF' from 1972, which had a looser network and a central leadership, 'Nei til EU' was built up as an ordinary political organisation. The central administration consisted of a board and a council, an annual meeting, and a control committee. There were also several subcommittees, such as a women's committee and an EEA committee. It actively cultivated grassroots elements, and had 442 local teams as well as 19 larger regional divisions, for which the centre organised study groups. The organisation also had a youth branch, 'Ungdom mot EU' ['Youth against the EU'] (Nei til EU, 1994a).

'Nei til EU' actively campaigned against the EEA agreement from very early on. In March 1991 it arranged its first national information campaign and action week against the agreement, and in January 1992 it produced a report on the EEA's implications for Norway. It tried to stop the ratification of both the original EEA agreement and the amended version following the Swiss 'No'. There was, however, some sharp internal disagreement on the issue, a fact which came to the surface at the 1992 annual meeting. There was also some difference of opinion about the leadership, and attempts were made to depose Kristen Nygaard as head. Another accusation against 'Nei til EU' was that it was in the pocket of the agricultural organisations. They provided around five million kroner of the organisation's total donations of 5.5 million kroner. Yet it was clear that the membership was wholly united in opposition to the EU. 'Nei til EU' proved very effective in putting its viewpoint forward, with May Day and March 8 – Labour Day and International Women's Day – being used in the fight against EU membership. Two million copies of the organisation's newspaper, *Standpunkt*, were distributed just before the 1993 general election. 'Nei til EU' also published leaflets, fact sheets and books, including *Lesebok 94*. This was a collection of writings, poems and short-stories by Norwegian writers opposed to EU membership and distributed to all Norwegian homes (Nei til EU, 1994a).

The main aim of 'Nei til EU' was to prevent membership of the EU. It worked to secure Norwegian sovereignty in areas vital to the Norwegian welfare state, to secure full freedom to administer resources and the environment responsibly, and to maintain solidarity with countries and groups of people dependent on international aid (Nei til EF, 1993, chapter 1). After 1993, 'Nei til EU' concentrated on three core themes: popular sovereignty, national and international solidarity, and a sound environment. It sought to establish that the European Union stood in opposition to government by the people, solidarity and the environment. The idea was that all arguments in the debate would fall under these three categories. Arguments on democracy, subsidiarity and control would be covered by the first category; this included documentation of how the EU system and market forces worked. The second category included solidarity, redistribution and the need to redress differences between regions, sexes, North and South, and other social and economic cleavages. The third category covered debates ranging from product standards to supranationality, and criticisms of growth theory. 'Nei til EU' advanced its campaign in the summer of 1994 by publishing a 'counter-report' ['motmelding'] to the government's report on membership (Nei til EU, 1994b). The counter-report covered EU policies generally and the specifics of the agreement with Norway.

Until October 1993 'Nei til EU' was the only organisation for EU opponents. It included members from all political camps. However, Labour party adherents had long been discussing the setting up of their own organisation. 'Social Democrats against the EU' (SME) was established in October 1993 by a group influential Labour Party politicians. In scope it was similar to the 'Arbeiderbevegelsens Informasjonskomité' from the early 1970s. This latter, however, was initiated by the labour movement; politicians joined later, including Bjørn Tore Godal (see Chapter 3). The SME's leader, Hallvard Bakke, was a former Cabinet minister and a member of the *Storting*'s foreign affairs committee. The deputy leader was Tove Strand Gerhardsen, another former Cabinet minister who had not been willing to stay on after the reshuffle in 1992. The leader of the Labour Party's youth organisation (AUF), Trond Giske, was another member of the interim board of the SME (*Dagens Næringsliv*, 28 October 1993; *Dagbladet*, 27 October 1993).

The SME was an important element in the subsequent campaign. It was formed without reference to the party leadership, which was first notified the day before its incorporation. The SME stressed, however, that it was not a faction within the party, but an independent organisation geared towards the referendum, after which it would disband. Unlike 'Nei til EU', the SME was wholly in favour of the EEA agreement. This meant that EEA adherents had their own organisation. For the SME, the actual negotiations with the EU were relatively uninteresting; their position was that Norway should not have applied in the first place.

SME's programme, published in April 1994, did not go into the details of the negotiated settlement. It argued that it would be impossible to carry out a social democratic policy if Norway joined the EU. They felt that Norway would have stronger international influence if it remained outside the EU. Norwegian membership would mean that the EU would have a stronger influence on Norwegian society than vice versa. These arguments were based on the consequences of the Maastricht Treaty, which SME interpreted as a recipe for a 'colder' society, with more competition, higher unemployment, and more crime as well as other dangers. Norway should instead follow its own path, and continue to give priority to solving environmental problems, the poverty crisis and the conflict between North and South (Gerhardsen et al., 1994, p. 3). SME worked actively to refute statements from the Labour Party's leadership, and described the leadership's campaign as propaganda intended to scare people into voting yes.

In the spring of 1994, institutional participants on the no side agreed to coordinate their activities. This meant closer cooperation between 'Nei til EU' and the SME, the Centre Party, the Christian Democrats, the Liberal Party, the Red Electoral Alliance, and the Workers' Communist Party. The Farmers' Association, the Small Farmers' Association, and several youth and environment organisations also joined in.

A little more than a month before the referendum, EU opponents on the right of the Norwegian political spectrum established a new organisation, 'Borgerlige mot EU' (which might be translated as 'Non-socialists against the EU'). This body originated among Conservative voters in Northern Norway and sought to provide an alternative to the Conservative Party's yes-propaganda. A number of smaller or less serious organisations saw the light of day as the referendum approached, such as 'Veterinary surgeons against the EU', 'The youth campaign against the EU', 'Hooligans against the EU', 'No for the sake of the EU', and 'Blondes against the EU'.

6.4 The Yes Movement

The pro-EU side also had a range of both serious and less serious organisations. The Labour Party was the most important actor, with all its resources, network and position in government. 'Europabevegelsen' ['The European Movement'], however, was the most important independent organisation. At its annual meeting in March 1992 it transformed itself into a campaign organisation, a year and a half after 'Nei til EF' had done the same. The organisation wanted credibility with the public, and needed a new leader with a broader appeal. The choice of Fredrik Vogt Lorentzen, with his background as a former director in industry with a substantial golden handshake, did not fall into this category. Even the NHO, the financial support of the organisation, was not impressed by the movement's work and held back finance. After the Danish no-vote to the Maastricht Treaty in June 1992, Vogt Lorentzen publicly advised the government to put on ice its plans of seeking EU membership. Gro Harlem Brundtland's reply was that the European Movement was scarcely fit to obtain a yes from the Norwegian people.

In 1993 the former rector of Oslo University, Inge Lønning, became the new leader of the Europabevegelsen. Tor Wennesland came in as secretary general, with the highly demanding task of making the organisation politically accountable and increasing its members. The organisation never became anything remotely as strong as the 'Nei til EU' was on the no-side, and had around 35,000 members at its height in the autumn of 1994.

'Fra Nei til Ja' ['From No to Yes'] consisted of converts to the cause, people who had changed their mind since 1972. Most cited the many changes that had occurred in Europe as the reason for their change of heart. Financial support came mainly from the employers' organisation, NHO. The majority of board members had connections with the Labour Party, and the leader was Arne Thorvik (*Arbeiderbladet*, 9 June 1994, p. 9).

'Ja-aksjonen for norsk medlemskap i Den europeiske union (EU)' ['Action for Yes'] was established in February 1994 as a more outspoken group. It was headed by a former leader of the Labour Party's youth organisation (AUF), Turid Birkeland, and was supported by a number of famous public figures. It strove to create enthusiasm and self-confidence on the yes side, rather than to enter detailed discussions on the settlement. Its prime target was to make clear what would happen if Norway did not join the EU, and to show that this would mean a break with Norwegian traditions.

'Europeisk Ungdom' ['European Youth'] was the youth organisation of the European Movement and originally a sister organisation of the international 'Jeunesse européenne fédéraliste' (JEF), being federalistic in its approach. A few years before, however, it had revised its policy in order to establish itself as a proponent of Norwegian membership of the EU. The new approach meant a wider selection of members and less emphasis on ideology.

Other organisations smaller in scope were established closer to the referendum, including 'Farmers for the EU', 'Women for the EU', 'Brunettes for the EU', and 'Lapps for the EU' (a branch of the European Movement). An organisation called 'Don't know' was also set up (*Dagens Næringsliv*, 21 October 1994).

6.5   The Political Struggle

The opinion polls indicated that support for EU membership varied, but that the proportion of those in doubt was surprisingly large and quite stable (*Arbeiderbladet*, 20 July 1994, p. 8). In the first half of 1994 as in the first half of 1991 one in three had not decided how they would vote in the referendum. In 1991 around 50% of those who had made up their minds, were in favour of membership, but the corresponding figure in July 1994 was only 35%. International events influenced this decline. In 1991, optimism prevailed generally in Europe, following the fall of Berlin wall, and the unification of Germany. Denmark's no to Maastricht in June 1992, however, brought a dramatic fall in support for the EU in all the Nordic countries. The Balkan war, economic crisis in Eastern Europe and problems with the Maastricht agreement all influenced the drift of public opinion towards scepticism about the EU. The July 1994 poll, with four month to go to the referendum, showed 10% fewer in favour of membership than at the corresponding stage in 1972, when 45% were in favour (EIU, 1994, p. 4).

The political parties played a more active role in 1994 than in 1972. The Labour Party was the main actor on the yes side, with Gro Harlem Brundtland as the chief exponent for the membership cause. Through the presentation of the negotiation result in April and the White Paper in May, the Labour Party managed fully to present its view on the EU question. Because of the roles the different ministers had played during the negotiations, they also became important yes campaigners, whilst the prime minister concentrated fully on the more general arguments in favour of EU membership, such as the need for international cooperation and supranational decision-making processes.

The no-side, on the other hand, emphasised democracy and self-governance. Although the 'Nei til EU' was a very strong organisation, Anne Enger Lahnstein of the Centre

Party was the public political face for the no side. She was presented by the media as Mrs Brundtland's rival, and several times just before the referendum the two party leaders participated in political duels on television and radio which were rated afterwards in phone-in responses. A number of times, especially in Lahnstein's speech on Labour Day 1994, the Centre Party pronounced itself as an adherent of old social democratic values, such as market regulation, social equality and social security (Jenssen, 1995a, p. 25). The battle was tough for the Labour Party.

The Socialist Left Party (SV) occupied a key position in the *Storting*. As an opponent of membership, its votes together with those of the Centre Party would provide a blocking minority in the *Storting*, even if the referendum result was positive. The party had declared that it would respect a yes majority only if there was a majority in at least ten of Norway's nineteen counties [*fylker*], an almost impossible condition. However, a number of leading SV politicians dissented from the party line, and constituted an SV network for the EU. One of their priorities was to persuade the party leadership to accept the referendum result, even in the event of a narrow yes majority (*Aftenposten*, 27 March 1994; *Aftenposten*, 6 August 1994; *Dagbladet*, 31 October 1994). During the autumn they gained the support of former *Storting* representative and SV spokesman on finance, Arent M. Henriksen. The SV leadership had endorsed the Centre Party slogan presenting Norway as a country with a difference ['*annerledeslandet*']. Henriksen reacted strongly to this. He felt that Norway would inevitably be influenced by the EU in any case, as almost all of its trading partners were EU members. The real question was whether Norway should seek to influence the developments from the inside (*Aftenposten*, 25 October 1994, p. 4).

As the SV positioned itself behind the Centre Party on the opposing side, so the Conservative Party took a secondary role behind the Labour Party on the yes side. Acknowledging the Labour Party as the best persuader of those in doubt, the Conservatives concentrated on their own sympathisers and stressed primarily the security political aspects of EU membership in the run-up to the referendum (Jenssen, 1995a, p. 21).

6.6   The Final Spurt

In a Norwegian opinion poll published just before the Finnish referendum, 46% said they would vote yes if Sweden and Finland joined, while 41% said they would vote no. Without the Nordic condition, the no side's lead was 10% down on the previous month; 45% would vote no, 35% yes, and 20% were undecided (*Aftenposten*, 15 October 1994, p. 4). The results were surprising, especially since the poll was taken after the LO convention's decision to recommend a no vote. It also contrasted with the success of a mass no rally on 25 September on the 22nd anniversary of the 1972 referendum which mobilised 25,000 people. That very same day, the government announced that Thorvald Stoltenberg would be the Norwegian Commissioner if Norway joined. The timing of the announcement was clearly intended to distract attention from the rally (*Aftenposten*, 26 September 1994, p. 2).

On 16 October Finland voted for EU membership with 56.9% in favour, on a 70.8% turn out. Norwegian opponents to membership presented the result as a narrow majority; adherents presented it as a clear victory. The majority for Finland's accession had shrunk in the run-up to the referendum. The densely populated south secured the yes victory, but there was no majority in the country north of Tampere. The result also showed a divide between urban and rural areas. In this respect it resembled the Norwegian referendum in 1972. Unlike Norway in 1972, however, the difference between yes and no votes in areas voting no was often not larger than 3–4% and never larger than 12%. Yet it was clear that northern farmers voted no, even though membership would bring them a generous subsidies package (Arter, 1995, pp. 361–387).

Surprisingly, the Finnish referendum seemed to boost the no side in Norway. Immediately after the Finnish vote, polls indicated 51% no, 31% yes, and 18% undecided. Even more surprising was the answer to the question of intentions in the event of Sweden voting yes: 48% would still say no, 41% yes, and 11% did not know (*Aftenposten*, 18 October 1994, p. 2). The Finnish referendum did not produce the positive momentum the yes side had hoped for. The majority of Norwegians were still sceptical about EU membership.

In *Arbeiderbladet* on 29 October, Gro Harlem Brundtland answered criticism that she was unwilling to say anything negative about the EU. Without going into details, she admitted to reservations about the policies followed by EU countries in many areas. She went on to stress the importance of creating a better future for Europe, being a realistic goal for European cooperation at that time (*Arbeiderbladet*, 29 October 1994, p. 7). This was an important step in the government's campaign, and one which could have been emphasised more strongly, preferably at an earlier stage in the process. In many ways the yes campaign had accepted the no side's premises. A main reason was that by the time the yes campaign started, there were many questions the no side had presented for answering. This led to an over-selling of the EU by the yes campaign, instead of leading a campaign independent of the no side's arguments.

Another problem for the government was that a number of questions were still unresolved at the conclusion of the negotiations in March 1994. The agricultural and the regional policies chapters both had open sections. The Norwegian government promised that these problems would be ironed out before the referendum. The outstanding items concerned support in general; the level of national supports in the transition period, the areas eligible for support under northern agriculture, and how much would be provided; and the measures needed to integrate Norwegian agriculture into the CAP (Stortingsmelding 40, 1993–94, pp. 194–196; *Dagbladet*, 9 June 1994, p. 10). Also outstanding were the levels of investment support to primary agriculture and of support to mountainous and disadvantaged areas (LFA), the areas eligible for disadvantaged area support and for EU rural development programmes, safety clauses for the food processing industry and the agricultural sector, the trade surveillance system for processed products, and investment procedures for the food processing industry (Stortingsmelding 40, 1993–94, pp. 197, 204–205). Most of these areas were duly finalised by the end of July, although some, like regional aid, dragged on into November.

The obvious result of these issues not being settled was to create uncertainty and confusion, leading those trying to make a choice to be even more wary. Opponents also used this fact to their own favour, pointing to the unfinished nature of the whole question. It therefore did not have a positive effect on the referendum result.

On 29 October, the incoming President of the EU Commission, Jacques Santer, announced the distribution of portfolios for the new Commission. Thorvald Stoltenberg of Norway was to be responsible for the fisheries directorate. Making the announcement,

Santer stated that the appointment was made in order to help the yes side (*Dagens Næringsliv*, 31 October 1994, p. 18). The news was welcomed by Stoltenberg himself and by the yes campaign. Gro Harlem Brundtland said that it was a signal that the Commission would emphasise responsible administration of resources and firm control in its fisheries policy (*Arbeiderbladet*, 31 October 1994, p. 8).[1] The no campaign, on the other hand, claimed the nomination of Stoltenberg as Fisheries Commissioner was a tactical move to induce a yes vote; and one which would not succeed. Kristen Nygaard, leader of 'Nei til EU', Oddmund Bye, leader of 'Norges Fiskarlag', Kjellbjørg Lunde of SV and Anne Enger Lahnstein of the Centre Party all rejected the idea that the nomination would have any effect on the November 28 vote. Oddmund Bye noted that Norway would have to adjust to the EU's rules and regulations in any case (*Dagens Næringliv*, 31 October 1994, p. 18).

On 13 November the Swedish people said yes to European Union membership, with 52.3% voting in favour and 46.8% against. The turn-out was 83.3%. The country was divided in two, with 12 of the 24 counties voting yes (Widfeldt, 1996). The vote was narrower than expected, but the Norwegian government still hoped that the 'Sweden effect' would help a favourable Norwegian decision.

Three days after the Swedish referendum Ivan Kristoffersen, the editor of *Nordlys*, recommended a no vote to his readers:

> We would be far from reality if we asked people to vote anything other than No. We would be extremely stupid to ask people to turn their back on their immediate environment, on the vulnerable ecology, and on the existing way of life for which Norway is responsible (*Nordlys*, 16 November 1994, authors' translation)

Yet he admitted that the choice would have been easier if Norway had obtained a different fisheries agreement. He criticised the government for not admitting that they had backtracked.

The yes side was not able to find a joint strategy before the Swedish referendum, and the 'Sweden effect' had lesser influence than expected, not least because the no side had prepared themselves and the people for a Swedish yes. In an opinion poll taken on the day of the referendum, only 7% had decided after Sweden's referendum, while 78% had decided some time before (Aardal & Jenssen, 1995, p. 37).

The negotiations, the referendum, and the *Storting* represented three hurdles for Norwegian membership. The outcome of the negotiations was contested. Mrs Brundtland managed to reach an agreement which her cabinet could endorse, including the three ministers most closely involved in the negotiations – those for foreign affairs, foreign trade and fisheries – and who had opposed membership in 1972. In the referendum campaign, the Labour Party campaigned hard for 'its' settlement. It was essential for any prospect of victory that the referenda in Sweden and Finland produced yes votes. 'The Nordic alternative' – a prominent theme in 1972 – would thereby no longer be an option, except within the EU. With a positive popular vote, the threat of the Centre Party and the Socialist Left Party continuing to block entry in the *Storting* would be lessened.

6.7   The Referendum Result

The result of the referendum on 28 November was 52.2% No and 47.8% Yes (Central Bureau of Statistics, 1995). The turn-out was an exceptional 89%, which was 9.7% more than in 1972. Otherwise the voting pattern was very similar to that of 1972, with urban–rural, centre–periphery, and town–country axes, and with the south against the north. While the stability in the pattern was evident, it also contained one important new element: a majority of women voted No. As much as 57% of the women did not want to join the EU, while 52% of the men were in favour (Bjørklund, 1994, p. 3).

The result was a clear blow for the Labour government. The yes campaign was the main responsibility of the Labour Party and the government. But the whole campaign had proceeded on the basis of the no side's arguments. It portrayed the issue as one of democracy against the Union, and claimed that Norway's sovereignty was at stake. This was not satisfactorily rebuffed by the government, which was pushed into a defensive stance, passively trying to claim that EU membership would lead to a vague 'additional democracy'.

The most striking aspect of the referendum in 1994 was the similarity it had to that of 1972. This was surprising because nearly half of the voters in 1994 did not have the right to vote in 1972. The great changes in society and in Europe had not changed the voting pattern. The result was, as in 1972, a clear division between town and country, and between centre and periphery, and between north and south Norway.

However, the opinion pollsters MMI made a survey on the day of the referendum which gave interesting results (*Dagbladet*, 30 November 1994, p. 3). It showed that the class perspective from 1972 was also valid in 1994. Workers were against membership and officials for, leading officials more for than the lower graded, and that lower-paid employees were more opposed than more educated and better paid ones. However, this does not show the whole picture, because of the vast growth in the public sector since 1972, and because the two sectors were seldom differentiated in surveys in 1972. Where it was surveyed, employees in the private sector had been a little more sceptical towards the EC in 1972 than those in the public sector. In 1994, however, the private sector was clearly the EU-proponents' sector: 57% of those employed in the private sector voted yes. Because the private sector was a large sector this was a quite substantial group. Close to four out of ten yes voters worked in the private sector, as compared with one out of four no voters.

Contrary to the public image, the significant no voters were not farmers and fishermen. According to MMI's survey, only six percent of the no voters were attached to the primary sectors. Women were a new no-resource as compared with 1972. Among the no voters women employed in public administration were four times as many as the no voters from the primary sector. This was the biggest change since 1972. Women in public administration had been a growing group since 1972. This provided the no voters in 1994 with one of its major differences from 1972. But women constituted a large no-resource not only as employees. The women's no-majority was larger than the men's yes-majority. 57% of the women in general voted no, whereas 52% of the men voted yes. This had also been the case in Denmark over the Maastricht Treaty in 1992, and in Sweden the yes-majority among men had been stronger than the no-majority among women.

The traditional party lines were erased. In the Labour Party only 65% of the voters followed the party leadership and voted yes. One element reflecting this was the LO's no-resolution, which had been partly ignored by the leadership. The result showed that the government's arguments had not reached out to the people. Opposition to the EU had become part of the culture in parts of the country.

An interesting element of the referendum result was that the southwestern coast of Norway still was against joining, in spite of the great influence oil had had there since 1972, indicating that involvement in the oil industry did not necessarily encourage support for EU membership. The decline of the yes-position in Bergen and Stavanger was clear. Opposition to the EU was still strong, in spite of the increasing density of populations in the towns since 1972. Clearly not only farmers and fishermen were against the EU.

6.8 Conclusions

What comparisons can be made between the 1994 attempt to join the EU and the 1972 attempt to join the EC?

There were notable similarities. The main issues were the same: agriculture, regional policy, fisheries, offshore oil and gas, and sovereignty. The most vocal opposition to membership came from the same quarters: the urban left and the rural voters. The farmers' and fishermen's organisations were still strongly against, and a grass-roots 'no' movement began its campaign well before the 'yes' organisation had an agreement which it could defend. Another similarity was that a minority Labour government was in power, nominally in favour of joining but with a number of opponents of membership among its ranks.

There were also significant differences. First and foremost, the international and European context had changed. The Cold War had ended and the EC had become the EU; the Union had decided to create a common foreign and security policy and indicated an intention to negotiate a common defence policy in 1996. The economies of the West European countries had become more integrated in terms of trade, capital and even labour. More decisions were subject to majority votes in the Council of Ministers, and the power of the European Parliament was increased by the Maastricht Treaty. In the years after 1972 the EC had developed new regional, social and environmental policies. It was also clear that the EU's agricultural and fisheries policies would undergo major changes in the coming decade. In 1994 the European Union included the United Kingdom and Denmark, as well as three southern countries which joined in the 1980s. In other words, it was a much different entity from the EC of 1972, and it was part of a totally changed European scene. The 1994 membership question was not just a replay of 1972.

Secondly, the Nordic dimension had changed. In 1972 none of the Nordic states were members of the EC, and the Norwegian referendum was held a week before that of Denmark. Opponents could thus claim that all the Nordic states could well remain outside the EC and could then strengthen their economic cooperation. In 1994, Denmark had already been a member of the EU for over twenty years. It was a founder member of the EU, though somewhat reluctantly. As the Norwegian referendum was scheduled to take place after those of both Finland and Sweden, it was always likely that those states would be on their way to EU membership when Norway voted. This was expected strongly to affect Norwegian voters, and particularly Labour Party supporters who felt solidarity with their sister parties in the other Nordic states. Nordic cooperation was among the arguments for a no vote in 1972; in 1994 it was an argument for a yes vote.

Thirdly, the negotiated settlement differed from 1972. The special position of Nordic agriculture was acknowledged, and the fisheries settlement was endorsed by the responsible minister, a self-confessed sceptic. Furthermore, three of the ministers who conducted the negotiations in Brussels were former opponents of membership.

Finally, the position of the Labour government was different from that of 1972. Mrs Brundtland went into the negotiations with a strong political base, after her government's gains in the 1993 election. This election also strengthened anti-membership parties; paradoxically, this seemed to help Norway's case in Brussels, in particular by showing the need to moderate Spanish demands on fishing. Key countries such as Germany and France realised that Norway had to have a settlement for which its government could win support. Perhaps the most important difference from 1972 was the Labour government's determination in the negotiations not to repeat the experience of 1972. This was the explanation for the new stress on the EEA; the cautious approach to the membership application; the choice of former opponents for the negotiating team; and the push for an 'acceptable' settlement.

Yet popular scepticism towards the whole process of integration as displayed in the EC and European Union endured in Norway. Bolstered by oil revenues and comfortable with a well developed welfare state, Norwegians felt able to pick and choose with respect to the integration menu. In the end they chose the option which they perceived would maintain their country's autonomy rather than attempt to exercise influence within a larger organisation, the European Union. In doing this, they pointed up the difference in approach between the Norwegian *nation* (or most of those that voted on this occasion) and the Norwegian *state* in the form of the political elite and administrators. The plans of the state representatives were thwarted by the disapproval of a majority of the nation.

Note

1   Fisheries has been a matter of Community competence (rather than national) since the adoption of the Common Fisheries Policy in 1983. The provisions governing the integration of Spain into the CFP allowed for a transition period, which was to be brought forward as a result of the 1994 negotiations.

PART II
NORWEGIAN ALLIANCE POLICY

7
The Road to Alliance: 1945–1949

7.1 Introduction

An important element in Norway's relationship with the rest of Europe has been the consideration of the country's security. According to perception, Norway can be seen as being in the most untroubled part of the 'quiet corner of Europe' or can be portrayed as a front-line state between two nuclear powers. The self-perception of Norway's strategic position by the security policy decision-makers has swung between the two stereotypes : during the 1920s and early 1930s, the country was seen in the former light, somewhat optimistically as it transpired. From the end of the Second World War until around 1989, Norwegian decision-makers – followed by most of the public – have increasingly seen their country in the context of the superpower rivalry known as the Cold War. It was realised within a few years of the end of the Second World War that the all-pervading contest between East and West would not pass by Norway. The only questions were how the country would respond to the new division of Europe and, once a choice had been made – to become formally allied with the Western side – what level of commitment was needed by Norway to maintain its security within the new NATO context. This chapter, and the following two, deal with the answers that Norway gave to those questions.

The development of Norway's security from 1945 to the end of the Cold War demonstrates important aspects of the country's relationship to the European integration process. First, it should be remembered that the Atlantic Alliance has itself been an important part of European integration. It has provided Western Europe with the institutional framework for the deepest form of defence cooperation between European states seen outside wartime, albeit undertaken in a North Atlantic context. Secondly, the security issue has been one of importance in the West European integration process. The Treaty of Dunkirk in 1947, through the Brussels Pact of 1948, the efforts to create a European Defence Community in the early 1950s, the creation of the Western European Union, the development of European Political Cooperation and the EU's Common Foreign and Security Policy have all demonstrated an enduring concern for security issues in the context of European integration. Thirdly, security requires a commitment of resources, whether defence-related or diplomatic. These can be national or – especially for a small state such as Norway – they can come from outside from institutions such as NATO, the United Nations or the Conference on Security and Cooperation in Europe (CSCE, later the Organisation for Security and Cooperation in Europe, OSCE), or through bilateral relations with other states, whether in an alliance or not. To obtain security benefits from outside, a country such as Norway normally has to make its own commitments, both to its own defence and to international arrangements. The nature and the extent of these commitments from 1945 are the themes of Part II of this book. They not only chart the re-establishment of Norway as a secure, sovereign state after the Second World War, but they demonstrate the involvement of the country in international security agreements at an Atlantic and European level. This demonstrates the sort of international involvement that the people and politicians were prepared – or were obliged – to accept, and those which were rejected. The preference structure in the area of security (see Table 2.1) gives some indication of the reasoning behind the approach to wider West European integration by Norwegian decision-makers and voters. It demonstrates a strong willingness to become involved with the United Kingdom and the United States – the Atlantic powers – though not at any price; a consideration for the Nordic neighbours, though with few formal links in the security field; and a wariness about connections to continental Europe.

The background to Norway's adherence to the North Atlantic Treaty can be seen in the country's foreign and defence policy since independence in 1905. There was the assumption that the United Kingdom, as the dominant sea-power in the region 'could be relied upon to prevent, in her own interest, any attempt by other powers to gain a foothold on the Norwegian coast' (Riste, 1984, p. 42). During the First World War Norway – together with Denmark and Sweden – remained neutral, though this policy was accompanied by a commitment of the sizeable Norwegian merchant marine to the allied cause.

In the inter-war years, although the three Scandinavian countries often had differing security political preferences, they developed their policies along similar lines until the mid-1930s. Belief in the idea of collective security, embodied in the League of Nations, was succeeded by a return to traditional neutrality when the ineffectiveness of the League became evident. Norwegian and Danish neutrality was marked by a degree of scepticism about defence, Sweden providing a sharp contrast to this by embarking on a major rearmament programme in the late 1930's.

In spite of their different war experiences, the three Scandinavian countries (including Sweden from November 1946), again chose collective security after the war, this time through the United Nations system. Confronted with escalating antagonism between the two big powers, however, the UN soon proved almost as impotent as the League of Nations, and a number of European countries again drifted towards neutrality. The Scandinavian response was a kind of bridge-building or non-bloc policy, and this inclination was strongest in Norway.[1]

The period between 1947 and 1951 represents for Norway the transition between its bridge-building policy and the formal turn to the West, typified by its entrance into NATO. Hence Norway's membership of NATO, and what it signified, has been a subject of dispute among researchers (Riste, 1985b). The Norwegian decision to join NATO was seen at the time as a fundamental change in Norwegian security policy. This viewpoint has both been confirmed, but also disputed by researchers.[2] Nils Morten Udgaard has regarded both the change to the 'Atlantic policy' during the war and the change to the 'bridge-building policy' as fundamental changes of policies (Udgaard, 1973). Olav Riste, on the other hand, has stressed the continuity of Norway's security policy from 1905 to the present: the basis for Norway's security has constantly been protection by a British, and later American, defence umbrella, even though the setting has changed over the years. He depicts Norwegian security policy as a two-stage rocket. The Great Powers' common interest in keeping conflicts away from Norwegian territory is the first stage, and the Anglo-Saxon Powers' self-interest in actively protecting Norway is the next (Riste, 1984).

7.2 Norway's Bridge-Building Policy

All declarations of neutrality and non-alignment lapsed after the German invasion on 9 April 1940, and in the autumn of 1940 the Norwegian government in exile launched its so-called 'Atlantic policy', based on close cooperation with the Western allies not only during, but also after the war.[3] This policy was softened towards the end of the war, in exchange for what was later termed the 'bridge-building policy'. The political leadership regarded good relations with the Soviet Union as necessary, not least because they wished for a smooth withdrawal of the Soviet liberating army from North Norway at the end of the war.

The concept of 'bridge-building' can be misleading, and is often interpreted as Norwegian aloofness towards the Great Powers rather than as an attempt at active mediation between them. However, when the United States introduced the Marshall Plan in July 1947 as economic relief to a war-ridden Europe, Norway was initially loath to participate. The best explanation for this attitude is a reluctance to choose sides in the Cold War, and thus undermine the 'bridge-building' policy by harming relations with the Soviet Union (Pharo, 1976, pp. 125–53). When it became clear that all the Western European states would participate in the programme, the government felt that non-participation would appear more suspicious. Norway thus accepted the Plan.

Norwegian researchers have debated the question of when Norway turned from 'bridge-building' to full adherence to the Western alliance. The traditional view, which accords with the perception of the contemporary foreign policy actors, was to date the shift to February/March 1948 (Lange, 1966). Tensions between the blocs increased throughout 1947–48, starting with the Soviet refusal to join the Marshall Plan. The Norwegian government regarded the subsequent expansionist Soviet policy as a threat, a view enhanced by the events of early 1948. The coup in Prague, the Berlin Blockade and the subsequent establishment of the Brussels Pact, the Soviet Treaty of Friendship, Cooperation and Mutual Assistance with Finland, and rumours that Norway would be offered a similar pact, all led Norway to consider entering an alliance. However, this view was revised by historians who claimed that many of the key politicians changed their stance even before February 1948 (Eriksen, 1972; Skodvin, 1971).

From the end of January 1948 to the end of March 1949, the professed direction of Norwegian foreign policy changed completely. The catalyst of this change was British Foreign Secretary Bevin's proposal on 22 January 1948 for a Western Union for European defence (Eriksen, 1972). The initial official reaction to Bevin's speech was very guarded, though a thorough reconsideration of Norwegian foreign policy by the government and within the Foreign Ministry was initiated. The speech also created public pressure on the government. When both the non-socialist opposition and activist circles within the ruling Labour Party showed signs of impatience in April 1948, it was time to rethink Norwegian security policy. However, the first response was not a move closer to the proposed Western Union.

7.3   Plans for a Scandinavian Defence Union

At a meeting of Nordic foreign ministers in late February 1948, Halvard Lange raised the issue of a Scandinavian Defence Union, a notion with roots in the 1930s and war period (Blidberg, 1987). Despite positive Danish and Swedish reactions, no decisions were taken (Skodvin, 1971, pp. 90–122).

Meanwhile, developments in Czechoslovakia and Finland, as well as rumours that something similar could happen to Norway, greatly worried Norwegians. Norway quickly decided to rebut any Soviet advance, and the situation eased a little during April 1948. Norway's security dilemma was still not resolved. A Western European solution was not of interest to Norway, as it entailed more intense cooperation with the continent and involvement in its conflicts. A closer connection to the Scandinavian countries and to Britain was seen as a better solution for Norway, perhaps through some sort of loose attachment to the Western Union (Skodvin, 1971, p. 122).

On 3 May 1948 Swedish Foreign Minster Östen Undén put a proposal for Scandinavian defence cooperation to Norway's Foreign Minister Halvard Lange, Prime Minister Einar Gerhardsen and Defence Minister Jens Christian Hauge. For the rest of 1948, Scandinavian defence cooperation dominated the political agenda. Negotiations began in the summer of 1948. The Swedish concept, as outlined by Undén, was of an alliance isolated from the West – in effect, Swedish neutrality extended to the Scandinavian area. For Norway the priorities were to secure weapons supplies from the United States and to establish a firm attachment to the West, while the Danes wanted a Scandinavian solution either way. The negotiations foundered. In January/February 1949, the three governments admitted that the conditions for establishing a Scandinavian defence union did not exist. The abortive attempt at comprehensive defence policy cooperation left Norway back where it started. However, the Scandinavian option had been shown not to be viable.

Varying explanations have been offered for the negative result. Most historians agree that domestic preferences, historical experiences and geostrategic positions generally explain the different choices of the three countries, rather than international pressures (Eriksen & Pharo, 1993, p. 13). The Norwegian historians Magne Skodvin and Knut Einar Eriksen both stress the lack of a common Norwegian–Swedish security interest, and thus the absence of a basis for a Scandinavian solution (Eriksen, 1972; Eriksen & Skodvin, 1981; Skodvin, 1971). The Swedish historian Kersti Blidberg follows this line, attributing the failure of the defence negotiations to the different foreign policy judgement of the three, a development that can be traced back to the 1930s or before (Blidberg, 1987). However, it has recently been revealed that Swedish postwar security policy leant more westwards that earlier assumed (SOU, 1994). In spite of this, however, the failure was clearly linked to differences in security policy structures and party political processes, differences which were developed in earlier decades and were accentuated during and immediately after the war.

When the defence discussions began in the spring of 1948, the main lines of Norwegian and Swedish security policy had already been set. Yet the details of Norwegian policy following the stabilisation of the postwar situation were not clear until the defence union negotiations ended. For Norway, and also for Denmark, Nordic defence cooperation also contained a threat of dominance by Sweden, given Sweden's economic and military superiority (Blidberg, 1987).

7.4 Choosing the Atlantic Alliance and the Norwegian Base Policy

At official level, little was said about the alternative of an Atlantic security scheme, which became a strong contender for Norwegian preference in the autumn 1948. But on 10 December Lange indicated that Norway might have to seek a solution to its security problem within a wider framework, should the Nordic alternative fail to provide a satisfactory answer.

However, the public was not officially informed about the contemplated alternative to the Scandinavian defence union until Lange made a major policy declaration in the *Storting* on 27 January 1949, when he revealed the differences of opinion that had emerged between Denmark, Norway and Sweden during negotiations. In view of Norway's exposed strategic situation, Norway regarded the likely effect of a Scandinavian defence union as an insufficient deterrent, while Sweden wanted an isolated pact, not linked to the Western Powers. After visits to Washington and London, Lange advised that Norway should participate in the Atlantic Treaty. Once the Labour Party and the *Storting* had accepted this option, Norwegian accession to the North Atlantic Treaty was formally approved by the *Storting* at the end of March (Eriksen, 1972, pp. 220–46).

Seen from the outside, the Norwegian government's decision to sign the treaty was made very quickly. The idea had, however, matured within the government for over a year, since the hectic days of February and March 1948. The Norwegian government in exile had concluded from its experiences on 9 April 1940 that the expected, but not officially declared, guarantee from Great Britain was not sufficient, and that assistance had to be prepared in peacetime. A similar judgement lay behind the 1949 decision to sign the North Atlantic Treaty. The need to formalise a security guarantee was based on two assumptions: first, Norway's strategic position was more exposed than politicians and officials had earlier presumed, and secondly, Western assistance had to be planned in peacetime, if it were to be effective in war, or to be a greater deterrent than in 1940.

In spite of the 'bridge-building' period, so-called 'functional ties' had existed between Norway and Great Britain since the war. Military cooperation included the stationing of Norwegian troops in Germany under British command, and training of Norwegian military personnel under British direction, and the procurement of British weapons (Archer, 1989; Eriksen & Skodvin, 1981; Riste, 1982). In other words, continuity was apparent in Norway's Western orientation. Riste's conceptualisation has been challenged by Tor Egil Førland (1988a), and this has led to greater precision about the concepts in question, such as 'change' or 'turning point'. There is still some disagreement about whether there was a shift in the Norwegian security policy in 1949, how great it was and what its nature was. The time perspective is relevant in this connection; different conclusions can be drawn depending on whether the starting point is 1905 or a later date. Whilst Riste is clearly correct about the long-term perspective, 1949 *was* a turning point in the sense that it *formalised* what had previously been assumed by Norwegian authorities. In terms of the nature of Norway's relations with the West, NATO membership was no radical innovation; in terms of formalities and institutions, it represented a new beginning, at least in peacetime.

Norwegian leaders constantly pursued a dual line: association with the West, whether formalised or not, and Nordic cooperation. The question of choosing between Nordic countries and the Atlantic Alliance did not arise until these elements appeared incompatible, at the end of January 1949. Within the Norwegian leadership, conflicting opinions persisted even after the decision to join the Alliance. The Labour Party had a strong commitment to solidarity. This had developed primarily during the 1930s in response to the threat to democracy, and gained further support during the war. After the war, the key position of internationalists in the Labour Party meant that what had earlier been a minority view became the party's main foreign policy line. The driving forces behind this change were Martin Tranmæl and Haakon Lie. In 1949, when this policy line was being formalised, it became apparent that the party's ranks included groups which clung to elements of the foreign policy of the thirties, including neutrality and a Nordic orientation (Blidberg, 1987; Eriksen, 1972).

Norway's rapid entry into the Alliance was preceded by a declaration by the government stating that it would not allow foreign bases on Norwegian soil in peacetime. The declaration was a response to a Soviet note that criticised the Atlantic Pact, inquired about the Norwegian government's relation to it and asked whether it intended to have foreign bases on Norwegian territory. The note was answered by the Norwegian government within a couple of days (Skodvin, 1971, pp. 333–6).

The Norwegian declaration on bases stated, 'the Norwegian government will not accede to any agreement with other states which commits Norway to receive bases for the armed forces of foreign countries on Norwegian territory as long as Norway has not been attacked or subjected to threats of attack.' (Gleditsch & Lodgaard, 1978; Wilkes, Gleditsch & Botnen, 1987). This statement did not constitute an internationally binding agreement; it was thus open to the Norwegian government to amend or interpret it as it saw fit. The declaration had two main motivations: to calm the Soviet Union and to pacify Norwegian opinion. Reluctance to bind Norway too closely to the United States was also a factor, as was consideration for any effect on Finland. Furthermore, the wartime German occupation was still fresh in the memory: the upset that foreign troops could cause small communities was fresh in people's minds (Lange, 1966, pp. 44–5). Norway was seemingly not asked to provide bases at the time of negotiating the Atlantic Alliance (Riste, 1985b, p. 145). Furthermore, it seems likely that, by early 1949, Norwegian decision-makers did not feel that their country was under an immediate threat of attack (Ørvik, 1986, p. 195) and thus the reasons against having bases prevailed.

During the twelve months following Norway's signature of the Atlantic Pact, the government sought to enlighten the public about the new shape of Western collective security. It stressed the commitment towards mutual assistance, and presented Norway as a likely recipient rather than provider of such assistance. When NATO's 'Strategic Concept' was introduced in December 1949, the Norwegian authorities were silent about the US insistence on an 'integrated defence' as a precondition for assistance. In the Norwegian text of the agreement, 'integrated' was translated as 'co-ordinated' (Tamnes, 1986b, p. 8; Tamnes, 1989, p. 206). Moreover, Norway was exempted from reciprocal assistance in relation to base rights, due to its 'no bases' policy, on which it had insisted upon from the start, as had Denmark. As for actual defence capabilities, little was said officially, probably for very good reasons. However, the Defence Minister, Jens Christian Hauge, stressed that Norway's adherence to the North Atlantic Treaty had removed its basic defence problem: the danger of being the isolated target of an assault.

7.5   Conclusions

The history of the development of Norwegian national security policy immediately after the Second World War is best described as a very gradual process. Norway – while safeguarding its special position as a front-line state – attempted to 'nail the Anglo-Saxon powers' to their presumed responsibility for the security of Northern Europe. Seen in this perspective, the decision to sign the Atlantic Treaty simply brought the prospect of external assistance closer (Riste, 1985a).

In the 1948 to 1949 period, Norwegian decision-makers were faced with three main security policy options. They almost seemed spoilt for choice : Norway could remain neutral as it had done in the inter-war period, but this time with the added nuance of UN collective security and the policy of 'bridge-building' between East and West; Norway could join a Scandinavian defence agreement; or the country could join the Western bloc, with the North Atlantic treaty being conveniently on offer. In fact, the menu for choice was limited by mainly international factors but also by domestic considerations. Internationally, the bridge-building option became less tenable in early 1948 with increased tension between East and West. As the two sides entrenched, the conciliator's role became more difficult. The fear of pressure from the Soviet Union tended to change Norwegian perceptions of the Soviets and made Norway a candidate for an agreement with the West. This also reflected the move of the Norwegian Labour Party away from being a coalition partner with the Norwegian Communist Party to being a deadly enemy. However, Norway did not immediately turn to Britain and the US. There was still a Nordic option in 1948, and this was considered for some nine months. In the end, the dynamics of Nordic cooperation failed here as they did in the area of trade. However much the Nordic states might have in common, their strategic positions and preferences – born partly from their varied war-time experiences – were different. The negotiations may have helped to change domestic thinking within Norway away from choosing between alliance and neutrality to one of deciding between different alliance options.

The security differences between the Nordic states may not have mattered so much had not events stressed these disparities, and the actions of outside powers pressed Norway to make its choice. The preference of the Atlantic powers – Britain and the United States – was to carry Norway with them into the new Alliance, though other states such as France had doubts. British and American viewpoints were not likely to be dismissed by a Norwegian government that owed its existence to these two countries. At the same time the reality of the USSR as a liberator and a neighbour had to be addressed. The outcome forged in 1949 was not ideal for Norway but it was seen as the best on offer. Signature of the North Atlantic Treaty at least could be seen as a deterrent because an adversary could not count on a negative US response under Article 5. At most it was the start of the process of tying the Atlantic powers more closely to the future defence of Norway. It brought no immediate credible promise of armed assistance, but neither did it heighten tension in the Nordic region by the presence of stationed troops or bases. It divided the Nordic countries into members and non-members, but left open the possibility of informal contacts on security matters and each Nordic state could still consider the interests of the others when arranging its own defence. It formally committed Norway to the Western side of the Cold War, but – partly because the country was not part of the central continental core of the Alliance – it could be allowed a certain latitude in pursuing more ameliorative policies towards the Eastern bloc. Indeed, Norwegian entry into Atlantic cooperation was not without qualms; the country's attitude has been labelled 'conditional' (Eriksen & Pharo, 1993). Domestic opinion pressed the government to undertake what could be regarded as a traditional Norwegian approach to conflict in international relations, one that sought to bring harmony and persuade all sides to negotiate wherever possible. How this approach fared during the progress of the Cold War will be seen in the following chapter.

Notes

1   Finland's fate after the Second World War has differed so much from the rest of the Nordic countries that they cannot be seen as a whole.

2   See Eriksen, 1972; Lundestad, 1980; Riste, 1985b; Skodvin, 1971; Tamnes, 1987; and Udgaard, 1973.

3   The Foreign Minister, Halvdan Koht, with his firm neutralist approach, was personally blamed for Norway being so unprepared for the German invasion, and was replaced in November 1940 by Trygve Lie, who initiated this 'Atlantic policy'. Halvard Lange succeeded Lie in February 1946, after the latter had been elected Secretary-General of the United Nations.

8

Norway in the Cold War: 1950–1962

8.1 Introduction

The creation of the North Atlantic Treaty in 1949 changed the basis for Norway's security policy. Not only had the country received promises of support from the other allies in case of attack – whatever that was worth at the time – but there was the prospect of developing a longer term security relationship with the Alliance members. However, Norwegian ministers had tried to make sure that, as far as possible, Norwegian preferences would be respected in any relationship. This was not always easy as Norway was the recipient of security while countries such as the United States and the United Kingdom were being asked to provide security for Norway. Nevertheless, as seen in Chapter 7, Norway had an existing relationship with these two countries, and this chapter will show how that developed within the period of the depths of the Cold War, that from 1950 to 1962. It will show how Norway, as a small but strategically significant state, developed its role within NATO, its ambivalence towards nuclear weapons and its participation in NATO's surveillance and communications activities. As will be seen, these aspects of Norwegian security policy were not without their domestic opponents, and their activities and influence will be noted.

The context within which Norway was acting during this period was one of hostility between East and West that sometimes was expressed in armed conflict – such as the Korean War from 1950 to 1954 – or in crises such as those over Berlin (1961) and Cuba (1962). Despite occasional thaws, such as that in 1954 after the death of Stalin, the relationship was one typified by ideological competition, mistrust and rearmament. The Soviet bloc faced NATO in a divided Europe and Germany. There was a cult of secrecy within the Soviet Union, and the US military was scarcely open about its activities. Technological change, especially that affecting weaponry, could give one side a lead in the arms race. Forces were deployed by both sides to reflect their particular military doctrines which themselves mirrored a number of factors, the most important being the perception of the other side's strengths and weaknesses, the state of technology, and bureaucratic, budgetary and domestic political elements. On the NATO side, the role attributed to members such as Norway depended on the demands of the prevailing doctrine, as well as the resources that country could offer. These might be in the form of military forces, but could also be command, control, communications and intelligence (C^3I) facilities, bases or diplomatic resources.

From 1949 to 1962 NATO played a vital part in Norway's security considerations. Membership brought obvious privileges such as the assumed protection of Article 5, but it also required certain commitments by member states. It is the attempt by Norwegian decision-makers to assimilate those demands with their own – and party and public – interpretation of Norway's security needs that will be recounted in this chapter.

Norway's foreign policy after 1949 has been seen as moving between four different circles: the Atlantic, the Western European, the Nordic and the global (Eriksen & Pharo, 1991, p. 193 – see also Table 2.1 above). Norwegian politicians have clearly regarded Atlantic cooperation as the most important, and NATO membership has been a cornerstone of Norwegian security policy. Norway's close attachment to Britain was gradually replaced by that to the United States after it joined NATO (Berdal, 1996, p. 5). In its defence concerns, Norway was constantly looking over its shoulder at the Soviet Union, and its border with that country gave Norway a special position within NATO, with which it had to cope. Relations with the other Nordic states on security matters were divided between those with Denmark and Iceland, which developed apace within NATO, and those with Sweden and Finland, which continued on a more tacit level.

After signing the Atlantic Treaty in 1949, Norway's security policy encompassed complementary elements; though given different labels by researchers, the basic content is the same. Johan Jørgen Holst described Norwegian policy towards the Soviet Union as a policy of *assurance* and *deterrence* (Holst, 1966). Closely linked to this analysis are Rolf Tamnes's concepts of *integration* and *screening*. Tamnes particularly examined Norway's policy towards the USA, which he characterised as one of integration with the West and NATO, while at the same time trying to keep some distance to the power which guaranteed Norway's security. This led to a policy of screening against the USA and NATO (Tamnes, 1987; Tamnes, 1991, p. 298). Geir Lundestad also attempted to pin down the conflicting elements in Norway's security policy. His description combined a wish for *integration* with the Western allies with *defence* against becoming too integrated. Towards the Soviet Union Norway's policy has been that of *screening*, though with obvious elements of *conciliation* (Lundestad, 1992). The official Norwegian line from the mid-1970s to the end of the Cold War was to use the concepts of *securing*, but *assuring* against the Soviet Union (Skogan, 1980). The following section traces the development of these elements in Norway's foreign and security policy in the 1950s, and demonstrates the pragmatic and parsimonious approach taken by Norway towards commitments within NATO.

8.2   The Organisation of NATO and Norway's Role

The outbreak of the Korean War in the summer of 1950 had a far-reaching effect on the world's military order. It created a more tense relationship between East and West, and spread a common fear of a new world war. It led to rearmament in Norway, and it contributed to the transformation of the North Atlantic Treaty into an organisation with an integrated command structure. After this, containment of the Soviet Union assumed a military aspect, and was no longer just economic and diplomatic. NATO's new structure was agreed in the autumn of 1950. The acceptance of the principle of forward defence meant a widening of Alliance responsibility up to its member countries' borders; defence was no longer based on the securing of key points. This in turn implied the strengthening of continental forces, because of the Soviet Union's strength as a land power. NATO's Continental Strategy caused Norway as a maritime country to be uneasy about its own position.

The militarisation efforts in NATO brought the two conflicting sides of Norway's security policy into sharp focus. On the one hand, Norway tried to draw the attention of

NATO and the Western powers to the Northern region or flank, while at the same time it maintained its base policy. Norway's special concern was the defence of Northern Norway. Norway was in many ways more important strategically than Denmark and Iceland, because of its border with the Soviet Union. However, NATO's principle of forward defence fitted well with the USA's view of NATO's flanks as springboards for defending the continent, and led to an emphasis on the Northern Flank in the years 1950–1952. The US wish for facilities in Norway – to sustain its nuclear policy, as well as to provide early warning and intelligence – further added to Norway's importance in these years (Berdal, 1996, pp. 14–16; Tamnes, 1991, pp. 64–7).

Norway's base policy was feasible in 1949 partly because the United States was not at that point interested in having bases on Norwegian territory. By 1950–51, on the other hand, the Americans regarded the gap in air cover in the Nordic area as more of a problem, and as detrimental to US interests. Norway had in effect come under the US nuclear umbrella when it signed the Atlantic Pact, and when it agreed to the Strategic Concept in December 1949 (Tamnes, 1986b, p. 8). In October 1950 the US Air Command offered to station about 200 tactical fighter aircraft at Norwegian airfields. Norway refused because of its ban on the stationing of foreign forces in the country in peacetime but Norwegian opinion was divided on the offer. The military authorities were in favour, the government was ambivalent, and the *Storting*'s enlarged foreign policy committee came out against the proposition. The aircraft were finally stationed in Scotland in 1953. Nevertheless, following an agreement between Norway and the Strategic Air Command (SAC) in 1952, they received frequent landing access to Norway, and the stationing of equipment and a limited number of American ground personnel was accepted. The Norwegian authorities had their misgivings about the SAC agreement, but they accepted it as long as it was compatible with the base policy (Beukel, 1974; Tamnes, 1991, pp. 71–4; Villaume, 1989).[1]

The Norwegian bases declaration of 1949 was not watertight, and left a certain margin for re-interpretation. In February 1951 defence minister Jens Christian Hauge made Norway's base policy more precise, arguing that the 1949 declaration was compatible with participation in NATO's military cooperation, and that it did not preclude specific kinds of collaboration. These were:

- the opening of bases for allied armed forces in the event of an armed attack on the North Atlantic area, or at a point when the Norwegian authorities might feel subjected to a threat of attack and might ask allied forces to enter the country;
- the conclusion of conditional agreements with its allies with the above situation in mind, in the required constitutional forms;
- the construction of military facilities in such a way that they would be suitable to receive and effectively support allied armed forces which were to be transferred to Norway in order to aid the defence of the country; and
- participation in allied joint manoeuvres or short visits by allied air and naval forces in peacetime (Wilkes, Gleditsch & Botnen, 1978, p. 281).

It was important for Norway to establish a clear Western presence during these first years of NATO. Norway tried, and partly succeeded, in committing the Western powers to the defence of the Northern flank (Tamnes, 1991, p. 11). Because of the British reluctance to provide extensive forces for the Northern flank, defence minister Hauge started instead to rely on the Americans. Norway and Denmark persuaded Eisenhower that this area was important, and the mark of this success was the establishment of a regional defence command for the North of Europe (Villaume, 1995). This Northern Command, based at Kolsås in Norway, had a British Admiral as Commander-in-Chief, and a US General became the Air Force Commander.

In spite of Norway's bases policy, close cooperation between Norway and its allies opened up in the military field, partly within NATO and partly bilaterally. The phrase 'the Norwegian base-policy has a firm basis' became something of a refrain over the years (Gleditsch, 1978). Yet it served also to conceal political disagreement over security issues. Norwegian decisions and statements were unilateral, and were formed in reaction to external events. They did not imply any obligations according to any treaty, and they could be withdrawn whenever Norway wanted. Ambiguity about the real content of the statements created a certain freedom of action for Norwegian governments.

8.3   NATO's Nuclear Weapons Policy: Norway's Ambiguous Attitude

In 1952 the United States decided to build up its tactical (short-range), medium-range and strategic weapons, and after 1952 'massive retaliation' was the NATO strategy in case of attack. From then on, USA and NATO policy in this respect towards Norway was not clear, though there was a general wish to place tactical and medium-range weapons in Western Europe. After the SAC agreement, however, Norway was seriously involved with NATO's defence strategy, and this strategy became more clearly nuclear-oriented after 1956–57. In 1956 NATO introduced a new strategic concept, giving less weight to conventional weapons and stressing its willingness to use nuclear weapons. The new principles were also known as 'the new weapons concept' (Tamnes, 1991, pp. 92–6).

The Norwegians had been discussing what line to take on nuclear weapons since 1955. That NATO was from the start based on US-produced nuclear weapons, was accepted by Norway when it entered the alliance, even though the political leadership downplayed this aspect for fear of public opinion. The political leadership was convinced in principle of the value of nuclear weapons for common defence. In 1955 foreign minister Lange stressed that NATO's strategic concept worked as a deterrent and was therefore an asset for the West (Stortingstidende, 1955, pp. 559ff). The question of the direct role of nuclear weapons in the defence of the Northern flank, however, was much more delicate (Tamnes, 1991, pp. 160–5).

The political leadership in Norway generally tried to avoid any major decisions concerning nuclear weapons. But from 1957, in the light of NATO's new policy decision, the government had to take a stand (Tamnes, 1989, p. 208). It accepted that allied air assistance could be armed with nuclear weapons, even though Norwegian consent had to be obtained in every case. From then on, simulated use of nuclear weapons was a regular element in the allies' exercises in the north of Norway. The Norwegian government had reservations about the use of nuclear weapons by the Norwegian armed forces. On this issue a split appeared on the political landscape, also within the government. The Liberal Party and the majority of the Labour Party were categorically opposed to nuclear weapons. The military authorities, Haakon Lie of the Labour Party, parts of the Conservative Party and the Agrarian Party wanted Norway to accept tactical nuclear weapons, and preferably medium-range missiles as well.

One of the two factions that emerged within the government was centred around Prime Minister Gerhardsen. The other centred on Foreign Minister Lange and Defence Minister Nils Handal. Both factions agreed that it might become necessary for Norwegian armed forces to use nuclear weapons in a war, and accordingly to store nuclear ammunition in the country in a crisis or in case of war. They also agreed that it was out of the question for Norway to store nuclear weapons in the circumstances pertaining at the time. The Lange/Handal faction, however, felt that this position left little room to manoeuvre. The situation might change, and they wanted Norway to have a flexible approach: Norway should be open to the possibility of stationing nuclear warheads already in peacetime (Tamnes, 1991, pp. 162–4).

The Labour Party convention in 1957 passed an 'ex auditorio' proposition which demanded a ban on nuclear tests and affirmed that nuclear weapons should not be stationed on Norwegian territory. In December 1957 Prime Minister Gerhardsen told the NATO Council meeting in Paris that stores for nuclear weapons or medium-range missiles on Norwegian territory were out of the question. With this, Norway placed a second important restriction on its own and allied activity on its territory in peacetime. This restriction came without notice, before any request to store such weapons. In this respect, Norway's nuclear policy from 1957 had much in common with its base policy. Both created deep divisions across party lines and within the government.

At its 1961 convention the Labour Party softened its line on nuclear policy, by accepting NATO's nuclear strategy. This opened the way in a war situation for Norway to call in American forces armed with nuclear weapons. NATO was at the time reviewing its strategy formulation of 1957 and debating whether it should be extended for another three years (Tamnes, 1989, p. 229; Ørvik, 1986, pp. 203–12). While the Labour Party resolution softened the Norwegian attitude towards nuclear weapons, it also rejected the idea of storing them on Norwegian territory in peacetime. As such it was a direct answer to the NATO challenge.

The 1961 decision can been seen as a turning point, partly because of the rejection of the storing of nuclear weapons; more importantly, it marked the end of the nuclear integration process in NATO which had started in 1954. The revision of this approach took time, and the concept of 'massive retaliation' remained the Alliance's formal strategy until December 1967. Norwegian political leadership, however, abandoned any thought of arming their forces with nuclear weapons (Tamnes, 1989, p. 232).

Interpretations of Norwegian nuclear policy, as of Norwegian security policy generally, vary. Was the international environment more significant than domestic considerations? Rolf Tamnes acknowledges the importance of international environment, while showing that domestic considerations heavily influenced key figures. The prime minister and the cabinet majority decided to limit the nuclear option and to continue its screening policy towards the USA and NATO (Tamnes, 1989, p. 232). Ørvik (1986, p. 206) places emphasis on the role of Gerhardsen and the left-wing of the party and saw the decision as a move to 'semialignment'. An explanation might be that while a new opportunity was created by the strategic changes, a positive response was needed to sign up to the new nuclear option and there was just not the willingness present in the Norwegian political system to so this. It did not reflect on the alignment of the country, more on the limitations of Norwegian involvement in the alliance.

While the debate on nuclear weapons continued, the Soviet Union in 1958 advanced the idea of a Nordic nuclear free zone (Hetland, 1985; Holst, 1966; Lodgaard, 1982;

Tamnes, 1983, p. 11). This was probably an attempt to loosen the ties between the USA/NATO and Norway and Denmark. Norway and Sweden bluntly rejected the idea, and it had little immediate effect. It was feared that the deterrence effect of Norwegian and Danish membership of NATO might be weakened. Yet the idea remained on the Soviet foreign political agenda, as will be seen below.

8.4   Loran C, U2 and Omega

Norway's base policy and nuclear policy both had a degree of ambiguity. The word 'base' was never authoritatively defined. It has been taken to mean an area with permanently stationed large armed units from foreign countries, or alternatively as a facility on Norwegian territory to which Norwegian authorities did not have access (Gleditsch & Lodgaard, 1978, p. 319). Olav Riste (1984) suggests that a base could also be a storage facility for equipment, fuel, etc., under the control of a foreign power.

The Loran C and Omega affairs were controversial in both the base and the nuclear debate. Loran C and Omega were two navigation systems built and operated from Norwegian territory mainly to deliver navigational data to US strategic submarines; Loran C was linked to the American Polaris programme (Gleditsch, 1978, p. 42). The US request to build a Loran C station in Norway was submitted in May 1958, with a transmitter being completed in October 1959, and a second one, on Jan Mayen, being operational in December 1960 (Berdal, 1996, p. 124).

The case of Loran C provides a good example of the flexibility of Norwegian base policy. It was American down to its wires. The Norwegians who operated it were, initially, trained by Americans, and its main purpose was to provide data for US weapons. It stood on Norwegian soil and was operated by Norwegians; Norway probably had the right to close the facility in case of war (Gleditsch, 1978, pp. 44–5).

The reaction to an American request in September 1964 to set up the Omega navigation system in Norway was more cautious than to the Loran C proposal. The defence minister assured the *Storting* in February 1965 that Omega would not serve Polaris submarines and in September and November 1971 the Cabinet and the *Storting* in turn consented to a permanent Omega station. Yet Norway had moved to a more careful attitude towards any project which might impair relations with the Soviet Union, in the wake of the U2 and the RB-47 affairs (Tamnes, 1991, p. 218).[2] The U2 affair – in which a U2 intelligence aircraft was shot down in May 1960 over the Soviet Union on its way to Bodø, provoking a formal Soviet protest to Norway – perhaps warned Norwegian decision-makers of the necessity of having strict control of their own policy.

The above episodes show that Norway has had strong concerns about US policies in the North, and that it tried to act non-provocatively towards the Soviet Union, while accepting the importance of a Western presence in Norway (Tamnes, 1991, p. 172). They also illustrate the two conflicting elements – integration and screening – in Norwegian security policy, in that Norway wished the security provided by the US-NATO equipment, but at the same time wanted control over it and the freedom to adjust its own relations with the Soviet Union. This was not an easy balancing act.

8.5   The European and Nordic Dimensions

The close Norwegian cooperation with the United States, outlined above, grew through-out the 1950s and 1960s. It was mirrored by a falling away of the previously intimate relationship with the United Kingdom which, mainly for economic reasons, could not sustain its presence in Northern waters. The one service that did remain committed to the defence of Norway in the early years of NATO was the Royal Navy (Archer, 1989, p. 23), though this presence started to fade after the Defence Review and budgetary cuts of 1957 (Berdal, 1996, p. 86). From then onwards the British naval effort in the North Atlantic was scaled down as a greater emphasis was placed on the nuclear deterrent. One indirect effect was to encourage the US to fill the gaps left by the British and to project their navy – including ballistic-missile carrying submarines – further north up into the Norwegian Sea. This 'brought Norway more directly into the nexus of superpower military confrontation in the late 1950s' (Berdal, 1996, p. 108). Sometime after the announcement of British cuts, the Norwegians persuaded the United States to finance half the cost of the renewal of the Norwegian navy to allow it to protect its own long coastline (Tamnes, 1991, pp. 153–4).

One possible extra source of assistance for Norway's defence during this period was Sweden. Though Sweden had maintained its neutrality policy after the breakdown of the Scandinavian defence union talks in 1949, it now seems clear that a close functional cooperation was maintained with NATO states, especially by the Swedish military (Cole, 1990; SOU, 1994). However, there were clear limits on intimate links with Sweden, as the Swedish government did not wish to compromise its neutrality. Nevertheless, Norway could take into account the very real presence of the Swedish air force when considering the defence of Southern Norway in particular, and the Swedes seemed to value functional military contacts with Norway as a means of maintaining links with the US and Britain (SOU, 1994, p. 290).

Another possible source of military support to Norway's position in the north of Europe, emerged by the end of the 1950s. This was the Federal Republic of Germany. The rearmament of the Federal Republic from the mid-1950s held potential benefits for Norway. In particular, the rise of the West German navy provided new partner for the revived Norwegian navy and assistance for Denmark and Britain in their naval operations in the Baltic Straits (Tamnes, 1991, pp. 147–8). However, care had to be taken on the political side. An effort was made in the late 1950s and early 1960s to alter the NATO command structure as a result of German involvement, but this met with some initial opposition from both Denmark and Norway, both of which were concerned about an erosion of their positions and the uncoupling of the Northern Region from the defence of Central Europe (Udenrigsministeriets Gråbog, 1969, chapter 9). In the end, it was decided to set up a Baltic Command (Commander Allied Forces Baltic Approaches) within the NATO command structure. Until 1959 the Norwegian government had resisted German representation at the Allied Forces Northern Europe headquarters at Kolsås, outside Oslo, on the grounds that public opinion, with its memories of German occupation during the War, was not ready for such a move. The Labour government con-tinued to be coy about the posting of senior German officers to Kolsås, and it was the centre–right coalition that changed that policy in 1965. West Germany had, by the early 1960, made an improvement to the defence of Norway by its inclusion into NATO and its rearmament (Jølstad, 1995). Close cooperation between the two countries started slowly at a low level and was hampered by political factors within Norway (Hermansen, 1980, pp. 223–37).

8.6   Domestic Political Opposition

Domestic opinion tended to be accepting of Norwegian membership of NATO throughout the 1950s. However, there was a higher percentage of opponents within the Labour Party than in any other party except the Moscow-oriented Communist party. An opinion poll in 1957 showed that 21% of the Labour voters who had heard of NATO were against Norwegian membership (Holst, 1967b, p. 242). There was also opposition to particular aspects of Norway's defence and again this was especially strong in the Labour Party. Rapid changes in the nature of NATO cooperation stoked disapproval. The main bones of contention were nuclear policy, defence spending and the length of the compulsory military service.

From the autumn of 1950 to the winter of 1954 the government tabled four separate proposals for extraordinary military expenditure at a time when NATO sceptics inside the Labour Party wanted to cut military spending. This group managed to obtain substantial compromises after opposition in the centre–right parties also became apparent. Most notable was the reduction of the length of military service (Meyer, 1989). Though Norway's defence expenditure rose sharply after the start of the Korean War, it also benefited from a series of deals with the US throughout the 1950s and 1960s, whereby the United States – and NATO – co-financed particular defence projects. While Norway had to pay its share, the leadership of the Labour Party realised that Norway's defence was being partly paid by other NATO countries. Public opinion seemed divided on the subject of defence expenditure (Holst, 1967b, p. 243).

The public was more opposed to other developments in NATO. In 1955, 74% of those asked were against German rearmament, and in 1959 49% were against (with 21% in favour of) German officers being stationed at Kolsås (Holst, 1967b, p. 244). As seen in section 8.5 above, the public view affected the government, especially on the question of West Germany and Norway. When military integration was put into practice, opposition was substantial; there was concern about German officers coming to Norway, and all political camps were hostile to the stationing of foreign forces on Norwegian soil (Hermansen, 1980, pp. 207–22). This gave a solid domestic foundation for the government's base policy.

The newspaper *Orientering* was a mouthpiece for views opposing official defence policy and had started life as a forum for opponents of NATO membership. The paper was not connected to any one party and its main ambition was 'to raise an unprejudiced debate on Norwegian foreign and domestic policy' and to propagate 'an alternative to steadily more one-sided power politics'. In practice, it condemned the persecution of the radical left and the limitations to the freedom of speech which accompanied the onset of the Cold War. Its preferred alternative to the bloc policy was neutrality, disarmament, the strengthening of the UN and the Nordic cooperation, the extension of cooperation with neutral countries, and an increase in development aid (Stenersen, 1977, pp. 379–81).

Until the start of 1958, relations between the Labour leadership and the group around *Orientering* were cool, but not bitter. The former saw little harm in the latter working off their opposition to government policies in the paper's columns. When some Labour

Party members tried to organise a more active resistance, a confrontation arose. The so-called 'Easter Rebellion' in 1958 featured a debate within the Labour Party on nuclear weapons and followed up a no-base resolution of the 1957 Labour Party conference. Radical students from the Socialist Student Group formulated a resolution that called upon the government to use its veto against West German rearmament (Eriksen, 1977, p. 246). It gained support from a number of Labour members of the *Storting* and from trade unions, and released neutralist, anti-militarist, and anti-German attitudes. While the resolution ultimately came to nothing, it was a warning to both the ruling Labour Party and to Norway's allies that care had to be taken in developing defence policy in the country.

In the end, several key figures in *Orientering* were expelled from the Labour Party in February and March 1961, and on 15 April the Socialist People's Party was founded. Norway's role within NATO's nuclear strategy and a fear of nuclear war was the issue that triggered the establishment of this new party. One influential group which shared these fears was called 'the 13'. This group was without party connections, but had a wide network of contacts. It campaigned particularly actively in the run-up to the Labour Party convention of March 1961. Yet 'the 13' exercised greater influence on public opinion generally than on the Labour Party's nuclear policy (Lindstøl, 1978).

8.7 Conclusions

Different explanations have been offered for Norwegian policy restrictions within NATO during the height of the Cold War. The bases declaration of 1949 stressed that Norwegian territory should not be used for any policy with an aggressive intent. On other occasions, the emphasis was on the wish not to provoke the Soviet Union. Much of the research on Norwegian base and nuclear policies addresses the significance of the international environment for the development of Norwegian security policy. In domestic terms, however, divisions on security policy in Norway were primarily within the Labour Party, in contrast to Denmark, where the divisions were predominantly between the various parties. Yet it is also clear that public concern about these issues was high, and this soon gave rise to the first of many grassroots movements.

During this vital part of the Cold War, Norwegian policy-makers managed a dialectic between various forces. On the one side there was what could be seen as the strategic requirements of Norway's position between two super-powers and of its NATO allies. This seemed to demand commitment in the defence field. It led to an increased defence effort by Norway to a level that showed such a sparsely populated country could maintain a reasonable national defence and could provide some facilities for outside assistance. It also meant that Norway became part of a US and NATO C^{3}I network and thus earned its spurs as a useful alliance member. The importance attached to Norway by NATO, and by the US in particular, changed with the prevailing doctrine. A start was made in defence relations with West Germany.

On the other side, there were pressures for restraint. At the international level, there was the desire to keep the Nordic area as one of comparative low tension within Europe. The absence of bases and nuclear weapons in the region during peacetime was consistent with this aim, as were constraints on NATO exercises in and around Norway. This was done partly in order not to provoke the Soviet Union, but was also part of a calculation about the security policies of the Nordic states as a whole. Each Nordic country considered the effect of its own security policy on those of the other Nordic states and there was a general avoidance of policies that could discomfort a Nordic neighbour and might upset the security pattern in the Nordic region. Finally, there were domestic considerations. The dominant Labour Party leadership had a clear idea of what was acceptable to party members and to the public. As shown in the Lund Commission Report, published in 1996 (Economist Intelligence Unit, 1996a, p. 8), the Labour governments during this period kept left-wingers under very close surveillance, but nevertheless nuclear issues sometimes played on the fears of the party workers – and a wider public – allowing the issue to become politically salient. This provided a constant reminder to the Labour leadership of the limits to their commitment to the North Atlantic Alliance. The nuclear aspect of the Alliance was either excluded from Norwegian soil or had to be undertaken in secret.[3] In the next chapter, the development of this commitment will be examined in the period when the Cold War – after some false starts – thawed.

Notes

1   Erik Beukel, 1977, sheds light, mainly from Danish sources, on Norwegian attitudes to the air forces of NATO states earlier attempt to procure bases and storage on Norwegian territory in 1951–53.

2   The RB-47 was a US reconnaissance plane shot down in international waters, according to the Americans, or in Soviet territorial waters, according to the Soviets, off the Kola Peninsula. The Soviet Union blamed Norway for aiding the 'spy mission' by permitting a Norwegian radio station to be used for communications. Norway denied the charge (Holst, 1967a, pp. 151–60).

3   There are indications that Norwegian air combat units were given training in the use of nuclear bombs in the 1960s. See statement by Martin Kolberg, State Secretary for Defence, *Norway Daily*, 1997, p. 1.

9

From Détente to the End of the Cold War: 1963–1989

9.1 Introduction

During the period from the end of the Cuban Missile Crisis in November 1962 until the fall of the Berlin Wall in November 1989, Norway's security policy was firmly fixed within NATO. The context for that policy was a series of events that led to first an easing of the Cold War, then a hardening in East–West relations and, finally, a mutual attempt to end the antagonisms of the previous forty years. With this changing strategic backdrop, Norway was able to manoeuvre substantially to improve outside commitments to the defence of the country. Yet it maintained the precarious balance between involvement in NATO defence arrangements and contributing to keeping the Nordic region as an area of comparatively low tension.

After the Cuban Missile Crisis, the feeling that nuclear war had been narrowly averted persuaded the two super-powers to place greater emphasis on the control of the weapons of mass destruction and on lowering international tension. Already the new Kennedy Administration was moving away from the threat of massive retaliation – that of launching an entire nuclear arsenal in response to any Soviet incursion into the West – towards a more measured and appropriate response, that of flexible response that called for a riposte at the level of the incursion but with the threat of further escalation (McNamara, 1962, pp. 16–17).

Even during the chilliest parts of the Cold War – in the Berlin Airlift Crisis of 1948–9, the Korean War and the Cuban Missile Crisis itself – the United States and the Soviet Union had maintained diplomatic relations and had continued to negotiate with each other over a range of issues. From 1963 until the end of the 1970s the two sides made a more conscious effort to agree on multilateral treaties – and some bilateral ones – that dealt with nuclear issues. In Europe, after a series of agreements involving the Federal Republic of Germany and its eastern neighbours, détente reached its symbolic climax with the Conference on Security and Cooperation in Helsinki in August 1975. This process recognised that, despite ideological differences, the European states – and the USA and Canada – had a common interest in a more peaceful Europe that also adhered to basic standards of human rights and fundamental freedoms (Archer, 1994c, Chapter 12).

The Soviet Union seemed prepared to take advantage of the opportunity of the US retrenchment after its withdrawal from South Vietnam and the subsequent collapse of pro-American forces there in 1975. Parallel to the arms control agreements, the Soviet leadership attempted to overtake the United States in the nuclear contest.

The period of détente came to an end and Ronald Reagan – elected to the US presidency in November 1980 – undertook to oppose the Soviet 'evil empire', to rearm the

United States and to embark on the Strategic Defence Initiative (SDI). The Reagan Administration instituted a New Maritime Strategy and also followed up President Carter's proposal to place updated intermediate-range nuclear forces (INF) in Western Europe as a balance to the seeming growth in Soviet and East European conventional and nuclear forces. The 'New Cold War' of the late 1970s and early 1980s reverberated in Europe. Acceptance of the INF decision by other NATO states became almost a test of loyalty. The maritime strategy seemed to threaten a naval nuclear conflict in Northern Europe. Sections of the West European public became wary of the rhetoric of the Reagan White House and of the apparent build-up of nuclear weapons in their midst. The Soviet leadership, ageing and dying, seemed unable to offer compromise, and the US president appeared unwilling to do so. The European members of NATO appeared to be caught between the contest of super-power wills, with rising defence expenditure as part of the price to pay.

In the end, the period of the 'New Cold War' turned out to be an interval between the era of détente and the deliquescence of super-power rivalry in the latter part of the 1980s. Mikhail Gorbachev's succession to the Soviet leadership in March 1985 and his introduction of 'new thinking' into his foreign and security policy, whereby the concerns and insecurities of the NATO countries about the Soviet Union were taken into account, did not go unanswered. Changes in the White House and the 1986 mid-term US elections, helped President Reagan to follow up the Reagan–Gorbachev Reykjavik summit of 1986 with disarmament agreements between the US and Soviet Union. The INF treaty of December 1987 was of the sort hoped for by countries such as Norway.

However the start of a disengagement process of the armed forces facing each other in Central Europe – which eventually led to the 1990 Conventional Forces in Europe (CFE) agreement – was not without problems for 'flank' states such as Norway, with the well-founded fear that the forces might be pushed out into the flank areas. Nevertheless, the CFE talks, from 1987 onwards, and the revival of the CSCE process seemed to indicate that a process of disarmament – so sought after by the Nordic states – was well under way (Holst, 1991b, p. 17). The collapse of the communist governments in East and Central Europe in late 1989 not only sped up that process but removed the ideological basis for the Cold War.

This chapter will examine the changing threat scenarios faced by Norway during the 1963 to 1989 period and will outline the relationship between Norway and its allies. It will consider another element that entered Norway's security calculations in the 1970s, that of the resources in and the defence of Norway's new offshore domain. Finally the effect on Norwegian security plans of the ending of the Cold War in the latter half of the 1980s will be examined. The chapter demonstrates the Norwegian preference for a strong Atlantic link in its security policy, its attempts to filter some aspects of that relationship, and the selective links with Western Europe in the security field.

9.2   The Soviet Union and the Northern Region

Even before Norway became a member of NATO in 1949, Atlanticism, as the basic element of its security policy, was seen as a bulwark against Soviet pressure, but was also combined with an active policy of assurance towards the Soviet Union which was continued in the periods from 1949 to 1962 and from 1963 to 1989.

The Soviet Northern Fleet was the smallest of the four Soviet fleets in 1950, but by the end of the 1960s it had become the largest and continued to grow during the 1970s and 1980s. The Soviet military build-up in the Murmansk area was already underway in the early 1960s after the Cuban Missile Crisis in 1962 and Khruschev's resignation in October 1964. This encouraged a re-evaluation of NATO's Northern Region both in the United States and NATO itself, which eventually led to a greater emphasis being placed on the West's defence presence there (Skogan, 1985, p. 45; Tamnes, 1991, pp. 238–69).

The Soviet expansion of its Kola bases was mainly a means of getting access to the Atlantic and was closely watched by Norway and its Allies. After the Cuban Missile Crisis, in which the United States had used its sea-power against the Soviet Union and Cuba, the Soviet leadership decided to expand the navy and, in particular, its presence in the North Atlantic. The aim was to allow the increasing sea-borne element of the Soviet nuclear arsenal to be deployed in submarines under the High Seas, and to produce a surface fleet that could have a global reach. One of the crucial areas that allowed the Soviet Union facilities to build its navy and ports with access to the open seas was the Kola Peninsula.

The result of the Soviet building programme can be seen in the Northern Fleet, which in 1950 had 30 submarines and nine destroyers, but by 1968 had 181 and 23 respectively. Throughout the 1970s the number of submarines remained at the 170–180 level and the number of major surface combatants (carriers, cruisers, destroyers, frigates and corvettes) in the Northern Fleet was between 40 and 70, often equalling the Pacific Fleet in size. In particular, the number of Ballistic Missile Submarines – hosting part of the USSR's nuclear deterrent – increased from 35 in 1969 to 53 in 1975. During the same period the number of attack submarines fell from 146 to 124. Also during that period, diesel-powered submarines were being replaced by nuclear-powered ones and torpedo-armed boats by cruise missile-bearing versions. Likewise the fleet of large surface combatants (carriers, cruisers and destroyers) grew from 29 in 1968 to 32 in 1975, with the Northern Fleet receiving four of the nine new cruisers built for the four Soviet fleets during this period. Also landing ships, absent from the Northern Fleet in 1968, started to appear in the Northern Fleet which had 14 by 1975 (Skogan, 1986; Weinland, 1986, pp. 23–8).

During the 1970s the Soviet Northern Fleet was still dependent in its submarine-based nuclear deterrent on vessels whose missiles had a range of 2400 to 3000 kms, though the newer type – the Delta class with its 6400 to 7600 km range – started to become more dominant after 1980. This meant that in the 1970s Soviet submarines had to deploy off the east coast of the United States in order to threaten major American cities. With the expansion of the Kola bases and the need for their submarines to exit into the North Atlantic, the Northern Fleet could not accept being 'bottled up' in their bases by the US navy. In a series of naval exercises – Sever 1968, Okean 1970, Okean 1975, Springex 1979 – the Northern Fleet projected itself out into the Norwegian Sea and started operations in the North Atlantic. If repeated in wartime, such operations could have threatened NATO's sea-lines of communications between North America and Western Europe with submarine attack. By the mid-1970s the situation was typified by a future Norwegian Minister of Defence and Foreign Minister, Johan Jørgen Holst as follows:

It is the intention of the Soviets to push their naval defence line outwards to Iceland and the Faroes. If this is a likely development, then it indicates that the Russians would, to an increasing degree, come to regard the Norwegian Sea as a Soviet lake, behind which, of course, Norway would lie. (cited in Berdal, 1974)

Though the growth of the Northern Fleet in the 1970s did not lead to the waters off Norway becoming a *mare sovieticum*, it did mean that the sea reinforcement of the country could be more expensive, should Allied navies be challenged by an active Soviet fleet.

The expansion and development of the Northern Fleet continued into the 1980s, with consequences for Norwegian security. As mentioned, the longer-ranged Delta strategic submarines became dominant in that fleet after 1980. These boats could deploy closer to their home ports – in the Barents Sea or the Arctic Ocean – because of their longer ranged missiles and could be more easily protected against Western hunter-killer submarines. By 1981 the Northern Fleet had introduced the Typhoon-class strategic submarine, specifically designed for under-ice operations, all of which were based on the Kola (Ries, 1988, p. 99).

At the same time as increasing its submarine presence in the Northern region, the Soviet Union had modernised its bomber force. By the mid-1980s the strategic Backfire bomber was being deployed and other intercontinental bombers such as the Bear H were being updated (Ries, 1988, p. 109).

The increased strategic importance of the Kola Peninsula and its surrounding seas for the Soviet Union meant that, though the Nordic region was not targeted by the intercontinental weapons there, a shadow was thrown across countries such as Norway by the consequent military build-up. Some of the forces deployed in the region had the task of air and sea defence of the strategic weapons and their military infrastructure, while others had theatre-level ground-offensive duties in the Nordic region to secure airfields and other key points which could otherwise be used in an attack on Soviet strategic forces (Ries, 1988, pp. 128–132). Even dressing these Soviet forces in their most defensive silk gloves, they still represented a sizeable military punch that could be used against neighbouring countries such as Norway. The importance of the Kola region for Soviet nuclear deterrence meant that, in a war or severe crisis, Soviet military action against the North Nordic region, especially Norway and Finland, could have been expected, if only to secure the defence of vital assets (Ries, 1988, pp. 128).

However, the rise of the Northern Fleet was not a story of unalloyed misery for Norway. First, as will be seen below, it did elicit a response from other NATO members and this was of such a magnitude that it may be said to have matched the Soviet expansion (van Tol, 1988, pp. 135–140). Secondly, as much of the fleet was constructed in the 1960s and early 1970s, it had a built-in obsolescence (van Tol, 1988, pp. 140-5). This meant that, by the mid-1980s, it was much older than the NATO ships and submarines that it was facing and, by the late 1980s, units were becoming redundant with little prospect of replacement as arms control agreements came into force and, more importantly, budgetary constraints began to tell.

Finally, it should be mentioned that during this period, Norwegian interest in the Soviet Union was not just associated with its military presence close to the Nordic region. It has to be seen in the wider strategic context outlined in section 9.1 above. Furthermore, there were other dealings with the Soviet Union over the two countries' offshore domains that did not always reflect the hostility implicit in the military situation (Sollie, 1988, pp. 31–43). After the advent of Mr Gorbachev, the military aspect started to wane and the economic, scientific and resource side of Soviet–Norwegian relations began to flourish (Scrivener, 1989).

In all its dealings with the Soviet Union, particularly in the 1963 to 1989 period, Norway was careful not to place itself in a position whereby it had to face its powerful neighbour alone. At a time when the strategic importance of the waters off Norway was perceived to be growing in the late 1970s, it needed little to persuade the United States to become more involved in the region, as will be shown below. It was clear that the European powers alone could not provide the sort of military presence to counter that of the Soviet Union, neither could they give Norway the powerful diplomatic and political support it sought in its negotiations with the USSR.

9.3 Norway and its Allies in the 1960s and 1970s

During the 1960s and 1970s NATO, under US leadership, underwent an important shift in nuclear doctrine from massive retaliation to 'flexible response' (McNamara, 1962, pp. 16–17). This suited Norway fine: massive retaliation had always been an unsatisfactory response to the threat of a Soviet move into an odd island off North Norway – 'salami slicing' – while flexible response allowed for such a move to be matched at the local level but with the threat of escalation.

This change presented challenges for Norwegian defence. If flexible response was itself to be credible, there had to be the forces either in place or ready as reinforcements to defend against a localised attack. Greater emphasis was placed by Norway on the defence of its northern areas and from 1961 Norwegian standing forces were airlifted once or twice a year to the north for exercises with local forces (Huitfeldt, 1985, p. 172). There was a cost for this greater defence effort: from 1959 to 1969, Norwegian defence expenditure as a percentage of gross national product averaged 3.7, compared with 2.9% for the previous six years (Brundtland, 1985, p. 188).

This national effort was backed by increased allied activity during the 1960s. Directly, the United States financed part of the cost of the re-equipment of the Norwegian navy and air force, and NATO infrastructure funds were used to modernise equipment and bases (Tamnes, 1991, pp. 203–4). The US stockpiled more equipment in Europe and improved its air-lift capability. The creation of NATO's Allied Command Baltic Approaches (COMBALTAP) in 1961 brought the Federal Republic of Germany more into the defence of the Baltic Straits which represented the 'soft underbelly' of Norway, though supply depots for the German navy had been made available in Norway from the late 1950s. NATO's rapid-reaction ACE Mobile Force (AMF) was established in 1960 and started to train in Norway in 1964. Also in that year, NATO's Atlantic Command began the TEAMWORK exercise series including naval forces from the United States, the United Kingdom, Canada, Germany, the Netherlands and Norway, and on land the EXPRESS series of exercises started. By 1965, the US Secretary of Defense was warning about 'pressure on the flanks [of NATO]' (Tamnes, 1991, p. 200). A Standing Naval Force Atlantic (STANAVFORLANT) was set up in 1967 and included frigates and destroyers from a number of NATO navies, including that of Norway. The same year a Canadian Air Sea Transportable (CAST) Brigade was committed to the reinforcement of NATO's Northern European Command, with a contingency option being Norway.

The rise of the Soviet navy in the North Atlantic during the 1960s and 1970s was matched by a decline in the US navy. The fleet of some 950 ships under President Kennedy in the early 1960s had shrunk to one of 459 ships by 1976 and the number of carriers from 24 to thirteen (Tamnes, 1991, pp. 253–5), though the fire-power of many of the newer vessels was greatly enhanced compared with that of their predecessors.

However, it was no longer seen as being realistic to expect US carrier task-forces to surge through the gap between the United Kingdom and Iceland towards the Norwegian Sea (Iden, 1986, p. 25). While the authorities in Oslo could do little to alter the new strategic balance in Northern waters, they could help to reduce the dependence of reinforcements for Norway on the threatened Atlantic shipping lanes. They did this by pre-stocking certain heavy materiel so that forces did not have to bring it with them across the Atlantic (or North Sea), and they made it easier to reinforce Norway by air. Furthermore, they supported an increase in the tempo of Allied exercises in and around Norway, allowing overseas forces to deal with the practical problems of reinforcement and to demonstrate Allied solidarity with Norway.

The 1971 Invictus agreement provided for storage facilities in Norway for spare parts, fuel, etc. for US maritime patrol aircraft. Also in 1974, the Collocated Operating Bases (COB) memorandum with the US allowed for the provision at Norwegian airfields of 'minimum essential facilities' for American fighter aircraft. The COB agreement initially foresaw ground spaces for aircraft, storage of fuel, ammunition and spare parts. These were subsequently supplemented by hardened aircraft shelters. A number of airfields, all in the south of Norway, were equipped to receive and support American fighter squadrons in an emergency. The squadrons could, however, also be transferred to airfields in other countries (Barth & Gleditsch, 1982; Holst, 1985a, pp. 66–7; pp. 237–8; Lundestad, 1992, p. 241; Tamnes, 1991, p. 248). The siting of the chosen airfields in the south of Norway can be seen as a response to the American wish to compensate for the lack of air bases in Central Europe, and as an effort to secure air supremacy over southern Norway, North Germany and the Baltic Sea (Tamnes, 1991, p. 237; Lundestad, 1992, p. 241).

The COB agreement, together with the installation of the Loran C and Omega systems, represented a development in Norwegian base policy as established between 1949 and 1951. In the preamble to the 1978 Defence Budget, the government listed activities deemed to be compatible with the base policy: the presence of allied military forces in Norway for short training periods or as a part of allied exercises; the establishment on Norwegian territory of facilities for command, control, communication, navigation or early warning for allied military forces; the establishment of depots for ammunition, equipment and provisions for allied military forces; and the participation of Norway within the integrated military organisation of NATO (Wilkes, Gleditsch & Botnen, 1987, p. 281). This adjustment removed the 1951 stipulation that facilities established in Norway had to be transferable to Norwegian control, while remaining in the hands of allied military forces. The shift lessened the distance between the de facto situation and the declared policy.

The Northern Region, including Norway, was important to the US as a base for early warning, intelligence, communication and navigation(Holst, 1985b; Tamnes, 1991, pp. 296–7; Wilkes, Gleditsch & Botnen, 1987). In the larger strategic perspective, however, NATO's Northern Flank and Norwegian military efforts had a relatively low priority for the Americans, especially during the 1970s.

These developments were made easier by an increased public awareness of Norway's strategic position. In February 1973 the major parties approved a report which stated that Norway's defence position had deteriorated seriously as a result of changes in Soviet deployments (Stortingsmelding no. 9, 1973–74, p. 17; Lundestad, 1992, p. 244). The report suggested that it would prove difficult to get allied support if the Soviet Union attacked, and hence it was important to maintain an allied military presence. Even though the report acknowledged that the Soviet military build-up was not directed solely against Norway, it led politicians and the military leadership to focus on the defence of the north of Norway. Both the Defence Commission's 1978 report and the Labour government's response stressed the North (*Forsvarskommisjonen av 1974*, 1978, p. 9; Stortingmelding 94, 1978–9), stating that Norway's own defence efforts gave priority to northern Norway.

After the initial few years of protest, support for NATO was high in Norway and opposition muted. Even the radical left was reluctant to demand withdrawal from NATO, reflecting a general concern at the Soviet naval build-up on the Kola Peninsula. The adverse effect on their country noted in 1973 by Norwegian politicians of the build-up in Soviet forces came at a time when Norway had decided to stay out of the EC. There was the fear that this could lead to Norwegian isolation from NATO, but this was far from the truth. In anything, the 'No' to the EC spurred a more reactive approach to NATO than previous to September 1972 (Tamnes, 1991, p. 265). The new opportunities offered by the Soviet activities in the North were to be matched by an increased willingness in Norwegian politics to react.

9.4   From New Cold War to a New Beginning

The cooling in East–West relations after 1979 and the subsequent toughening of American policy changed Norway's strategic situation within NATO and affected domestic opinion.

President Reagan sped up the rearmament begun under Carter. His administration thought in terms of prolonged war, in which case the sea lines of communication (SLOCs) between Europe and North America would play an important role. President Carter had already instituted an increase in ship numbers. Reagan's New Maritime Strategy (NMS) posited maritime superiority and forward sea control, also in the Norwegian Sea. This meant a dramatic increase in the significance of the northern flank as the US Navy contingency plans for war emphasised carrier battle groups being placed forward to threaten Soviet strategic bases such as those on the Kola Peninsula (US Naval Institute Proceedings, 1986; Tamnes, 1991, pp. 278–84; Lundestad, 1992, p. 247).

The plan was to place the Soviet sea-based deterrent in greater jeopardy, thereby forcing their navy to bring most of its attack submarines closer to home. This was presumed to ease the threat to NATO's reinforcement effort in the North Atlantic. In order to implement this forward strategy, the United States needed the support of Allied navies, particularly those of Britain and Norway, and it needed to secure control of the Norwegian bases in North Norway. In the words of the British First Sea Lord, 'the defence of Norway and the control of the Norwegian Sea are inseparable' (Staveley, 1986, p. 4). This meant the early deployment of Allied aircraft and amphibious capabilities to that area, and once again Norway's preparedness to receive such units was stressed. NATO's adoption of the Rapid Reinforcement Plan in 1982 increased the dedication of reinforcements to North Norway, in particular improving the availability of air support (Huitfeldt, 1987, pp. 121 & 139).

The 1971 Invictus agreement was extended in 1980, when it was agreed that in an emergency these aircraft could be transferred to bases on the mainland. This would allow US carrier-based aircraft to use Norwegian airfields should their carrier be badly damaged in war (Holst, 1989, p. 20).

The 1981 pre-positioning agreement for the American Marine Amphibious Brigade (MAB) provided another pillar of Norwegian-NATO cooperation, even if it had been under negotiation from the start of the 1970s. Agreement over the thorny question of the positioning of the heavy equipment for the Brigade was ultimately reached, with Trøndelag in central Norway being chosen. It was explicitly stated that the agreement would not conflict with Norwegian base and nuclear policies and the agreement was included in NATO's regional plan for the Northern flank in 1982. Nevertheless, while this new regional plan devoted greater attention to the Northern flank, it was still clear that NATO's main interest was the continent proper.

The renewed US interest in Norway posed some problems for the Norwegian government. With President Reagan in the White House and an intransigent Soviet leadership, strategic matters increasingly became a matter of public interest in Norway as in other European countries.

Even during the decision concerning the pre-stocking in Norway for the US Marine Corps from 1979 to 1980, a political debate arose – and leaked into the public domain – concerning the siting of storage and the possible use of the nuclear-capable A-6 aircraft. The Norwegian concern was that – apart from military considerations – the placing of Marine Corps materiel in North Norway, as originally suggested by the Americans, could be seen as provocative by the Soviet Union, as could the use of the A-6. In the end, the Norwegians got their way and the pre-stocking was placed in central Norway, while the Skyhawk replaced the A-6 (Tamnes, 1991, pp. 266–9).

NATO's 'Dual Track' decision, taken in 1979, led to the introduction of new nuclear missiles into Western Europe. This followed a heated public debate in Europe about the placing of so-called neutron bombs in Europe that had led to their deployment being cancelled. The publicising in July 1980 of a US Presidential Directive on nuclear policy (P.D.59) which some interpreted as plans for war-fighting and winning in Europe did not help (Evensen, 1983, p. 28). Jens Evensen, then a Foreign Ministry official but previously a Labour minister, advanced the idea of a Nordic nuclear-weapon-free zone, a notion that was supported by the Labour Prime Minister, Oddvar Nordli, in his 1981 New Year's speech. The proposal for a nuclear-weapon-free Nordic region had previously been advanced by President Kekkonen of Finland and had received some support from the Soviet Union (Archer, 1984, pp. 17–27). The idea was somewhat watered down by mid-1981 by the leadership of the Labour government under its new prime minister, Gro Harlem Brundtland, and appeared in the government's Long-Term Programme as being part 'of the work to reduce nuclear weapons in a wider European context' (Stortingsmelding 79, 1981, p. 22, authors' translation). This seemed to fit more comfortably with the ideas of other Social Democrat parties in West Germany and the Benelux countries, with which the Nordic Social Democrats had been discussing the matter (Tamnes, 1991, p. 269).

The Labour Party lost power to a centre–right coalition in September 1981 and the new government resisted Labour attempts to press its opposition to nuclear weapons (especially the INF ones) in parliament in November 1982, and March and November 1983. After the Labour Party regained power in May 1986, it again raised the question, and in 1987 the Nordic Foreign Ministers instructed a group of Foreign Ministry experts to study the idea. Their report appeared in March 1991, but did not bring the zone any closer to reality. Events had by then overtaken the idea, which had also lost its public appeal (Brundtland, 1986; Tamnes, 1991, pp. 289–90; Utenriksdepartementet, 1991). The question also arose whether navy vessels – including those from NATO members – visiting Norwegian ports should be required to declare that they were not carrying nuclear weapons. The new Labour government side-stepped the issue by referring to an earlier declaration which assumed that Allied vessels did not carry such weapons (Tamnes, 1991, p. 290).

The Labour government of 1986 also added a 'footnote' to a NATO communiqué concerning the American SDI programme which had provoked much opposition in Norway. The Norwegian 'footnote' annoyed the United States, and the Pentagon responded by leaving a greater share of the costs of certain defence agreements to Norway. The following NATO Defence Ministers meeting revised the text, and this allowed the Norwegian side to drop the controversial footnote. After the Reagan administration showed more interest in East-West cooperation, the Labour government became a strong supporter of the INF agreement and played down its opposition to the SDI programme (Melby, 1986). However, the INF treaty's ban on land-based missiles accelerated the deployment of American and Soviet sea-based cruise missiles in the seas to the north of Norway.

Another issue of contention between the Labour government and the United States was the Kongsberg affair. In 1987 it was discovered that submarine-related technology had been exported illegally from Kongsberg Våpenfabrikk – a state-owned Norwegian munitions company – to the Soviet Union over many years, in contravention of COCOM regulations. COCOM (the acronym comes from Coordinating Committee) was established in 1949/50 to deal with the multilateral strategic export control towards Eastern Europe. It was a US initiative, and Norway was a member from the start. After threats of retaliations, Norway went to great lengths to restore confidence, and the episode created only temporary damage to US–Norwegian relations (Førland, 1988b; Wicken, 1988).

These various episodes demonstrated the political problems experienced by Norwegian governments from the late 1970s to the late 1980s. Defence issues had a higher profile internationally and were more salient on the domestic political scene. This particularly affected the Labour Party, partly because it was in power in the crucial years from 1979 to 1981 and from 1986 to 1989, and partly because it had an active left-wing that was outspoken on nuclear and defence issues. Furthermore, in the early 1980s it was affected by some of the alternative defence ideas coming out of Germany and the United Kingdom. At the same time US governments were anxious that there should be little NATO dissent on nuclear and related issue, especially from countries such as Norway that relied so heavily on American defence support. Norwegian governments – particularly Labour ones – had to tread a tightrope on defence issues whereby established Norwegian principles, such as the base policy, were not transgressed; public opinion – especially that in the Labour movement – was not alienated; and yet the United States could still be persuaded that Norway was a good defence partner. The debates that wracked the Labour Party during this period must have encouraged the leadership not to raise security issues without very good reason. They also seemed to benefit the party at the polls very little and certainly did not enhance its standing in Washington or London. The connection with the European Social Democrats on this issue seemed to have brought little return.

9.5   The Offshore Domain and Defence

Securing fisheries resources has always been an important element of Norwegian foreign policy, and the delineation of fishing zones has repeatedly brought Norway into conflict with other foreign states. Territorial waters, however, were not such a big problem. Norway had a 4 nautical mile zone from 1812 until 1961, compared to the international standard of 3 miles. In 1961 Norway extended its territorial waters to 12 miles; Iceland had done the same in 1958 (Frydenlund, 1982, pp. 53–69; Holst, 1985c, pp. 350–65; Lundestad, 1992, pp. 244–5; Tamnes, 1991, p. 240). In 1974 a Norwegian government statement of principles argued for a 50 mile fisheries zone around the coast. In autumn 1976, the government went further and claimed a 200 mile exclusive economic zone (EEZ). This was a new concept, and it was a response both to technological change that allowed, for example, exploration for offshore minerals and over-fishing, and to the greater demand for resources, especially petroleum. Within an EEZ, the coastal state did not gain full sovereignty over the continental shelf and the sea column, but it gained jurisdiction over the resources within the zone. Territorial waters were still limited to 12 nautical miles.

In January 1977, five months after Norway claimed a 200 mile economic zone, the Soviet Union followed suit. This created problems of demarcation in the Barents Sea. Norway and the Soviet Union had been in negotiations on the Barents Sea since 1970, the question having arisen earlier in 1963. In 1977, the two parties were far apart. Norway favoured the median line between the two coastal states, which was advantageous to Norway and which had been used in disputes with Great Britain and Denmark. The Soviet Union favoured a continuation of the sector principle by which they claimed jurisdiction over a sector of the Arctic seas and which was to their advantage. Talks continued for years. The Grey Zone Agreement of January 1978 set down provisional rules for the regulation of fishing in parts of the Barents Sea. It allowed the Soviets to fish an area of 23000 sq. km. within Norway's offshore domain, and Norway to fish within 3000 sq. km. of Soviet waters. Either could allow third countries to fish in their own waters without notifying each other. The Agreement originally ran for six months, but it has been regularly renewed (Churchill, 1988; Hoel, 1994; Scrivener, 1989).

Norway and the USSR also disputed waters around Svalbard (Spitsbergen), although the two countries agreed that Norway had sovereignty within 4 nautical miles of the archipelago. This was set down in the Spitsbergen Treaty of 1920, which followed the principle of equal access to economic exploitation and allowed for a special tax regime for Svalbard. The Norwegian position on waters outside the 4 mile limit was that the shelf was an integrated part of the mainland; accordingly, it came under Norwegian legislation, rather than the Spitsbergen Treaty. Most other signatories of the 1920 Treaty disputed this view. The Soviet Union considered that Svalbard had its own continental shelf and fisheries zone which fell under the provisions of the 1920 Treaty. Despite this disagreement, the international community did not intervene when Norway in June 1977 declared a provisional, non-discriminatory fishery zone around Svalbard, stretching southwards to the 200 mile zone from the Norwegian mainland. For the time being this settled the regulation of fishing in this area (Ulfstein, 1995, pp. 439–54).

The creation of a 200 mile EEZ from 1 January 1977 was of importance for Norway in terms of resources and security. Though offshore petroleum exploration had already begun before that date, the EEZ helped clarify the legal status of some of the related activities and, with the creation of a Norwegian coastguard, provided surveillance and protection. The EEZ also saw the establishment of a defined, for the most part, and massive fisheries zone off Norway, which again was to be protected by the coastguard. Norway not only confirmed its growing status as an oil and gas producer, it also established itself as Europe's largest fishing power. A country that already had extensive global merchant shipping interests further increased its maritime dimensions and involvement in products – oil, gas, fish – that had both a European and a world market. Fish and oil had already played a role in the 1972 referendum and were to do so in that of 1994. In 1976 the Norwegian state showed itself willing to exercise national control of these offshore resources.

9.6   The Scaling Down of Defence Expenditure

As the NATO and USA contribution to the defence of Norway increased during the 1970s, so did Norway's own defence expenditure. The 1974 Defence Commission, reporting in 1978, recommended a 3% annual increase in the defence budget for the following 15 years and this figure was more or less maintained by Norway. Thus the Norwegian defence budget was relatively high throughout the 1980s, as Table 9.1 shows. Yet, the Norwegian Air Force had too few planes and too few experienced pilots, and Norway found it difficult to provide adequate command and control for allied air operations. This raised questions about the traditional concept of 'national balanced forces', and drew criticism within the alliance throughout the 1980s (Tamnes, 1991, pp. 288–9).

On 3 June 1988 the government presented a new defence report dealing with the period 1989–93 (Stortingsmelding 54, 1987–8), the last five-year period covered by the 1974 Defence Commission report. This report presented the political leadership's views on national and international development and outlined the priorities of Norwegian defence policy over the following five years. Given the favourable international situation, the 1988 report signalled a cut in the defence budget. This shift also reflected the country's weaker economic situation after a period of falling oil revenues which made expenditure reductions a necessity. The cuts also meant emphasis on efficiency, in order to maintain

Table 9.1   *Norwegian Defence Expenditure 1970–1996*

	1990 per capita	% of GDP (current prices)
1970		3.0
1975–79		2.9
1980–84		2.7
1985–9		2.9
1990–94		2.8
1993	773	2.7
1994	803	2.8
1995	700	2.3
1996	760	2.4

Source: NATO, 1997, pp. 5–6.

overall defence capability. The basic aims of Norwegian security policy remained unchanged: 'to prevent war in our area, to secure our sovereignty and freedom to act and to contribute to a peaceful development in the rest of the world' (Stortingsmelding 54, 1987–8, authors' translation). Whereas earlier long-term reports listed defence duties in order of priority, the 1988 report did not give specific priority to any single goal (Dalhaug, 1989, p. 45).

The 1988 report resulted in a 2% real increase in the defence budget, compared with the usual 3% or 3.5%. Personnel was to be reduced by 1%. Productivity, however, was projected to rise by 1% to 2% a year. Though budgetary considerations were uppermost, it is also clear that the reduction of the defence budget would not have been possible without the better climate in East–West relations, embodied in the INF treaty and the CFE negotiations.

Norway's military leadership, not unsurprisingly, were unhappy with the cuts and with the figures presented in the long-term report. The Chief of Defence (*Forsvarssjefen*), Vigleik Eide, maintained that the report's proposals would weaken Norwegian defence both quantitatively and qualitatively (Dalhaug, 1989, p. 47; Eide, 1988). The political and military leaderships were divided on how defence duties should be maintained and on the level of resources needed. The military leadership believed the long-term report was over-optimistic in its assessment of the potential for greater efficiency in the Norwegian defence system.

The proposed spending cuts did not have immediate effect. As can be seen from Table 9.1, Norwegian military expenditure decreased steadily from 1970 to 1984 as a proportion of GDP, reaching a low point in the 1980–84 period. It then rose again, reaching a high point by the end of the 1980s, but from 1991 the trend has been downwards though irregular.

Defence expenditure in Norway has reflected the seriousness with which security issues were taken, especially at a time when the Soviet Union built up its forces on the Kola Peninsula. There tended to be cross-party agreement on the defence budget, though the military often asked for more. Its own national effort and NATO support, especially from the USA, meant that, in the course of the 1980s, 'the defence of North Norway gradually reached a satisfactory level' (Molvig, 1994, p. 16).

9.7   Conclusions

As seen in Chapter 8, Norwegian Atlantic policy in the 1950s was closely related to fears about Soviet intentions after the outbreak of the Korean War. Norway therefore kept a low profile vis-à-vis the USSR. The Soviet Union, on the other hand, sought to extend its relations with Norway after Prime Minister Gerhardsen's state visit in 1955, though these plans were revised immediately after the U2 affair in 1960. The improved climate in US–Soviet relations in the early 1960s allowed Norwegian foreign policy to take advantage of the onset of détente, and to exercise some political freedom on wider security matters. Similarly, NATO and American military interest in Norway lessened from the middle of the 1950s up to the early 1960s and again in the late 1970s. Rolf Tamnes sees the main explanation for this as the rise of the intercontinental missile and the conviction of the US political and military leadership that emphasis should be placed on the Central Front in Europe (Tamnes, 1991, pp. 238 & 296–7).

From the end of the 1970s until the mid-1980s, the United States' adoption of a 'continental strategy' in Europe – a preparedness to fight the Soviet forces in continental Europe – and a 'New Maritime Strategy', led to a greater NATO interest in Norway (Tamnes, 1991, pp. 272–294 & 296–8). Once more, this activated the ambiguous elements in Norway's security stance. As seen, the Norwegian leadership was anxious to receive assurances of American assistance but a closer relationship brought out points of disagreement.

The onset of the end of the Cold War from the mid-1980s gave Norway and other smaller states a freer hand within NATO. The new agenda of arms control and disarmament was to their liking and the pressure for increased defence expenditure eased. However, the emphasis on moving forces from Central Europe caused Norway some concern. Likewise the reversal of the American naval build-up off Norway's coast meant a possible weakening of the Atlantic link so important to Norway. The re-emergence of the Western European Union during the 1980s provided an extra forum for discussion of West European defence issues, but Norway was neither invited nor wished to participate in it at that stage.

The concept of screening towards the United States was especially noticeable in Norwegian policy in the late 1970s and early 1980s, when the New Cold War was at its coldest. NATO's nuclear policy was criticised, creating some difficulties in relations with the United States. The thrust of Norwegian policy had two key elements. One was to strengthen defence and deterrence through integration in NATO and through national effort; the other was to encourage détente with the Soviet Union. Public opinion supported this combined approach, even though it could be argued that the general public was not well informed about the extent of Norwegian integration into NATO's defence structure. Despite any reservations, Norway remained Atlantic in its security outlook during the 1963 to 1989 period. Attempts to produce a Nordic aspect faded, and the European element in Norway's defence was placed in the NATO context. Norway was prepared to consider wider aspects of security through the CSCE process – but as part of the NATO grouping – and was eager to cooperate with the diplomatic initiatives of the EC countries in European Political Cooperation. Yet the reality of Norwegian security policy was based on the need for a US presence in Europe, not least in Norway's part of the continent.

During this period Norwegian decision-makers were faced with a menu for choice of some complexity. Emergence from the depths of the Cold War seemed to expand the room for manoeuvre for small states such as Norway. There were new security fora such as the CSCE and a range of arms control and disarmament issues were discussed internationally. This was not the vision seen by most Norwegian decision-makers whose thoughts were dominated by the increased Soviet presence on their northern border. They had to deal with domestic concern about allied nuclear policy in particular. In the end they largely took a preserving stance, balancing what they considered to be the needed response to Norway's precarious strategic position with the restraints of public opinion and consideration for their Nordic neighbours. This policy can be judged a success by the standards of the decision-makers themselves. However, this very success meant that the Norway was only able to respond slowly to the changes of 1989.

10
Norway's Strategic Position after 1989

10.1 Introduction

By the mid-1980s a good deal of uncertainty had crept into Norway's security policy. As outlined in Chapter 9, Norway had become a frontline state, in the northernmost part of the Central Front of Europe, as the forward-most part of NATO's maritime defence, and as one of the Arctic frontiers between the Soviet Union and NATO. The New Cold War of the late 1970s and early 1980s had seen a renewed American interest in the seas off Norway. The Norwegian desire to balance deterrence and defence with an element of détente became more difficult. The United States was central to the defence of Norway, but the Norwegians looked increasingly to their European colleagues – especially the United Kingdom and the Federal Republic of Germany – to contribute to the defence and deterrence side of Norwegian security, in a way less threatening to the détente aspect. Both the need for, and the form of, Norwegian defence was a matter of political consensus in Norway, and certainly support for Norwegian membership of NATO was solid. This consensus was periodically challenged by issues such as INF emplacement, the pre-positioning of military stocks and plans for a Nordic nuclear-weapon-free zone. Even these issues were managed in a less divisive way than in Denmark, for example.

From 1989 until the end of 1994 Norway faced a sea-change in its security position and in the options available to deal with its security needs. There were improvements in both compared with the days of the Cold War, but the developments were by no means all beneficial. Norway confronted a proliferation of possible insecurities but was also faced with a variety of institutions that could assist national means in the search for security, none of which, however, seemed to be as effective as NATO membership had been in the Cold War period. Furthermore, those in government in Norway could only look forward to this situation becoming less satisfactory (Archer, 1994b).

The developments that took place internationally and in Europe from 1989 to 1994 threatened change in the five elements that were the main influences on Norwegian security policy: the overall global situation; the power and intentions of the Soviet Union, and then Russia; the interest and involvement of the United States in Northern Europe and Europe generally; the policies of the European members of NATO; and the preference structure of Norwegian domestic opinion. The first four elements underwent major changes from the end of 1989 to the beginning of 1995, which this chapter will outline insofar as they affected Norway. What can be noted is the way that the developments seemed to contribute to the increased feeling of the marginalisation of Norway from the mainstream of European security. The final sections will deal with the response of the political elite and population of Norway to the ending of the Cold War.

10.2   The Global Strategic Position

As outlined in Chapter 9, the coming to power in the Soviet Union of Mikhail Gorbachev led to a change in the relationships between the Soviet Bloc and the West and a rethinking of the Soviet approach to foreign and security policy more generally. The Soviet leadership started to see security issues in terms of a non-zero sum game and advocated forms of Common Security as well as a Common European Home, to which the Soviet Union would belong (Warner, 1989, pp. 13–34). A number of arms control deals were concluded with the West, with the agreement to withdraw INF weapons from Europe and the subsequent agreement on Conventional Forces in Europe being of greatest significance for Nordic public opinion. Together with the general reduction in tension achieved by 1989 and the move towards a strategic arms reduction treaty, the INF agreement helped reduce one of the main causes of 'nuclearphobia' in Norway and Denmark. The détente and arms control process also reduced much of the suspicion – present in some sections of public opinion – about the superpowers witnessed in the early 1980s. The threat-image was fading, but was still there in outline.

With the collapse of the Warsaw Treaty Organization and the Soviet Union, the international system ceased to be a predominantly bilateral one. Russia was still an important power – and a nuclear one – but it no longer had the international reach of the Soviet Union and was anyhow pre-occupied with its own economic and social problems. For a while, the United States seemed to be the only super-power and, in taking the lead against Saddam Hussein in wresting Kuwait from Iraqi control in 1991, appeared to be ready to put a New World Order in place (Bush, 1991, pp. 161–3; Kissinger, 1991; Sloan, 1991).

By 1992 it was clear that there would not be a New World Order worth the name. Russia was neither able nor, often, willing to participate in such a venture and the dissolution of Yugoslavia saw US–European disagreement followed by a degree of inaction (or, at least, inappropriate action) by both parties. The United States military intervention in Somalia proved disastrous. Both the election of President Clinton and the 1994 mid-term victories by the Republicans indicated that the United States would be selective in its world role and would probably follow an 'America First' policy. The bipolar world of the 1980s seemed, by early 1995, to have turned into an international situation with one failed superpower and a reluctant one (IISS, 1994, p. 5).

The fall of the Soviet Union also meant an end to the ideological element of the Cold War. Again the seeming victory for the remaining partner – capitalism – turned out to be somewhat hollow as the West descended into deep recession. By the mid-1990s, a number of the former communist countries started to retreat from the march towards the market economy (IISS, 1994, p. 122).

Furthermore, the end of the ideological dispute – at least that of capitalism versus communism – was soon replaced by an increased Western fear of the spread of Islamic fundamentalism and by national and ethnic-based conflict. The latter phenomenon provided the fuel for new wars, not least civil ones, with little restraint being exercised by hegemonic powers and with only fairly weak regional or global institutions brokering for peace (IISS, 1994, pp. 5–12).

Agreements such as the Strategic Arms Reduction Treaty (START), the Conventional Forces in Europe (CFE) treaty and the arrangements on confidence and security-building within the CSCE, helped to 'build down' the conventional forces in Europe. Perhaps their most important aspect was the way in which they took the sting out of the nuclear weapons of both sides. The number of weapons and their delivery systems were cut by the START process, but the end of the Cold War anyhow meant that the nuclear confrontation between East and West was over. No longer were the forces facing each other, ready to strike at a moment's notice.

This stand-down did not mean an end to the nuclear threat. The break-up of the Soviet Union brought its own nuclear problems, not least those of the sharing out of the former Soviet Union's nuclear resources and also the danger of nuclear weapons and technology falling into the wrong hands (IISS, 1994, pp. 50–9).

The above developments were ones that formed the framework for Norwegian security from 1989 to early 1995. They portray a period of rapid – if not revolutionary – change both in the relationship between the superpowers and in the policies of those two countries. The ending of the Cold War, the attempt to create a New World Order and the stalling of that process created a new series of opportunities for governments. These have been felt most by those states that were most restrained by the Cold War, either by the presence of a hegemonic power or by the perception of a direct outside threat. In the case of Norway, the presence of a hegemonic power – the United States – was one that was on the whole welcomed by Norwegian governments and public opinion, and the nature of the direct outside threat may have changed for Norway with the end of the Cold War, but – as will be seen below – there is still a feeling that Norway has been comparatively less freed of this imposition than other European states.

Norwegian governments were used in the Cold War period to manoeuvring within the diplomatic confines set by East-West confrontation. It does seem that the post-Cold War world has changed the context within which Norway acts, but that the room for manoeuvre has not increased as much as could have been expected, nor has the change been as great as for many other European states.

Indeed changes in world politics were by no means seen as being all positive. In March 1992, the Norwegian Defence Commission of 1990 reported (Forsvarskommisjonen av 1990, 1992). As the name of the Defence Commission suggested, the report had been some two years in the making. The Commission was chaired by the former Conservative prime minister, Kåre Willoch, and originally had Johan Jørgen Holst, Director of the Norwegian Institute of International Affairs, as its vice-chairman, before he became Minister of Defence in the Labour administration that took office in November 1990. The members of the Commission consisted of nine representatives from the six political parties (Centre, Christian Democrats, Conservative, Labour, Progress and Socialist Left) in the Norwegian parliament (*Storting*) and five experts drawn from the defence community and research institutes. The Commission's report outlined other general threats to security, such as the spread of conflict and the potential for increased use of armed forces, the proliferation of nuclear weapons and weapons of mass destruction, trade divisions between economic blocs, religious and cultural-based divisions, the pressure of the growth in over-population, the political consequences of control over the exploitation, sources and transportation of energy, environmental issues, and the differences between the rich and the poor areas of the world (Forsvarskommisjonen av 1990, 1992, pp. 44–52). All these factors were seen as having potential security consequences that could undermine stability. So, even by early 1992, developments in the international environment within which Norway had to work were by no means seen in Norway in an optimistic light.

Developments since the publication of the 1992 report until 1995 only underlined the reason for such caution. Relations between the Russian Federation and the West, especially the United States, cooled. The prospect of nuclear proliferation increased with Iran and Iraq continuing their nuclear programmes, and with North Korea scarcely being restrained from manufacturing nuclear weapons. Trade divisions between the US and the European Union and Japan widened. Little was done to ease the pressures of over-population, threats to the environment or the division between rich and poor. Banditry and drug-trafficking seemed to have spread.

Meanwhile the United Nations and other international agencies were unable to fulfil the early promise of the 1989 to 1992 period. The UN signally failed in its peace enforcement operation in Somalia and its peacekeeping activities in former Yugoslavia had only limited successes and were later superseded in many areas by NATO-run activities under the 1995 Dayton Peace Accord.

As at the time of the 1992 report, it was possible to imagine an improvement in the international environment within which Norway acted. Indeed, the world economic situation improved generally from 1992 to 1995. However, little was achieved in entrenching increased international cooperation, strengthening the international institutions that treated conflict, and dealing with the basic causes of socio-economic problems.

10.3   The Fall of the Soviet Union

The general effect of the coming to power of Mr Gorbachev and of the end of the Soviet Union on the international system has been noted above. However, there were specific consequences for Norway, a small North European state with a border to the Soviet Union and the new Russian Federation. These effects can best be seen over two periods – that of the shrinking Soviet power from late 1989 to the start of 1992, and that of an unstable Russia from 1992 to 1995.

An evaluation of the possible effects on Norway of events in the Soviet Union in the first period was provided in the report, in March 1992, of the Norwegian Defence Commission. In particular, they saw the danger in security terms of the break-up of the Soviet Union and the crises of authority and of economic reform in the successor states of the Commonwealth of Independent States (CIS) (Forsvarskommisjonen av 1990, 1992, pp. 39–40). Comparison was made with inter-war Weimar Germany.

The Commission's evaluation of the pros and cons of the end of the Soviet empire placed some weighty points in the latter category. It could lead to chaos, anarchy and conflict, with many danger signals already being seen by early 1992. Thus the dangers inherent in the dissolution of the Soviet Union were recognised, especially with the squabble between the Ukraine and Russia over the Black Sea Fleet, the break-up of the common command system for the CIS armed forces, the dispute about Russian control of ex-Soviet nuclear weapons, and the adverse consequences of the disintegration of the Russian armed forces brought about by social and economic factors (Forsvarskommisjonen av 1990, 1992, pp. 54–8).

The positive side of the dissolution of both the USSR and the Warsaw Pact, and of the unification of Germany was that the military basis for an overwhelming and massive conventional attack against NATO in Central Europe no longer existed (Forsvarskommisjonen av 1990, 1992, pp. 61).

What then of the security of Northern Europe? The report pointed out that this was decisively tied to military security, typified by the connection with the United States. Dealing with Norwegian security concerns in the New Europe, Norway was said still to have a special position in Europe tied to the former Soviet Union:

> The situation in East and Central Europe and the former Soviet Union creates a risk for Norway being more directly affected than the continental European countries by the trend of maritime military developments and possible instability in Russia. (Forsvarskommisjonen av 1990, 1992, pp. 84)

The report said that the North was experiencing lesser change than in Central Europe, a fact that had both political and military-strategic consequences. Norway continued to be neighbour to the large base-complex on the Kola Peninsula. The military situation was dominated by the navy and the airforce, with the army playing a more limited role. Furthermore, arms control agreements had not always had a positive effect on Norway's strategic situation. In 1989 the Soviet Union transferred Fencer long-range attack aircraft from Central Europe to the Leningrad Military District, apparently in preparation for the outcome of the CFE negotiations then being held in Vienna (Ellingsen, 1991, p. 2).[1] Also the US–Soviet Strategic Arms Reduction (START) agreement of July 1991 meant that all the Soviets' remaining strategic submarine force would be based in the Kola Peninsula (Ellingsen, 1992, p. 12).

According to the report, the extent to which the Russians wished to maintain a large Northern Fleet was an open question. The new Russian authorities had not taken over the world role for which the fleet was needed, and Russia – a different country both economically and politically from the Soviet Union – could have different interests arising from its smaller geographical extent. The loss of harbours on the Black Sea and the Baltic meanwhile meant that the bases on the Kola had a relatively increased importance for the Russians, even if their maritime forces had been reduced. A possible economic and social collapse of Russia could have consequences for the Northern Fleet and, to the extent that Russian military forces were maintained in the North, this could represent a future challenge to Norwegian military security.

The chapter headed 'Consequences for the main elements of Norwegian security policy' continued the theme of Norway being different from the states of Continental Europe because of its propinquity to Russia. The stress was constantly on the instability of and the uncertainty about Russia, which anyhow remained a European great power. The requirement of a security guarantee by Norway was tied to allied interests in Norway's oil and gas reserves which in themselves made Norway more liable to outside pressure (Forsvarskommisjonen av 1990, 1992, p. 96). A few pages later there was the warning that Norwegian security must be based on the possibility that Russia would be affected by a long period of instability (Forsvarskommisjonen av 1990, 1992, p. 99), and a reminder that local Russian forces in the North could act independently of the central political and military authorities, adding another risk for Norway (Forsvarskommisjonen av 1990, 1992, p. 107).

Events in the second period – from the publication of the report to the end of 1994 – demonstrated the precarious political position of and in the Russian Federation. The attempted coup d'etat against President Yeltsin was followed, in December 1993, by the election of a parliament dominated by nationalist and former-communist forces. The Russian government responded by moving away from a policy of close co-operation with the West to one of stressing Russian national interests. The suppression of Chechen nationalist forces from 1994 led to a further distancing of the Yeltsin government from the West.

The mood in Moscow was partly reflected in the Russian areas bordering Norway. The Northern Fleet seemed to be in disarray after the break-up of the Soviet Union, with Norwegian sources reporting 160 combat vessels out of service since 1989, with the surface fleet being reduced by fourteen vessels down to 150, and the submarine fleet being cut by 22 to about 130 (Forsvarsdepartementet, 1994, pp. 7–8). By 1994, it seemed that the problem for Norway was that of the nuclear reactors of decommissioned vessels (ibid., p. 6). Social and economic problems among the armed forces on the Kola Peninsula were also identified as destabilising factors (Ministry of Defence, 1994, p. 21). Attempts at cross-border cooperation in the region had their limits and Norwegian investors in Russian enterprises found themselves eased out (*Aftenposten*, 11 April 1995).

Clearly the security situation for Norway had improved with the end of the Soviet Union. However, the feeling of greater security was not without some reservations, particularly in the north of Norway. Nor did developments in Russia necessarily add to the confidence that Norway had in its 'new' neighbour.

10.4   The United States and Europe

Only the United States had – and still has – the maritime force to counter Russian strength, which could otherwise dominate Norway's neighbourhood (Forsvarskommisjonen av 1990, 1992, p. 8).

Norway was seen as being affected by the dominant military land power in Europe, which at the same time was the major sea-power near Norway. In a crucial sentence the Commission considered that Norway's connection to the USA will to a great extent be a function both of the form of Norway's link with Europe and of Norway's special strategic position in connection to Central Europe (Forsvarskommisjonen av 1990, 1992, p. 8). Large-scale change on the Continent and lesser changes in the North created a complicated security situation for Norway. As long as the Soviet forces in the North had some meaning for the situation in Central Europe, Norway and its neighbouring area were of importance. 'After the great changes in Central Europe, Norway is no longer of the same interest' (Forsvarskommisjonen av 1990, 1992, pp. 85–6) The danger was not just an unstable, well-armed neighbour, but also abandonment by allies.

This fear was to a certain extent realised from 1989 to late 1994. Generally, the United States started to disengage from Europe. Under President Bush plans were made to bring down the US army's presence in Europe from 150,000 to 104,000, and under President Clinton the figure was 84,000 by 1994 (Ellingsen, 1994, p. 33; IISS, 1993, p. 27). While most of these cuts affected continental Europe, there was an effect on Norway. As stated above (section 9.3), Norway depended upon the United States to provide reinforcements as well as air and sea support in the case of a crisis or an attack. That the United States would arrive was made more sure by pre-positioning of stocks and collocated bases. However, by 1994 the US government's defence cuts and change in strategy had resulted in proposals to reduce the number of Collocated Operating Bases (COBs) in Norway, though it was stressed that this was not to be seen as a signal of a reduction in or a drawing back of other reinforcement of Norway (Ellingsen, 1994, p. 188). Despite this, concern was expressed about the effect of the reorganization of the US Marine Corps on its commitment to reinforce Norway, and, by the end of 1994, the Canadian government had warned that budget reductions would lead to the withdrawal of its infantry battalion group from the NATO Composite Force, the one allied reinforcement force that had Norway as its only placement area (Ellingsen, 1994, p. 189).

10.5   The European States and Northern Europe

The events in Europe from mid-1989 to the start of 1995 totally changed the international context of Norway's security.

At the same time, the rapid change in Europe produced potential candidates for new threats to security. These generally were the fear of the spread of the type of ethnic conflict that was already evident in former Yugoslavia and parts of the former Soviet Union; the consequences of economic and social unrest in East and Central Europe, including the possibility of large-scale migration; and the international aspects of the breakdown of law and order in East European countries – in particular the fear of renegade groups gaining control of armaments, including nuclear weapons. The very uncertainty as to what may be a threat to security – even in the near future – in itself undermined a stable peace.

Another factor in this theatre of change was the development within the European Communities (EC). Negotiations for the Maastricht Treaty of European Union in the latter half of 1991 can be seen as the high-water mark of the latest round of West European integration in which the EC sought to complement the completion of the Single European Market by 1993 with a rush towards an Economic and Monetary Union, further institutional development, and a move to a Common Foreign and Security Policy. With this vitality, it was perhaps not surprising that, in the early 1990s, the EC became a centre of attraction both to the newly-liberated states of Eastern Europe and to the richer and more established EFTA democracies. At the same time, Germany was unified and the West Germans took on the task of trying to rebuild the economy of the former German Democratic Republic while the Western world was experiencing a cyclical recession. Together with the political uncertainty experienced with the Maastricht Treaty on European Union and the European Economic Area agreement (Archer, 1994c, chapters 6 & 7), this gave a double edge to the attraction offered by the European Communities.

According to the report of the Norwegian Defence Commission, by 1992 Europe was changing from being stable and divided into a fragmented, complicated continent, troubled with ethnic and national divisions and deep-seated economic problems. Further disintegration in Eastern Europe could make the establishment of a common authority even more complicated. The situation in Europe could also be negatively affected by factors outside the continent: economic problems, religious differences, population increases and regional conflicts being among those that afflict countries south and south-east of Europe (Forsvarskommisjonen av 1990, 1992, p. 37).

The Cold War had made it difficult to establish common norms and rules for inter-state relations in the postwar period, according to the report. The possibility of establishing a new European order – with all participating states accepting common norms of behaviour – would to a certain extent depend on a suitable coordination between the main international organisations such as the UN, NATO, the EC and WEU, the Council of Europe and the CSCE/OSCE. However, the variety of organisations also seemed to typify a lack of clarity, with the lines of authority and responsibility being blurred (Forsvarskommisjonen av 1990, 1992, p. 38).

10.6   Norwegian Domestic Opinion

The report of the Norwegian Defence Commission of 1990 came in March 1992, at the time the changes outlined above were beginning to have their effect. The Commission's mandate was to lay down the basis for the preparation of the framework for defence after 1993. That was to be the end of the fifteen year planning period (1979–93) that had been the subject of the Defence Commission of 1974 (reporting in March 1978). So the existence of the Defence Commission was not determined by international events but by the needs of Norwegian politics. The Commission was tasked with evaluating the security-political, technological and strategic developments affecting Norway, in the light of the ongoing political developments in Eastern Europe and the East-West relationship, and of the positive tendencies in disarmament negotiations (Forsvarskommisjonen av 1990, 1992, p. 11). This perhaps explains why, while the work of the Commission was over-shadowed by international events, a mere page-count of its report shows that – excluding the introduction and summary – external events and factors were covered in 62 pages while Norwegian aspects took up 98 pages.

Indeed, security questions and membership of NATO were scarcely contentious political matters by the 1990s. Security affairs were mostly determined by political consensus – as in the Defence Commission of 1990 – and support for NATO was high. By October 1991 69% of those asked in an opinion poll considered that Norway's membership of NATO led to further security for the country (Den norske Atlanterhavskomité, 1991, p. 25).

The main internal constraint on Norway's security policy was in the field of the emerging European Union. Once it became clear that the EU would have a Common Foreign and Security Policy and as the Western European Union increasingly became the arm of the EU in defence cooperation matters, the Labour government – supported by the Conservatives – gave this as a reason for closer links with the EU. While this view was challenged by the Socialist Left Party and the Centre Party, it did not stop Norway from taking up associate membership of the Western European Union. The main domestic constraint on Norwegian security policy in the post-1989 period was more in the form of a general desire for a 'peace dividend' and thus cuts in the defence budget, but otherwise – outside the EU debate – the traditional consensus and broad 'liberal institutionalist' hopes remained.

10.7   The Response After 1989

Norway, like other NATO countries, was caught unawares by the events of late 1989 that led to the collapse of the communist bloc. Even by January 1991 – in the year that was to see the end of the USSR – a well-informed publication based on official sources in Norway was making a fairly standard appraisal of what had previously been called 'the Soviet threat' (Ellingsen, 1991). Indeed, it made sobering reading. The build-up of the Soviet Northern Fleet had continued, with an arsenal of ballistic missiles and of cruise missiles that could target NATO surface vessels. A more forward air defence of Soviet territory was being established, allowing them an increased capability to protect naval and air landings in North Norwegian territory (Ellingsen, 1991, p. 3).

The Norwegian response to what was seen as a continued military threat was not to make any major changes in their dispositions but to build on their existing policy. This was partly a result of what could be called 'bureaucratic inertia' – the fifteen year planning period covered by the 1978 report of the 1974 Defence Commission was coming to an end in 1993; a new Defence Commission was to be established in early 1990; and the main elements of the defence budget for the 1989–93 period had been agreed across the parties without any major changes (Forsvarsdepartementet, 1987), in particular to weapons acquisition programmes which were difficult to undertake at short notice. On top of this, there was the belief that while the Soviet Union (and later Russia), from 1989 to the end of 1992, no longer had any 'intention of using military force against NATO or any of the Nordic countries', its vast military capacity remained. Intentions could change rapidly and it had to be assumed 'that the capability to use military force is present' (Ellingsen, 1992, p. 2). In view of this, prudence dictated a 'military insurance designed to block future offensive options inherent in the substantial military capabilities which remain in Russia and the Soviet Union' (Holst, 1991a, p. 5).

Thus for the time being, Norway's official response to the above developments was to reiterate its previous policy of building up its own defence and its ability to receive reinforcements. The linkage with NATO remained vital, though it was clear that the Organization's strategy would have to change after the demise of the Soviet bloc.

Once again the emphasis was on the forces in North Norway where the Finnmark Land Defence (FLF) had equipment pre-positioned for rapid reinforcement within Norway. Brigade North in Troms, with some 5,000 men, then constituted the Norwegian Army's standing force in the area. Norwegian forces in North Norway – the standing forces in FLF and Brigade North – were upgraded to Brigade 90 and Brigade 90 armour-reinforced standard respectively (Ellingsen, 1991, p. 5), demonstrating Norway's continued commitment to defending its northern areas. The Norwegian Air Force maintained its five military airfields in North Norway with tasks ranging from maritime surveillance and coastguard rescue to air defence and an anti-invasion role. The Norwegian naval presence in the region was very much unchanged (see Chapter 9) with the emphasis being on the ability to reinforce North Norway within a short period. However, the essential element in Norwegian defence remained that of reinforcement, both from southern Norway to the north and from outside Norway.

Though the intention of the military was to continue the programme of defence build-up started in the late 1970s, resources proved to be strained. By 1992 the effects of financial stringency at a time of economic retrenchment meant that some defence plans had to be stretched. Pre-positioning of equipment for the second Norwegian reinforcement brigade in North Norway, previously promised to be in place by the end of 1991, was – by 1992 – to be ready by the end of 1993. Furthermore the economic guidelines in the 1991 and 1992 defence budgets meant measures to reduce running costs, including an end to the previous 50% readiness of all standing units in North Norway (Ellingsen, 1992, p. 8).[2]

In this context, the US II Marine Expeditionary Force (2.MEF) and in particular the Norway Air Landed Marine Expeditionary Brigade (NAL MEB) were of continued importance. In 1991 NAL MEB practised taking out its pre-positioned equipment from

Trøndelag in a field-training exercise in North Norway, 'Battle Griffin'. This represented a successful step in the conversion of an important element of the US reinforcement from a sea-borne to an air transported brigade, felt necessary by the increased Soviet naval presence in northern waters during the 1980s (Ellingsen, 1991, p. 21).

An issue concerning the Norwegian authorities in the early 1990s was a replacement for the Canadian CAST brigade as the only reinforcement exclusively earmarked for deployment to Norway after the ending of that status in November 1989. By the beginning of 1992 a NATO Composite Force (NCF) had replaced the CAST brigade in its exclusively Norwegian role, though work continued on the composition of the new force. Norwegian defence officials were concerned that the reinforcement of Norway should be held at its previous level, if not improved. The Canadian move could have provided the first sign of an unravelling of the network of reinforcements put together by the Norwegians and the allies in the previous two decades. It was therefore important that the change made to the CAST brigade should not be seen to create a 'hole'. By 1992 the plans were for the force to consist of a German and an American Field Artillery Battalion, a Canadian Infantry Battalion Group (taking over some of the equipment pre-positioned in North Norway by the CAST brigade), and a Norwegian Helicopter Squadron. Clearly this array could not be deployed as an integrated force but elements were intended to be attached to Norwegian brigades, which would also be responsible for their supply and support. The flexibility of the NCF was stressed, thus making a virtue out of a necessity. This fitted in with the developments in NATO doctrine seen during this period, with the wider emphasis on flexibility. As the Norwegian Minister of Defence pointed out, 'NATO's new force structure . . . will have many points of similarity to the structure already developed for our area' (Ministry of Defence, 1991a, p. 16).

The air reinforcement of Norway remained vital to Norwegian defence plans in the early 1990s with some 200 to 300 British and American aircraft earmarked for deployment to Norway (Ellingsen, 1992, p. 4). The disposition of allied naval forces were also of great importance for the Norwegians. However, an attempt to extend the range of the Invictus agreement (see section 9.3) for logistical support and ship repairs of Allied ships was held up by the Foreign Affairs Committee of the *Storting* in 1990, as it was felt that agreement could send the wrong signal at that time. This was one of the few times during the 1989 to 1992 period that Norway consciously moderated its defence effort in order to stress the element of reassurance rather than that of insurance and reinforcement.

On the whole then, the response of the Norwegian defence to the changed situation in Europe after 1989 was cautious and considered. Military plans and budgets took time to revise and implement, but the feeling within defence circles was anyhow that Norway's security had not benefited as much as that of Central Europe by the changes. There seemed every good reason to maintain the policy as before, that of a considerable defence effort by Norway being matched by reinforcements from outside, particularly by the United States and United Kingdom.

However, the political changes in Europe and between the superpowers had an effect on Norwegian defence in the years immediately following the events of November 1989. The United States might still wish to maintain that capacity for other reasons, but the specific emphasis on the northern region of Europe seemed to have lost its former raison d'etre. This was recognised in October 1991 by the then Norwegian Minister of Defence, Johan Jørgen Holst. He considered that the end of the Cold War reduces to some extent the strategic importance of Norway to the security of Europe at large, since that importance has been very closely linked with the need to protect the trans-Atlantic sea lines of communication in order to contain the danger of a Soviet military drive for mastery in Europe... Norwegian bargaining power and influence in NATO may appear to be on the decline. (Holst, 1991a, p. 26)

Holst feared that there was an acute danger of 'marginalisation and isolation' for Norway, with the changes in NATO created by the end of Cold War being compounded by Norway's 'self-imposed isolation in Europe'. Holst's answer to this dilemma was already clear in 1991:

If the issue of membership in the Community [EC] were to be decided solely on the basis of foreign and security policy considerations, a membership application would surely be forthcoming from Oslo. However, such policy interests must be weighted against other policy interests . . . (Holst, 1991a, p. 27)

This statement was perhaps the most overt expression of an 'internationalist' in the Labour government of the need to be part of the European integration process for security reasons. Holst went on to predict a chain of events in a manner which, in retrospect, could be seen to hint of a future campaign strategy for proponents of Norwegian EC membership:

Nevertheless, the issue of marginalization and isolation from the emerging architecture of the new Europe will cause strong bells to toll, and applications for membership from more EFTA countries could create band-wagon effects which would compel Norway to overcome the divisions from the bitter referendum campaign of 1972 . . . (Holst, 1991a, p. 27)

This was to see the question of isolation in a wider context than that of military security, namely that of Norwegian separation from the major centre of decision-making in Europe, the European Communities, and the European Union that was in the making at that time.

Also present in governmental statements in this early post-Cold War period was a wider appreciation of the concept of security. In mid-1989 the Foreign Ministry had already noted the new challenges resulting from faster change and saw Norway's security in broad terms (Stortingmelding 11, 1989–90, p. 6). The Minister of Defence, Mr Holst, placed some emphasis on the arms control and 'shared interests' between states (Holst, 1991b, p. 1). However, he noted that the stability upon which arms control was predicated had been destroyed by the end of the Cold War (Holst, 1991b, p. 5). He saw that the change in the nature of the security landscape in Europe would mean that arms control would become integrated into a wider agenda and broader strategies 'for the prevention, amelioration and resolution of conflicts' (Holst, 1991b, p. 9). Holst also stressed that the Soviet Union should be included in the 'network of institutions and commitments shaping the future security order in Europe', and that its constituent republics should be included in the CSCE when they emerged as sovereign states (1991a, p. 4). He considered that the Nordic area's 'rapprochement with the European Community' (Sweden had already applied for membership) reflected a 'search for stability and linkage with the West in the context of increasing uncertainty in the East' (1991a, p. 6), with the EC being 'the principal framing institution in the new Europe' (1991a, p. 11).

The themes in this more discursive view of European security at the end of 1991 were ones that saw the future stability of Europe resting on a wider understanding of the term 'security', and which considered the European Community and the about-to-be-conceived European Union as central institutions in the creation of a more stable Europe. That the Nordic region should make its peace with the EC had consequences for Norway. Once again EC membership was implied as the best choice purely for international security reasons. It should be recognised that Holst had his background in strategic studies and was an Atlanticist. He also had been a cautious advocate of Norwegian EC membership in the 1980s (Holst, 1984, p. 15). Being on the right-wing of the Labour Party and an intellectual, he had little 'grass roots' following, though his later work as Foreign Minister in bringing together the Israelis and the Palestinians earned him respect within the Labour Party and across the political spectrum.

10.8   The Wider Policy Response

Many of the wider themes that had appeared in Mr Holst's speeches in 1991 can be seen in the Report of the Defence Commission, issued early in 1992. The Report also dealt with the more defence-related response to the new situation in Europe, established as it was to set out guidelines for Norwegian defence until into the 21st century.

In the defence field the Report showed a good deal of continuity from the previous position. Support of the concept of Total Defence was reiterated, with its dependence on conscription and utilising the civilian resources of society (Forsvarskommisjonen av 1990, 1992, p. 19). The main tasks of Norwegian defence were given as those set out in the proposition to the *Storting* for the 1992 defence budget (Forsvarskommisjonen av 1990, 1992, p. 21). Indeed that budget had already set the framework for the first five years of the period covered by the Defence Commission by introducing a structure of objectives for the Defence Establishment which would be adapted over a five year period 'to achieve a balance between goals and budgets' (Ministry of Defence, 1991b). The zero growth in the 1992 defence budget (in relation to that of 1991 but adjusted for inflation) suggested that the Defence Establishment could not look forward to the sort of funding it had enjoyed until 1990. It was clear that the ambitions outlined in the Report to the *Storting* in 1987, and covering the period 1988 to 1993, would not be achieved and that long-term guidelines were lacking as the Defence Commission of 1990 still had to report (Ministry of Defence, 1991c, p. 3).

When it came, the Report produced a number of options for Norway's defence structure over the years from 1995 to 2012, ranging from a 'high level' involving a 2.5% real increase down to a 'low level' which involved a reduction to 80% of the 1991 base. The Chief of Defence rejected the idea of cutting the defence strength, saying that this would involve a great degree of risk for the nation's security (Forsvarskommisjonen av 1990, 1992, pp. 171–2). It was this aspect of the report – and the subsequent cut of 2.4% in the defence budget announced in September 1992 – that caused debate among military circles in Norway (Forsvarsdepartementet, 1992, p. 3). The government gave the downturn in the economy as the main reason for reductions (Forsvarsdepartementet, 1992, p. 3), though clearly the prospect of a 'peace dividend' affected political calculations. The defence establishment saw cuts as being short-term and not justified by continued international uncertainty (Forsvarskommisjonen av 1990, 1992, p. 171–2; Bull-Hansen, 1993, pp. 10–19).

One of the main aspects of the Defence Commission's Report was the weight that they gave to the non-military response to international events. Their evaluation of the context for Norway's security gave what can be called a 'liberal institutionalist' or pluralist view of events in Europe since the Second World War.[3] The lack of a common international authority was seen as contributing to insecurity and unpredictability in international politics. In recognition of this, states 'have sought to reduce insecurity by attempting to establish a common authority . . . The tendency to international anarchy is sought to be counteracted by organizing a comprehensive pattern of cooperation' (Forsvarskommisjonen av 1990, 1992, p. 37, authors' translation). Whilst accepting that a genuine international authority with a set of common rules and laws that all states follow all the time was an unrealistic goal, the establishment of a certain level of norms and rules that most countries consider worth following and which none oppose, was regarded as a desirable and achievable aim (Forsvarskommisjonen av 1990, 1992, p. 37).

The building up of new forms of cooperation between East and West and the further development of existing institutions to establish common authority and stability would be necessary after the dissolution of the Soviet Union. The Commission saw the example of how age-old rivalries had been dissolved within an institutionalised framework in Western Europe as a possible model for Eastern European states, with the aim having 'security in community' for all European countries (Forsvarskommisjonen av 1990, 1992, pp. 38–9). The 1990s for Europe was characterised by three trends: that of the western part developing a closer cooperation in many areas; an eastern part where division and the creation of smaller states led to more unpredictable developments; and a tendency to regionalisation and increased nationalism. The development of arrangements that could include the eastern states into a common structure, creating greater order and predictability, was seen as being a major task for European politics in the coming years. Norwegian action in response to the Commission's evaluation can be seen in two particular areas.

The Barents Sea region was an area where Norway faced Russia across an unsettled maritime frontier and, according to the Norwegian Defence Commission report, where Russian military forces could provide a challenge to Norwegian military security (Forsvarskommisjonen av 1990, 1992, p. 89). This led to a continued Norwegian stress on their maritime links with the United States. However, they also attempted to defuse the situation. In 1992 Norway's then foreign minister, Thorvald Stoltenberg, inaugurated discussions about a multilateral forum, the Council of the Barents Euro-Arctic Region (BEAR), which was created in January 1993 with representatives from the Nordic states, Russia and the European Commission. Observer states included Canada, France, Germany, the United States and the United Kingdom. A Regional Council was also established with representatives of county authorities with interests in the region (Stokke & Tunander, 1994a, pp. 1–3). This was an attempt to involve Russia in a functional network in northern Europe that would give added value to their economic and environmental relations with the Nordic states – and the European Communities – and, by implication, would de-emphasise their military strength. Thorvald Stoltenberg described the Barents initiative by Norway as a wish

> to replace the previous hostility in the North with an active form of cooperation. We wished to build peace-promoting and confidence-building structures by linking the northernmost parts of the Nordic area in a new cooperative region. (Stoltenberg, 1994, p. ix)

Mr Stoltenberg made a comparison that underlined the 'liberal institutionalist' agenda of the Norwegian foreign ministry and politicians:

> Just as the EC cooperation was established in the 1950s in order to build confidence between the hereditary enemies Germany and France, so we wished to establish a network of positive contacts across the East-West border in the North that could promote growth and affluence and make future conflicts less likely. (Stoltenberg, 1994, p. ix)

The logic expressed here was that of the functionalist approach, which, to cite David Mitrany, 'circumvents ideological and radical divisions, as it does territorial frontiers' (Mitrany, 1975, p. 226). Thus functionalism 'treats the promotion of welfare as an indirect approach to the prevention of warfare' (Claude, 1968, pp. 34–5). Stoltenberg's reference to the change in Franco-German relations and the 'network of positive contacts' had resonances of Karl Deutsch's work on security communities in which he analysed the absence of 'significant organized preparations for war or large-scale violence' between international political communities. Deutsch examined 'security communities' in the North Atlantic area that had eliminated 'war and the expectation of war within their boundaries' and where there was the 'real assurance that the members of the community will not fight each other physically, but will settle their disputes in some other way' (Deutsch, 1957).

Pluralistic security communities – ones where the separate governments maintain their legal independence – need three conditions for their success: 'the compatibility of major values relevant to political decision-making'; 'the capacity of the participating political units or governments to respond to each other's needs, messages and actions quickly, adequately, and without resort to violence'; and the 'mutual predictability of behaviour' (Deutsch, 1957, pp. 66–7). Deutsch emphasised the need for increased transactions (such as trade, transport but also political transactions) between the units, which in turn would bring mutual dependence. These heightened transactions must also be accompanied by mutual responsiveness, with each side's demands being treated sympathetically. This would lead to a greater feeling of trust and security.

At the time of the establishment of the Barents Council, none of Deutsch's three conditions were sufficiently present between the Nordic states and Russia to the extent that a security community existed. The proposal was aimed at changing this situation over time. Mr Stoltenberg's reply to those who asked about achievements of the Council was to come back in ten years' time (Stoltenberg, 1994, p. x). A co-founder of the Council, Andrei Kozyrev, the then Russian Foreign Minister, described how the cooperation promoted by the Council itself contributed

> to strengthening stability and good-neighbourly relations in the North and overcoming psychological prejudices left over from the era of confrontation and Cold War with regard to this region of strategic importance. (Kozyrev, 1994, p. 28)

In other words, this cooperation was of value not just for the material benefits it brought but also for the positive contribution it could make to mutual perceptions. In time this could affect behaviour and expectations.

Johan Jørgen Holst, the successor to Stoltenberg as Norwegian Foreign Minister, placed some emphasis on the regional aspect of Barents cooperation which, though it did not replace the nation state, added 'a new set of players' to the European equation (Holst,

1994, p. 22). The Barents Council was seen as something that could 'draw Russia into Europe', making a contribution 'to the efforts to create stability in the border areas in the East, which is the primary task of the Nordic countries in a European context' (Holst, 1994, p. 23).

Barents cooperation thus represented for the Norwegian government an alternative approach to military means for creating security. It also formed an essential part of the Norwegian government's approach to the European Union as it provided Norway with a foreign and security policy 'dowry' to take to Brussels. It institutionalised not only Norwegian but EU relations with Russia in the High North.

The second area was that of the Baltic Sea, where the Nordic states generally had a particular interest. The fear here was that the instability outlined in the Norwegian Defence Commission report could manifest itself in the east end of the Baltic – in disputes between the Baltic republics and Russia or because of an economic and social collapse of Russia – and have adverse consequences for all the Baltic littoral states. Again, the response of the Nordic states was not a purely military one: indeed, Nordic ministers decided not to sell arms to the Baltic republics, though they did agree to train and clothe some of the forces of those states (*Aftenposten*, 23 September 1993). The Nordic countries sponsored and involved themselves in the building of an intense network of links, both governmental and non-governmental, throughout the Baltic region, as typified by the Baltic Sea Council of States (Archer, 1997; Joenniemi & Wæver, 1992, pp. 12–16).

The final area of involvement that showed a Norwegian response along the lines of the Defence Commission report was in the area of former Yugoslavia. Norway was involved in UNPROFOR and the Nordic countries collectively sent a battalion to Macedonia to help prevent hostilities breaking out. This seemed to fit in with the history of Nordic support for UN peacekeeping operations and with the perception of the main threat to peace in Europe coming from instability and ethnic disputes. Of relevance here for defence cooperation within the European Union, was the ability of the Nordic states (excepting Iceland) to work together in Macedonia, despite their previously different defence doctrines. Sweden and Finland were willing to accept the operational experience of Norway and Denmark gained through their NATO membership (Archer, 1994a, pp. 367–386).

10.9   Conclusion

The Norwegian response to the new uncertainty after 1989 was one that had, after all, served them well since the Second World War, and it was to re-affirm and attempt to strengthen its defence links with NATO generally and with the United States specifically. All that had been built up from the 1970s – reinforcement agreements, collocated bases, host-nation support and the pre-positioning of stocks – remained in place, but by the end of this period it was beginning to be eaten away. The Canadians looked unlikely to stay in Europe and US forces in Europe were being rapidly reduced. The United Kingdom started a reappraisal of its armed forces. Germany, which had been increasing its defence involvement in Northern Europe during 1980s, had other, more pressing, interests after the unification process.

The Norwegian response was threefold. The main reaction of the decision-makers was to re-confirm their belief in NATO and their traditional policy of reinforcement.

However, it was soon clear that this policy could be based on shifting sands. A policy element that ran parallel was that of 'liberal institutionalism', very much a Nordic approach to international security dilemma. This involved stressing the need for a collective approach to security threats, and thus an emphasis on a multilateral institutional response that did not just involve military action. The idea was to tackle the very basis of insecurity in the international system and to create more of an international society.

The third element followed on from the second, and it was the reconsideration of the European Communities as a source of security. While the EC was not a security institution as such, it contained the most important European allies of Norway and its members were developing their foreign and security policy cooperation. It seemed likely that the European Union, which emerged from Maastricht in early 1992, would take forward the development of a common security policy, and that the EU could be a major force for stability in Europe. It thus had much to offer in the non-defence aspects of security, just those areas that could, according to Norwegian thinking, bring a more solid and lasting peace than purely the resort to a military-based security policy. By the time of the signing of the Maastricht Treaty, the European Union – purely in security terms – appeared an attractive proposition for a sizeable number of the Norwegian decision-makers. It is the role of the security question in the Norwegian debate on EU membership that will be covered in the following chapter.

Notes

1   Despite the CFE treaty clarification in June 1991, a similar fear was expressed by the Minister of Defence, Johan Jørgen Holst, in his Defence budget speech in October 1991 (Ministry of Defence, 1991a, pp. 30–1).

2   Compare with Ellingsen, 1988, p. 8 and see also Ministry of Defence, 1991a, pp. 2–3.

3   Such a view would contrast with a realist or power politics interpretation which stresses state-to-state relations, seen as being marked by conflict, balance of power and security problems. Liberal institutionalists place greater importance on international institutions, on society-to-society relations and on non-military issues such as trade and the environment. They also accept the notion of progress in building an international community. See Michael Banks, 1985, pp. 16–7; and Ole Wæver, 1992, p. 1.

11

Security and the Referendum Campaign

11.1 Introduction

As shown in the previous chapter, Norway's international security environment changed considerably from 1989 to 1993, and the response of the political establishment in the period following the tearing down of the Berlin Wall was originally one of caution. However, soon Norway's defence effort was eroded by an economic downturn and by the pressure for a 'peace dividend'. What came to the fore was the development of a traditional Nordic approach to security, one that stressed the more diplomatic and less military side. As the new situation in Northern Europe still left Norwegians feeling exposed, and as the United States presence was on the decrease, some of the politicians in Oslo turned to Brussels as a possible source of future security. European Political Cooperation and the emerging Common Foreign and Security Policy (CFSP) seemed to share many elements with Norway's wide understanding of security.

This chapter is an account of the involvement of the security element in the 1994 referendum campaign. Its intrusion into the debate is explained in terms of both the nature of the European Union and the wishes of the pro-membership politicians. The whole issue seems to have been a major element in the Labour leadership's application for EU membership. Its failure to make an impression on the campaign can be seen as a result of its lack of saliency for most of the electorate and their refusal to accept that the question of EU membership had a substantive security implication.

11.2 The European Union as a Security Institution

Why was international security an issue in the 1994 referendum campaign? The prime answer must be that Norway was applying to join the European Union and not just the European Communities (EC). It could be argued that the EC was mainly an economic and trading institution that had some competence in other domestic policy matters such as environmental affairs and social policy. However, even the Common Commercial Policy and Common Agricultural Policy of the EC had security implications as they allowed EC states to be more dependent on each other – but also to rely less on the outside world – in a crisis. Indeed this was given as one of the reasons for Sweden not applying for full membership of the EC as far back as 1961.[1] Parallel with the first extension of the EC in 1973, the member states began to develop their own form of cooperation over matters outside the remit of the Communities' treaties, including foreign policy matters. Foreign policy was defined to include international security questions, though not defence issues.[2] The Single European Act of 1986 associated EPC more closely with the European Communities, while still keeping the two sets of institutions separate. One aspect of the negotiations for the European Union, as they developed during 1991, was the uniting of EC and EPC elements into one Union, though with three 'pillars', the EC, the Common Foreign and Security Policy, and Justice and Home Affairs (which had also been discussed previously by EC ministers, partly under EPC and partly in other fora) (Stortingsmelding 40, 1993–94, pp. 61–4, 100–6). In 1994 – unlike in 1972 – Norway was applying for membership of an institution that would have competence in foreign and security policies.

The response in Brussels to Norway's application for EU membership in November 1992 showed that a Norwegian subscription to the Common Foreign and Security Policy was not seen as a problem (Council of Ministers, 1993, Conclusions). After all, the country had been a founder member of NATO and could very easily become a full member of the WEU once it had joined the EU. Norway had had informal consultations with EPC since 1980 and a bilateral consultation agreement since 1988. Soon after Norway submitted its application for EU membership, this contact was broadened and was continued within the process of the CFSP once the European Union came into existence. Norway also had a more organised contact with EU states through the 'troika' of the EU presidency in such international organizations as the CSCE (later OSCE) and the United Nations (Stortingsmelding 40, 1993–94, p. 337). During the negotiations with the EU, the CFSP proved not to be a matter of contention for Norway (Stortingsmelding 40, 1993–94, p. 343).

The inclusion of the CFSP in the Maastricht Treaty meant that international security would be an issue in the negotiations between the EU and the applicant states during 1993–4 (though it proved to be a non-issue in the case of Norway). Why should have it become an issue during the referendum campaign? The answer to this question lies in the importance attached to the security aspect of membership by the leading members of the Norwegian Labour Party government.

11.3   Security: the Golden Thread

The international security framework outlined in Chapter 10 was one that presented a dilemma for Norwegian decision-makers in the years following the destruction of the Berlin Wall. The dramatic changes in Norway's broad strategic context not only brought improvements and a greater feeling of safety. Some of the old nervousness about Russia remained and new instabilities threatened international peace. Internally, public opinion expected something of a peace dividend and certainly no extra spending on defence. The Norwegian response to their new situation, as covered in Chapter 10, was to re-confirm their traditional NATO-oriented policy, but also to pursue more energetically another age-old policy, that of taking a wide 'liberal institutionalist' view of security. A final strand was to look to Europe as a growing source of security, broadly defined. The last two approaches implied Norwegian membership of the European Union. The re-emphasis on NATO could paradoxically have lead to a greater stress on defence links with the EU members through the Western European Union in its role as the European pillar of the Atlantic Alliance. These aspects of government policy from late 1992 to November 1994 will now be traced.

Elements of this policy can be seen in the short statements made by the Norwegian prime minister concerning Norway's application for membership on 16 November 1992, and by the trade minister, Bjørn Tore Godal, at the opening of Norway's membership negotiations on 5 April 1993. Norway's Atlantic connections were stressed, as was the country's position in the broad pattern of Atlantic and European cooperation (Stortingsmelding 40, 1993–94, p. 432). The Barents Euro-Arctic Region, in which the EC had been involved, was mentioned as a means to normalise relations with Russia after the Cold War (Stortingsmelding 40, 1993–94, p. 434). The ability to deal with problems such as environmental ones in the Far North was seen to be dependent on a recognition that these were also EU problems (Brundtland in Stortingsmelding 40, 1993–94, p. 426). Finally there was the view that, in previous years, the EC had become the core organization for cooperation in Europe (Brundtland in Stortingsmelding 40, 1993–94, p. 424) and that it would be the central institution in shaping the continent's future (Godal in Stortingsmelding 40, 1993–94, pp. 435–6).

Such general statements were fairly uncontroversial and scarcely represented a full-blown argument in favour of EU membership on the grounds of international security. However, they provided an early outline of this case, with a much fuller statement being made in the 1993–1994 defence budget proposal in September 1993 (Ministry of Defence, 1993b).

This discursive account, given by the then defence minister, Jørgen Kosmo, contained the three elements that represented the considered Norwegian response to the end of the Cold War:

- There was to be a confirmation of Norway's Atlantic links, especially those with the United States through NATO. However, there was a recognition that the United States might not provide the level of support that had existed previously.
- Security was to be widely defined and Norway would contribute to the building of an international society in Europe, not least through the institutions.
- The EU was seen as *the* core institution in Europe, membership of which would allow Norway to participate in the moulding of events in Europe and would prevent the country from becoming marginalised.

All three of these arguments – which were often inter-twined – led the Norwegian government to the conclusion that membership of the EU was necessary for Norway in security terms.

The Atlantic link through NATO was stressed as still being essential for Norway's security. The majority recommendation of the Defence Commission of 1990 and the conclusions of the 'Long-Term Report' of December 1992 (Ministry of Defence, 1993a) were reiterated. Despite the changes after the end of the Cold War 'military security guarantees and Allied commitments to assist Norway remain a necessary element of our security policy in combination with a solid national defence effort' (Ministry of Defence, 1993b, p. 6). Assistance could be sought through NATO which retained 'its decisive importance for Norway's security since NATO represents an underlying guarantee through its capacity to mount credible collective defence and provide Allied reinforcements' (Ministry of Defence, 1993b, p. 10).

It was recognised that NATO and the Atlantic link had changed and that Norway could not 'base itself on the status quo – neither in NATO nor in other ways' (Ministry of Defence, 1993b, p. 31) The '*new* NATO' would be one in which the European members would assume a larger share of the burdens and responsibilities, with the North American presence in Europe reduced. The WEU would be the European pillar in NATO as well as the defence component of the EU, and there would be growing importance attached to burgeoning bilateral links between the EU and the United States (Ministry of Defence, 1993b, p. 18). The report dealt with the fear that the development of the EC and WEU 'might contribute to "pushing" the United States out of Europe', by doubting whether the WEU would be able to develop separate from NATO and stressing that European cooperation within the WEU would be complementary to that in NATO. The United States would expect to see the Europeans assuming more responsibilities 'and a larger number of tasks' (Ministry of Defence, 1993b, p. 18).

An alternative posited was that of the United States leaving Europe, regardless of what the Europeans did. In this case the WEU, developed as a defence institution, could take over NATO's military structures 'if . . . there should be a need to do so'. The 'Europeanisation' of NATO would be an alternative to the 'renationalisation' of defence. Should the US leave Europe, it would be unlikely to treat Norway as a special case, thus it would be important for Norway to be 'a fully integrated part of the European pillar in NATO that has WEU as its institutional core'. This would 'give Norway the largest possible *influence* on the evolving security relationship between the United States and its European Allies' (Ministry of Defence, 1993b, p. 20). Even though by total desertion of the United States was seen as an unlikely scenario, it was deemed necessary to insure against it. Nevertheless, the continuation of NATO involvement in the security of Norway was seen to point increasingly in a European direction with full Norwegian involvement in the WEU, which meant EU membership.

As if to back up fears about US desertion, an agreement made in Washington in March 1994 reduced the number of US Collocated Operating Bases (COBs) in Norway from nine to five. However, four of these remained in North Norway and the final total compared well with the original American intention to reduce the number of COBs to two (Helgesen, 1994, p. 6). Nevertheless, it was becoming clearer that the end of the Cold War, budgetary constraints and internal political developments meant that the US commitment to the defence of Norway was weakening in material terms and would continue to decline.

The budget proposal also outlined a *wider security approach*. It reminded the reader that '(t)raditionally Norway has applied a broad approach as the basis for its security policy', that the country 'quite early tried to integrate more political instruments as part of a more *comprehensive* security policy' and that, since the end of the Cold War, it was more urgent than ever to pursue such a policy (Ministry of Defence, 1993b, p. 2). NATO's new strategic concept had itself taken up a broad approach to security that added dialogue and cooperation to collective defence. Likewise Norway had re-evaluated its instruments of policy, finding that the political aspects had gained in weight 'at the expense of the military ones' (Ministry of Defence, 1993b, p. 5).

A 'liberal institutionalist' view was advanced in the Report, whereby the road to European peace and security could be found through common security, though this was being challenged by a series of antagonisms that could lead parties 'into a vicious circle of competitive security' which 'represents a significant explanation of why the nation-state system in Europe has, historically speaking, been characterised by war to such an extent' (Ministry of Defence, 1993b, p. 8). It was thus in the interests of Norway that the 'norms, rules and standards' contained in CSCE documents were complied with, as their undermining could result in tragedies such as that seen in former Yugoslavia (Ministry of Defence, 1993b, p. 8).

The agenda for the new emphasis on collective security meant that the international norms of behaviour must be extended, the national military sovereignty reduced, mutual transparency of the military dispositions of the states ensured, and measures for collective security and collective defence taken (Ministry of Defence, 1993b, p. 14).

In undertaking the economic and political aspects of security 'the process of European integration, or EC, is at the core' (Ministry of Defence, 1993b, p. 14).

The Report also brought in a concept that has already been referred to in connection with Thorvald Stoltenberg's writings on Barents cooperation (see section 10.8), that of a *security community*. It was considered that '(t)he Nordic region, NATO and the EC are today to be considered as security communities' and that the area should be expanded to include as much of Europe and 'the adjacent areas' as possible (Ministry of Defence, 1993b, p. 12).[3] In doing this, a key role was ascribed to NATO and the EC. It was felt that the CSCE, though important, was not then ready to replace either (Ministry of Defence, 1993b, p. 12).

In its appreciation of the situation in Russia, the Report noted the conventional and nuclear armaments of that country. While the strategic balance had to be maintained, it was also necessary to pursue a policy of dialogue and cooperation with Russia. Multilateral cooperation in the Barents and Baltic regions was mentioned. Emphasis was placed not just on the Russian state but also groups within it, so that a 'fundamental goal for Norway (was) to connect major interests in Russian society to peaceful cooperation with its Nordic neighbours'. In particular, 'the social situation for the armed forces on the Kola Peninsula' was increasingly a matter for concern (Ministry of Defence, 1993b, p. 22). This approach contrasted with a traditional state-to-state view of international security and also fitted in with the notion of creating a security community extending east from the Nordic region.

In all the plans for a strengthening of international society in Europe, the EC (the EU had not then come into being) was given prominence. A greater emphasis on economic and political factors pointed to the EC. The notion of a security community was one that was typified by the EC. The institutional framework in Europe had the EC as its core. Even cooperation with Russia in the Far North was best undertaken with EC support.

It is thus not surprising that the third arrow in the Norwegian security quiver was *membership of the European Union*, the EC's successor. The fletching on the other two – as seen above – was already coloured with the familiar twelve gold stars on a blue background.

With the need for collective security to help defend Northern Norway and with the emphasis on building common security throughout Europe, Norway had to be 'willing to contribute to security, stability and possibly collective military defence in other parts of Europe' (Ministry of Defence, 1993b, p. 9). If nothing else, this was a quid pro quo for the readiness of allies to make a similar commitment in Northern Europe. The European members generally had to bear a larger share of 'the burdens and responsibilities which European security entails' (Ministry of Defence, 1993b, p. 10). Though NATO was of key importance here, the WEU and the CFSP of the EU represented the intersection of 'the European and Atlantic (Ministry of Defence, 1993b, p. 10).

Should the United States become more isolationist, the European imperative would strengthen, with Norwegian membership of the EC/EU and full participation in the CFSP being decisive. Should Norway not be so involved, then 'the very motivation of our

European Allies to be concerned about Norway's security may be expected to diminish over time' (Ministry of Defence, 1993b, p. 21).

It was considered that the WEU would play an increasing role in the division of labour and role specialisation among NATO's European members (Ministry of Defence, 1993b, p. 44). Norway was only an associate of WEU and was not represented in the military Planning Cell, though the Chief of Defence, Minister of Foreign Affairs and Minister of Defence participated in meetings with their WEU colleagues (Ministry of Defence, 1993b, p. 33 & 35). However, it was made clear that associate member status was '*not* satisfactory' and that '(o)nly full membership will provide the basis for full and equal participation, and full right to take part in making decisions' (Ministry of Defence, 1993b, p. 36, emphasis in original). This meant membership of the EU.

Specifically referring to Norway's relations with Russia, the Report stated that:

> Today it is desirable and correct to couple Norway's relations with Russia as closely as possible to Russia's relations with the EC and Continental Europe, in order to ensure close and equal cooperation between Norway and Russia.

It continued:

> Norway should not risk that Russia may pursue one kind of policy towards Continental Europe, based on Russian needs, and a different policy in the north, based on Russian demands. . . . (T)o enter into close and multi-dimensional cooperation with Russia, Norway will need to be an integrated part of a larger Western community. (Ministry of Defence, 1993b, p. 15)

Norway should not be considered 'a small northern European buffer state, but rather a part of the political and economic mainstream'. EC membership would safeguard 'the *political* and *economic* dimensions of Norway's security policy vis-a-vis Russia' (Ministry of Defence, 1993b, p. 15, emphasis in original).

In the end, the security case for EU membership lay in the fear – often expressed by Norway in the context of its NATO membership that it might otherwise be left alone to face an uncertain and unstable Russia: if Norway were to sit on the sidelines during the process of European cooperation, in the next round one might risk ending up on the sidelines in transatlantic cooperation as well. In the Norwegian debate on security policy, this has been referred to as the danger of 'political marginalisation' (Ministry of Defence, 1993b, p. 11).

All this laid the ground for the use of the security card in the Norwegian referendum campaign. At the start, international security was only a minor theme in ministers' speeches, though the Conservatives were more prepared to include it in their attacks on the left-wing opponents of membership. However, the issue was introduced to centre-stage when Mrs Brundtland made a speech on 15 August 1994 in Måløy which stressed peace and security as one of the main reasons for Norwegian membership of the EU. (Brundtland, 1994b, pp. 1–2; see also section 6.2).

In her Måloy speech, Mrs Brundtland pointed out that NATO, the traditional basis for Norwegian security, was increasingly affected by the view that the European members should take on a larger responsibility for their own security, and that the EU and WEU would have a more important role in security matters. The prime minister stated that it was clear to her that Norway should not be 'a second rank security policy nation in Europe' and there were therefore strong foreign and security reasons for Norway becoming a full member of the EU (Brundtland, 1994b, p. 9).

This approach was supported by the Conservatives who saw membership of the WEU, through full EU membership, as being desirable because of its links to both the EU and NATO. EU membership would allow greater influence within NATO at a time when the EU countries were increasingly coordinating their policies within such fora as NATO. The Centre Party considered the WEU as unnecessary as it was the US – through NATO – that provided Norway with its security (Eide, 1996, pp. 82–3). This was in line with the arguments advanced by the Centre Party in the 1990 Defence Commission (see section 10.6).

The Social Democrats Against the EU (SME) faced the security issue head on. They recognised that the supporters of membership had pushed security policy as a main argument for Norway being in the EU, and talked about them using fear and uncertainty to frighten Norwegians into acceptance. However, they saw no reason why Norway's security would be weakened outside the EU (Gerhardsen et al., 1994, p. 28). They considered the challenge in Europe as that of integrating the new democracies in the East, including Russia, in a form of cooperation that could secure peaceful solutions for conflict. They did not think that the EU could fulfil that role within a short period: more realistically NATO and the CSCE/OSCE were likely to do so.

They complained that opponents of EU entry were called unrealistic when they supported the building up of CSCE/OSCE, though in this they felt themselves to be in line with the rest of Europe. Militarily Norwegian security was secured through NATO, but the yes-side had sought to place this in doubt, according to the document. The authors considered Norway never to have been more secure. They cited Bengt Westerberg, a former Swedish Liberal Party minister and EU supporter, in saying that the Russian war machine was a fragment of its former self. Neither was there any reason to think that NATO allies would not stand by their commitments. The reduction in the US presence in Europe was a result of the end of the Cold War. If doubts were to be raised about Allied commitments within NATO, these could just as well be brought up in the context of the EU. On the question of having a military side of the EU through the WEU, the writers considered that new organizations excluding the East European states should not be encouraged. Whilst association with WEU meant that Norway could not veto action within that organization, neither was Norway bound by WEU decisions (Gerhardsen et al., 1994, pp. 28–9).

The government had rightly identified international security as an issue which both sides of the campaign saw as a pro-membership argument (Ringdal, 1995, p. 49). This was the case in 1994 as it had been in 1972. However, it was not a key issue in determining the votes of either sceptics or waverers in the campaign. As one commentator remarked, traditional security policy did not have a particular meaning for the question of Norwegian EU membership (Østerud, 1994, p. 96).

11.4   Security in the Margins

The failure of the security issue to affect the referendum debate in a major way can be explained in terms of it not being salient for much of the electorate. Why was this the case? The answer lies partly in the nature of the discourse on security matters during this period.

The essence of the government's argument ran thus: Norway cannot defend itself, it must always have outside help available. To attract such help it must not appear to be marginal to the interests of its potential protectors, otherwise it might be discarded. It can make itself more attractive by taking defence seriously (it cannot expect its allies to be more enthusiastic about its defence than itself) but in the end the defence of Norway has to be important to its allies. In the post-Cold War situation, the direct threat to Norway had seemed to have diminished and the US willingness to aid Norway may also have been seen to falter. The official response was partly to stress that Norway was in fact not as well off as other states in Europe – it still had a threat on its doorstep. As American help might decrease over time it was necessary to replace it – or at least supplement it – with EU assistance. The other strand in the argument was that the new security situation in Europe was predominantly one of diverse insecurities. These could best be dealt with by a collective effort and by non-military as well as military means. The EU was the main source of non-military instruments – the diplomatic and the economic – and the WEU (seen as the EU's defence arm) could become an important element – alongside NATO – in the military effort. Norway had to participate fully in both in order not to be marginalised in the new European security order. A European discourse was thus called in to buttress the more familiar Atlantic one.

Most of the Norwegian electorate clearly did not either understand or accept this argument. Why? There had been the suggestion after the 1972 referendum that Norway – after rejecting EC membership – would become marginalised within the Atlantic community, but the opposite had happened. During the late 1970s and early 1980s the United States and other NATO members had become *more* interested in the defence of Norway and the seas off its coast. By 1994 neither the idea of a continuation of a Russian military threat at previous levels nor that of American abandonment seemed to have been accepted by most of the electorate. After all, the level of threat or abandonment had to be high to attract voter interest. Those who were the potential opponents of EU membership – people in the regions and in the primary industries – did not see their country as being marginal in the Atlantic context. Indeed, Norway's central involvement in the Middle East peace process during 1993 suggested otherwise.

Furthermore, when it came to the new security agenda – the one that stressed the need to respond to uncertainties and instabilities – there seemed little acceptance that this was now a European discourse. Indeed, the EC/EU's involvement in former Yugoslavia gave the impression that this was not then the case. The security instruments involved – as in the Gulf War – were those of the United Nations Security Council and NATO, with ad hoc coalitions being formed around them. The 'softer' security agenda – human rights, minority issues and the like – were catered for by CSCE/OSCE and the Council of Europe. It seemed hard for the Norwegian public to accept that there was an emerging European security complex with the EU as its core and from which Norway absented itself at its peril. The attempt to use the EU as a golden thread that could be woven through all Norway's security concerns was bound to fail in a country with such an Atlanticist view of its position in the strategic world. Neither was the case helped by the inability of the EU and its EC-EPC predecessor to be seen to act effectively in many of the main foreign and security issues from 1992 to the end of 1994.

The government's strategy of linking the security issue with EU membership was risky. If joining the EU was the way to avoid marginalisation, then the implication was that staying out could court trouble. Would not EU members accept Norway's own definition of itself as an 'outsider', even in the security field? Who would offer assistance to Norway should the United States step down its commitment even further? Did not a 'marginalised' Norway make itself vulnerable in bilateral relations with its Russian neighbour? The security consequences of the Norwegian 'no' will be examined in the next chapter.

Notes

1   See the speech in 1961 by Tage Erlander, then Prime Minister of Sweden, (Erlander, 1992, pp. 120–122) in which the argument was that Sweden had wider international obligations than those encompassed by the EC and that the country would have to be self-sufficient in a crisis. Many parts of this speech, *mutatis mutandis*, could have been used by Norwegian Labour Party opponents of EU membership in 1994.

2   For the development of European Political Cooperation (EPC), as this process was called, see Archer and Butler, 1996, chapter 12; Ginsberg, 1989; Nuttall, 1992.

3   Whether Greece and Turkey, both members of NATO, can be considered as part of a security community seems doubtful. They may not have gone to war with each other since 1945, but the possibility of such conflict can by no means be ruled out.

PART III
AFTER 'NO', WHAT?

12

Norway: Secure at the Margins?

12.1 Introduction

The most immediate security policy effect of the Norwegian refusal of EU membership was that full membership of the Western European Union (WEU) was closed to Norway. However, Norway still remained an associate of WEU and a full member of NATO, as well as a member of the United Nations and the OSCE, the successor to the CSCE.

What are the longer term consequences of staying outside the EU for Norwegian security policy?

It is difficult, if not impossible, to estimate the effect on the security policy of a country of one variable, namely that of membership or non-membership of an organization, the involvement of which in security matters is as yet unclear. However, an attempt can be made to answer the question by two differing approaches. The importance attached to EU membership by the decision-makers can be examined and their response to non-membership seen (see sections 12.2 and 12.3 below). Some likely scenarios for European security can be outlined, with some estimation of what each may mean for Norwegian security policy (see section 12.4 below). These scenarios will vary according to the Russian, American and European security situation, and according to other more strategic and systemic changes.

12.2 The Immediate Policy Response

As mentioned at the end of the last chapter, the government's decision to stress the importance in security terms of Norwegian EU membership held some risks. The negative response in the referendum meant that the basis of the country's security policy might have been called into question. What did the government say and do to ameliorate the situation after 1 January 1995?

As before that date, Norway had to face a wide and complicated security agenda in a period of change and uncertainty. The Norwegian State Secretary at the Ministry of Foreign Affairs, Siri Bjerke, identified the three main requirements to meet the security challenges as a stronger and more effective Europe, continued substantial American involvement in European security, and the inclusion of all European countries and Russia in security cooperation (Bjerke, 1996a, p. 29). The immediate response of the government to the security challenge can be placed under the three headings of the US in Europe,

Europe's role, and the role of Russia and Central and East Europe. More generally there was also a concern about Norway's international engagements, such as those in the UN.

These issues were addressed directly by the then Minister of Defence, Jørgen Kosmo, in a speech to the Oslo Military Society on 9 January 1995 when he called for a building up of Norwegian bilateral links with European and Atlantic allies and a more active Norwegian international engagement in order to look after the country's security interests. In his address to the same group in October 1995, Bjørn Tore Godal, the Foreign Minister, reiterated the country's security priorities outlined by his colleague at Defence some nine months earlier. There was perhaps a greater stress on using 'a more varied set of political and institutional instruments' to meet broad security challenges which could not be dealt with 'by military means alone' (Godal, 1995a, p. 14), but this might be only natural from the minister who was expected to use such instruments. Generally the message from the two ministers was not one of isolation or of Norway being apart, but one of engagement and commitment. However, the form of Norwegian involvement in enhancing international security had to be by means other than those allowed by full EU membership.

Kosmo considered that preserving security, peace and stability would depend on encouraging increased contact and cooperation between East and West, especially in the North where closeness to Russia gave Norway 'a natural capacity to play such a role' (Kosmo, 1995, p. 3, authors' translation). A critical factor was the need for solid cover from allies in Europe and the US which would allow Norway to take the risks needed (ibid.).

Indeed a continuing and strong *interest of the US in Europe* was recognised by both ministers, though a reduction of the American military presence was also seen. Kosmo considered it to be in America's interest that the European states together took a greater share of responsibility for security requirements, especially through the WEU, described as NATO's European pillar. Particular tasks for Norway were to ensure that the USA continued its commitment to Norway and Europe, and Washington recognised that Norway's defence-related question was different than that on the European continent. The credibility attached to Norway's defence against invasion produced a special requirement of allied activity, and thus it was important that the USA did not view Norway as just a part of Europe, but as a country with which it was in their self-interest to continue to have close bilateral relations (Kosmo, 1995, p. 6).

Kosmo underlined this strong Atlanticist theme: the most important security-political task for Norway was to secure its close political cooperation and military agreements with the US. Continued dependence on the NATO security guarantee meant first and foremost the USA. It was important to increase contacts and cooperate militarily with a range of different states, but this should not be at the expense of Norway's connection with its most important ally. The meaning of prepositioned materiel and regular exercises for the credibility of Norwegian defence was stressed by Kosmo and the reduction of Canada's involvement in the defence of North Norway strongly regretted. In particular the notice given by Canada that its reinforcement obligation to Norway with its materiel contribution to the NCF would be repatriated, caused concern (Kosmo, 1995, p. 6).

The importance of the United States for European security was later stressed by Godal at a time when the US administration became more involved in the settlement of the conflict in former Yugoslavia, leading to the Dayton Accords (Godal, 1995a, p. 16). Somewhat paradoxically it was recognised that, while there would be a 'continued reduction of the

US military presence in Europe', new security challenges had enlarged 'the scope of continued US involvement in Europe' (Godal, 1995a, p. 16). This seemed to recognise that the Clinton administration had started to become more involved in issues such as Bosnia, Northern Ireland and the Greek-Turkish dispute, showing less of the hesitancy displayed during the first two years of office. Broadly, what Norway might see as negative trends in trans-Atlantic relations had, by the end of 1995, been reversed in the defence and foreign affairs field. Of direct interest to Norway was the US Air Force taking on the Chief of Staff position at Stavanger Allied Headquarters North, providing more than a symbol of continued US strategic interest in the region.

In the area of *Europe's role*, there was some change in the emphasis given to particular institutions. One of the immediate results of the referendum was the increased weight given to the WEU in the Norwegian government's security policy. In his statement on foreign policy made to the *Storting* on 19 January 1995, the Foreign Minister stated that 'the government is . . . now considering whether to earmark Norwegian forces which the WEU can employ in planning rescue, humanitarian and peacekeeping operations' (Godal, 1995b) (see section 12.3 below). Later in 1995, Godal went into further detail about the possible development of the WEU. His view was that it should take on some of the new security tasks – such as those mentioned in his *Storting* statement (the 'Petersberg tasks') – and that the associated Central and East European states, as well as countries such as Norway, should become more involved with the WEU in such tasks. Norway therefore wanted to maintain the WEU as an organisation separate from the EU and, should the WEU become closely linked with the EU, 'Norway should be given an opportunity to become linked or associated with this part of the EU cooperation.' (Godal, 1995a, p. 25). However, in the context of security, there was a warning against 'exaggerated "Europeanisation", which could in reality call into question the entire notion of the transatlantic community' (Godal, 1995a, p. 25).

Godal again stressed the importance of a trans-Atlantic dialogue but considered it crucial that this should embrace all North American and European allies. The European voice should not be limited to the EU states (Godal, 1995a, p. 18). Whereas in the referendum period, the connections between the EU and NATO had been assiduously made, the necessity was by 1995 to make it clear that, while Norway may have exercised the 'exit' option in the case of the EU, it certainly remained a loyal member of NATO and expected its voice to be heard. Having failed to become part of the European pillar, Norway had to make sure that 'marginalisation' did not become a self-fulfilling prophecy.

In order to counter the impression that Norway's rejection of EU membership meant that it would be standing outside of European integration, Kosmo said that Norway would make known its viewpoint that support should be given to develop the 'traditional and positive elements in alliance cooperation' at the same time as supporting the new tasks the Alliance had taken on (1995, p. 3). He stated bluntly that it would not be in Norway's interest should NATO develop 'from a military alliance to only a security-political institution' (ibid.). It was recognised that economic limitations would have a negative effect on NATO's infrastructure programme, from which Norway had benefited over the years and which had helped to make credible plans for reinforcement (Kosmo, 1995, pp. 4–5). It was also accepted by the minister that these traditional aspects of NATO had to be balanced with the new activities such as Partnership for Peace agreements with the Central and East European states which might eventually lead to the extension of membership to these states, bringing Norway into a new security situation (Kosmo, 1995, p. 5).

Some months later, Mr Godal turned to the difficult question of NATO enlargement encompassing states from *East and Central Europe*, a process seen as 'primarily political, not exclusively military' (Godal, 1995a, p. 19). Norwegian official statements about the enlargement of NATO to include Central and East European states tended to be cautious. It was recognised that the process was about bringing those countries into binding security and defence arrangements, that it would help democratic control of their armed forces, help avoid re-nationalisation of security and reduce the impact of regional conflicts. However, some of the reservations in the study on enlargement were recognised: the process must 'contribute to increased security for all states and for Europe as a whole' (Bjerke, 1996a, p. 30) and should not bring 'new dividing lines or the resurrection of old ones' (Godal, 1995a, p. 19). One concern here was that of the attitude of Russia which was seen as 'clearly seeking to reassert its position as a major power' and in 'a difficult transitional phase' (Godal, 1995a, pp. 20–1). Emphasis was placed on including Russia in international cooperative arrangements.

Specifically it was mentioned that there was 'no military rationale for the stationing of foreign troops or nuclear weapons on the territory of the new members' (Bjerke, 1996a, p. 31). This reflected Norway's existing position within NATO, though the point was that the prospective members should be free to choose their arrangements. A warning was given about acting prematurely over enlargement, safeguarding – and developing – the 'political and military qualities that are unique to NATO' (Bjerke, 1996a, p. 31). In the 1995 Defence statement to the *Storting*, concern was expressed that new tasks and an eastern enlargement of NATO should not be realised at the expense of core functions, which themselves should not be interpreted in too narrow a way (Forsvarsdepartementet, 1995, p. 9).

For Norway, any precipitous enlargement of NATO could rebound on its relations with Russia and also detract from the trans-Atlantic nature of the organisation that has been – and is – so valuable to the country. It could also re-focus the Alliance's concern on the central area of continental Europe at a time when Norway has been trying to get the members to pay attention to the situation on the 'flanks'. For these reasons the Norwegian government has been one of the more cautious members of NATO concerning membership enlargement.

The extension of EU membership to the Central and East European states was seen by Norwegian ministers as being more unreservedly beneficial as this could strengthen democracy, help resolve environmental problems and bridge the prosperity gap (Forsvarsdepartementet, 1995, p. 9; Brundtland, 1996, p. 16). It was hoped that the Intergovernmental Conference of EU governments should decide on the changes needed for a larger membership, as EU enlargement was 'in the interest of Norway'(Bjerke, 1996b, p. 3). Even though it was recognised that the enlargement of NATO and the EU to the east were parallel processes, Norway seemed to prefer that the more indirect road to security – that of EU membership – take precedence. After all, the Norwegian government had ventured down that road until forced to turn back by the electorate in November 1994.

Russia continued to be central to Norway's security. The situation there was typified as unstable and insecure, not least as a result of the way that the Russian authorities dealt with conflict within its own borders and with its relations to the lands of the former Soviet Union. The conflict in Chechnya could, according to Kosmo, lead to a strengthening either of the military or of democracy within Russia, though it was too early to tell which. Russia's insecurity again underlined the NATO connection (Godal, 1995a, p. 7). The 1995 defence statement to the *Storting* gave an ambiguous account of Norway's troubled neighbour. It was admitted that the insecurity of Russia, together with a 'more considerable military capacity near Norway's territory', would to a great extent influence Norwegian security policy and planning in the coming years (Forsvarsdepartementet, 1995, p. 4, authors' translation). The considerable armed might of Russia on Norway's border was rehearsed. However, the cooperation potential with Russia was linked to a high Norwegian profile in East-West relations, with Norway acting as a catalyst and 'door opener' for contact across the former bloc division in the North. Partnership for Peace exercises and multinational cooperation in dealing with nuclear contamination in the North were mentioned. In policy terms, it seems that – once left outside the EU – Norway's response was to portray its propinquity with Russia as an asset, just as it had done with the creation of the Barents Euro-Arctic Council before applying for EU membership. This time the appeal was made to a wider Western audience, with the United States receiving particular attention (Forsvarsdepartementet, 1995, pp. 5–7).

Norway's *international engagement*, especially its participation in UN peace opera-tions, also received comment from ministers. Defence Minister Kosmo stressed the importance for a small country of the upholding of international norms and legal prin-ciples. Norway had to reckon with participating in the new generation of peacekeeping operations that had a wider mandate than the traditional ones. He voiced strong Norwegian support for a political solution to the conflict in former Yugoslavia, not least because it would provide a boost for the establishment of cooperative arrangements in the security-political area in Europe (Kosmo, 1995, p. 3). He also pointed out that Nordic defence and security cooperation had developed from just being in the UN context to covering a number of issues. In particular the joint Nordic activity in establishing a Baltic battalion was cited (Kosmo, 1995, p. 8).

This aspect of Norwegian security policy also found a central place in the Defence Report to the *Storting* in October 1995 with particular attention given to OSCE, cooperation with the Baltic states, Partnership for Peace and UN operations (Forsvars-departcmentet 1995, pp. 2, 4, 7, & 14–17). There was little change from 1994 except that this approach to international security was then seen as one that Norway, together with the other Nordic members, could bring into the EU councils as a distinct contribution.

In the period following the rejection of Norwegian EU membership, the Norwegian government had to remake its security policy not so much in points of substance but more in the way it was presented. The 'golden thread' of the EU as both an instrument and a forum for security policy was replaced by a commitment to involvement in a wide range of institutions, with special emphasis being placed – as ever – on the trans-Atlantic link. Rejection of membership had not meant a growing distance between the EU and Norway – indeed Norway expressed interest in having the closest possible relationship with the EU on foreign and security matters – but policy had to be pursued in a vigorous fashion at a number of points to demonstrate that Norway was not about to sink into the margins.

A more specific case of the liberal institutionalist approach brought to bear on a secu-rity matter was that of Norway's approach to the Baltic states and Barents regional cooperation. Norway continued to deal with its security problems by non-military means in these areas (see section 12.3). Barents cooperation had been developed for a number of reasons and had provided Norway with an important foreign-security dowry that it could have brought with it into the European Union. Norway's decision to stay outside the EU meant a change in priorities. Its absence from the EU – and Denmark, Finland and Sweden's presence – meant that less emphasis was placed on the Barents compared with the Baltic in the Union's policy towards the Russian Federation in the North. As a Norwegian Ministry of Defence document stated: 'In parallel with the weakened western focus on the North, increased interest is being shown in the Baltic region, both within the EU and in a Nordic context' (Ministry of Defence, 1995b, p. 5).

Nevertheless, Norway was prepared to become a good Baltic country as it recognised that the security of this region – and the relationship of the Baltic republics to Russia – was crucial for its own security and the Baltic countries were defined as being in an area 'of immediate interest to Norway' with stability in the Baltic region being a prerequisite of stability in northern Europe (Ministry of Defence, 1995a, p. 6). However, Norwegian interests were still strongly directed to the north-west area of Russia. In his annual address to foreign ministry station heads in August 1995, Bjørn Tore Godal, the Foreign Minister, devoted the equivalent of two and a half pages to Barents region cooperation, including environmental cooperation, but one short paragraph to Baltic cooperation (Godal, 1995c, pp. 6–7 & 10–11). Norway still found its policy towards Russia concentrating on the north-west part of that country, though Sweden and Finland's presence in the EU drew the Nordic flock towards an emphasis on the Baltic region.

The arguments advanced in the government's defence policy documents in the lead-up to the referendum have been typified in the last chapter as containing a 'golden thread' tying security to membership of the European Union. The direct involvement of the EU in security matters was matched by its importance in the other two legs of the Norwegian security tripod, 'liberal institutionalism' and the Atlantic Alliance. After the referendum, the 'golden thread' had to be unravelled, and Kosmo's speech started that process. While the EU and WEU were still seen as important and institution-building was mentioned in the context of UN peacekeeping, the main stress was on NATO, the WEU and the United States. There was some recognition of the inherent difficulties that such dependence may bring, but they were not emphasised as strongly as before the referendum. A further element received attention, that of Nordic cooperation in the defence field. This was not new at the start of 1995, though attention to it was perhaps greater than before.

The nuances found in the development of Norwegian security policy since the referendum were partly a result of Norway being outside the EU and partly a response to new security developments, such as those in former Yugoslavia. One aspect that allowed the government some freedom of manoeuvre was the lack of any domestic challenge to its policy. After the confrontations of the referendum debate, the then Labour government found that it had a broad political consensus behind its general security policy line. The Centre Party criticised the government for coming too close to the EU, but mainly in the area of justice and home affairs and the Schengen border agreement. The Conservatives regretted the loss of influence resulting from non-EU membership but broadly supported the government. On the question of NATO's expansion, the Centre Party and the Socialist Left Party were more cautious than the government and the Conservatives more in favour (UD Informasjon, 1996). The general configuration of domestic political forces has, however, given the minority Labour government a hand free from domestic constraint in following its post-referendum security line. The change to a centrist-based minority government after the September 1997 election is thus unlikely to bring any great change in this position.

12.3 Security Policy Outcomes

The above section has provided an overview of the main developments in Norway's international security policy since the referendum. How were these policy aims translated into outcomes? There have been a number of developments that have demonstrated Norway's security priorities and, in particular, have shown the country trying to respond to the situation created by self-exclusion from the EU.

The first policy area where there was a notable development was that of the *Western European Union*. Norway, as an associate member of WEU, has no formal input into WEU policy but has been active in its support of the organisation and has opposed its integration into the EU. It was recognised that this would limit even further Norway's ability to influence the development of a European security policy, but collaboration would be closer should Norway declare forces to the WEU – in effect announcing their availability for WEU action – especially if these forces took part in a particular action (Forsvarsdepartementet, 1995, pp. 13–14).

Norway declared a number of forces to the WEU for tasks described in the June 1992 Petersberg Declaration, often called non-Article 5 tasks.[1] These consist of one infantry battalion (the Telemark Battalion), one F-16 squadron, one mine-clearer, and the 2,000 or so personnel, three naval vessels, two C-130 Hercules and four helicopters that make up Norway's on-call force for peacekeeping. The operational headquarters, Defence Command North Norway, was also declared for WEU tasks (Ellingsen, 1996, p. 19).

A more practical opportunity for Norway to participate in multilateral security cooperation came with the implementation of the *Dayton Peace Accords* which, in November and December 1995, had seen the end to the warring in former Yugoslavia. The agreement in Bosnia-Herzegovina was to be overseen by a new NATO force, the Stabilisation Force (SFOR). All NATO members contributed in one way or another to SFOR, as did non-NATO states, and it was to be led by the Commander-in-Chief Allied Forces Southern Europe. Norway contributed about 740 personnel as part of the Polish/Nordic Brigade in the US led division and an 'HQ defence company/immediate reaction force for the SFOR commander' (Ellingsen, 1997, pp. 18).

Norway's regional policy was aimed at creating as low a level of tension as possible in its immediate area. This referred not only to the Nordic region but also to its links with the Baltic states and to Russia in the Barents region.

Norwegian implemented its policy towards the Baltic states in three main areas. First, it supported the strengthening of their sovereignty. For example in December 1994 a fast patrol boat was transferred from Norway to each of the Baltic states (Forsvarsdepartementet, 1995, p. 17). Secondly, it helped tie the three republics more closely to the West through cooperation with either the Nordic states or the EU. Norway itself signed framework agreements on cooperation in the defence sector with Estonia, Latvia and Lithuania in August 1995, and seminars were held between the defence ministers of the Baltic and Nordic states (Forsvarsdepartementet, 1995, p. 17). Norway was also involved with the other Nordic states in the BALTBAT project whereby the three Baltic states were encouraged to create a Baltic battalion for peacekeeping tasks (Forsvarsdepartementet, 1995, p. 17). Mrs Brundtland encouraged the Baltic states – specifically Lithuania – to see integration with the European Union as a source of security and to advance with their application for full membership. Thirdly it tended to preach restraint to the Baltic states both in their treatment of minority groups and in their dealings with Russia. In this context, it seemed to be Norwegian practice to advise caution in relation to expectations about NATO membership (Brundtland, 1996, pp. 15–16).

Norway continued to implement a policy of building cooperative links with Russia in the Barents area. *Barents cooperation* had a value for Norway in itself and was pursued not just through the Barents Euro-Arctic Council but also by bilateral and trilateral cooperation involving Russia (Godal, 1995c, pp. 10–11; Press Release, 1995). Norway was able, with Finland and Sweden, to participate in the establishment of the EU INTER-REG Barents programme which stretched across the former East–West division (Aas, 1995, p. 35). It seemed that a practical consequence of Norway staying out of the EU was that Barents cooperation was pursued through more various means, with some emphasis placed on engaging the USA.

A further aspect of policy implementation was the growing *Nordic* involvement in Norwegian security policy. With Finland and Sweden in the EU but not in NATO and observers in the WEU, Denmark in the EU and NATO but only an observer in the WEU, and with Iceland and Norway in NATO but not the EU, there has been the danger that the Nordic security situation could become even more fragmented than before. However, these differences were seen as 'good opportunities for the further development of collaboration in the fields of security policy and foreign policy' (Ministry of Defence, 1995b, p. 5). In practical terms substantive meetings of Nordic foreign and defence ministers were held and Norway strengthened its defence contacts with Sweden and Finland, all giving the Nordic states the opportunity 'to develop a more closely correlated security policy than was possible during the Cold War period' (Ministry of Defence, 1995b, p. 5). The Nordic/Polish Brigade in NATO's Stabilization Force and exercises such as Nordic Peace in Troms, May 1997, in which forces from the four main Nordic states participated (Ellingsen, 1997, p. 18), represented a strong reflection of that new collaboration.

During the period after the referendum, Norwegian defence experienced changes arising from the new international situation, those resulting from decisions made by allies and those consequent on the internal process of military reform.

As a result of reduced budgets, new force structures and the Partnership for Peace structures, NATO decided to revise its exercise programme. Meanwhile Norway's reinforcement and exercise obligations were anyhow undergoing changes. After the renegotiation of the COB agreements in 1994 (see section 11.3), Norway – responding to an American initiative – revised its NALMEB (Norway Airlanded Marine Expeditionary Brigade) agreement covering the prepositioning of materiel for the US Marine Brigade so that Norway would pay a larger share of the operational and maintenance costs for the stockpiles. Following the Canadian withdrawal of its prepositioned equipment for the NATO Composite Force (NCF – the sole NATO force with Norway as the only potential area of operation), the United States completed its prepositioning of materiel for the US artillery battalion in that force (Forsvarsdepartementet, 1995, pp. 12–13).

The Ministry of Defence's budget proposal for 1996 contained suggested adaptations on Norway's self-imposed restraints on Allied military activities in Norway to meet the new situation whereby former adversaries could carry out such activities under the

Partnership for Peace or possibly in the context of the OSCE. Still, the strategic situation in the North had to be given due regard and military activities would not be permitted that could be seen as provocative or create tension among neighbours (Ministry of Defence, 1995a, p. 2). There was to be an easing on the restraints on exercises in Finnmark county, allowing small allied and 'other foreign military units' to conduct exercises and training there, especially in relation to NATO's Partnership for Peace. Allied aircraft would be allowed to fly over Finnmark for visits to and inspections in Russia. Foreign military and passenger aircraft could go to Kirkenes and a zone would be established near to the Russian border in which foreign combat aircraft 'will not normally be permitted'. All military aircraft in Finnmark would be strictly supervised, and there would be no large-scale allied exercises in the county (Ministry of Defence, 1995a, p. 2). New general guidelines would be drawn up for the admission of foreign warships and military aircraft to Norway.

Organisational changes undertaken by the Ministry of Defence were consequent on the Defence Commission of 1990 and the Main Guidelines for the 1994–1998 period (Forsvarskommisjon av 1990, 1992, Part IV; Ministry of Defence, n.d.; Kosmo, 1996, p. 6). The latter, in particular, attempted to redefine the Norwegian military structure for the post-Cold War world by maintaining a balanced defence but by shifting expenditure from operational to investment spending. This had the effect of cutting the peace-time size of the armed forces and greater emphasis had to be placed on their flexibility and effectiveness. Reliance was still to be placed on allied reinforcement, though the assumption was that the changed international situation meant that Norway was unlikely to face an invasion without little or no 'lead time'. Cuts in the army were foreseen with a greater differentiation in standards between units (Ministry of Defence, n.d., pp. 15–17). At the same time, the general increase in international instability could require Norway to contribute to peace-keeping and peace-making forces.

By 1996 it was recognised that the follow-up Long-term Report to that of 1994–98 would have to address the question of flexibility of the armed forces in face of 'new tasks' that typified the international situation and their need to maintain their basic anti-invasion capabilities (Kosmo, 1996, p. 6).

The new Long-Term White Paper had to tackle some hard decisions for Norwegian defence. On the one hand, the failure of the Soviet Union to transmute into a fully democratic Russia with a stable economy and which implemented all its Conventional Forces in Europe obligations,[2] meant that Norway felt it necessary to keep anti-invasion tasks as the priority for its armed forces. This had certain consequences in terms of balanced forces, conscripts, and host nation support, all of which required resources. On the other hand, the unstable international situation, typified by conflict in former Yugoslavia, made demands on countries such as Norway that felt that they should contribute to the maintenance of a well-functioning international society. However, the military aspects of such activities were stringent; not least they required the application of international standards (Kosmo, 1996, p. 7). It is not surprising that the Long-Term review that will take Norway into the next century will examine the very basis of the country's anti-invasion capabilities and, indeed, the question of conscription. These issues will have to be seen in the context of an increased bill that Norway may have to pay, in terms of host nation support, for the maintenance of American reinforcement promises, its extended engagement in the Baltic and Barents region, and a possible contribution to a follow-on to SFOR. The cost of maintaining a high level of activity that helps prevent the feared marginalisation of Norway outside the EU has begun to show in the defence budget. In 1996 that budget saw a 1.6% increase, reversing the cuts of previous years, partly because of SFOR-related expenditure (Kosmo, 1996).[3]

12.4   The Options for the Future: Factors Affecting Choice

In order to examine the possible development of Norwegian security policy beyond the Long-Term White Paper and into the next generation, it is necessary to consider the main factors that will shape that policy. This section will examine the possible 'opportunities' available to Norwegian decision-makers, on the basis that these will primarily be fashioned by (1) the overall strategic situation, (2) US policy towards Europe, (3) the attitudes and actions of Russia, (4) the development of the European Union and the Central and East European states, and (5) broader developments in the international system. As it is impossible to cover all scenarios, the best case (A), the worst case (Z) and two intermediate cases – a return to the Cold War (C) and a continuation of the status quo (Q) – will be mentioned (see Table 12.1 below). Of course any evaluations of 'best' and 'worst' are bound to be subjective and are not intended as prognostications but more as aids to understanding what might be the range of international restraints within which Norway may have to formulate its security policy during the next 25 years.

It is not too difficult to imagine what could be the worst sort of development in the wider strategic context for Norway (1Z), as it is implicit in the Report of 1990 Defence Commission. It would involve a collapse of international order with widespread conflict based on religious, ethnic and cultural differences and caused by the pressure of population growth, economic divisions and a battle for control over energy and resources. Global warming and the thinning of the ozone layer would continue and environmental degradation could become a source of conflict. Nuclear weapons and other weapons of mass destruction would proliferate, falling into the hands of dictators or of terrorist groups (Forsvarskommisjon av 1990, 1992, pp. 44–52). Methods of international control would break down, with international relations becoming Hobbesian.

Table 12.1   *Scenarios for the Future*

	Strat	US-Eur	Russia	EU/CEE	Int Sys
	1	2	3	4	5
Best A	1A	2A	3A	4A	5A
C W C	1C	2C	3C	4C	5C
SQ Q	1Q	2Q	3Q	4Q	5Q
Worst Z	1Z	2Z	3Z	4Z	5Z

The worst case in the context of US policy towards Europe (2Z) would mean not only the US withdrawing all its troops from Europe but entering into harsh economic and commercial competition with Europe. This could eventually preclude the United States from offering Norway the sort of military assistance that has been available, in one form or another, since the Second World War.

In this scenario Russia (3Z) would descend into civil war and outbreaks of nationalism, with perhaps the military finally taking over some form of control. It would be difficult, if not impossible, for Norway to build up a 'non-zero sum' relationship with Russia, partly because of the chaos and confusion and partly because of the negative attitude of any Russian rulers. The borders between Norway and Russia and between the Baltic Republics and Russia would become areas of tension, with perhaps some form of armed incursion by Russian forces in the latter's case.

A negative view of the development of the European Union (4Z) would be one in which the Union started to fall apart. Economic and Monetary Union would not be achieved (though some may not view this as negative) and this failure would adversely affect other economic cooperation between the member states. A Common Foreign and Security Policy would not be developed, with each country carrying out its own policy, even to the detriment of other member states. The Central and East European states would either be barred from membership in acrimonious circumstances or some might become members then fail to make the necessary adaptation to membership. In such a case, Norwegians may be glad that they did not join the EU, but there would be little to rejoice about. The collapse of the EU could see a re-nationalisation of policies which, if undertaken by Germany, could spread concern among neighbouring states. There could be a return to the coalition-building of the inter-war period. Norway would, presumably, try to encourage a common Nordic response and would tend to look to its traditional ally, the United Kingdom, for some leadership. However, this might not be forthcoming and Norway could find itself feeling the cold winds from Russia in the north and Germany in the south without the option of shelter from its Atlantic allies, the United States and the United Kingdom.

Broader developments in the international system (5Z) would be ones that saw greater societal conflict in the Third World affecting Europe with greater refugee flows and more terrorist action. In such a harsh world Norway could do little but build up its own defence potential and try to attract allies, possibly because of its position as an oil producer. Whether Norway had joined the EU would mean little, indeed non-membership could even prove to be an advantage if the members of the EU squabbled among themselves.

An optimistic view of the development of the strategic framework over the next 25 years (1A) can also be extrapolated from the Defence Commission's Report and would involve the creation of an international society within which small nations could comfortably exist. International norms and rules would not only be accepted but respected and conflict controlled (Forsvarskommisjon av 1990, 1992, p. 37). International organizations would take on increasing importance, the level of armaments held by states would be reduced and the causes of conflict would be tackled on a global basis. The world would reflect the sort of progress made in the Nordic region from the nineteenth to the twentieth century.

In this scenario, the United States would remain on friendly terms with Europe (2A). Though there would be commercial competition between the US and the EU, trade disputes would be settled in the World Trade Organisation. The United States would keep a presence in Europe to allow it to make a more effective contribution to UN or OSCE or NATO-led peace-keeping or peace-making operations. In such a case, Norway could keep some of its defence arrangements with the US.

In a best-case scenario, Russia (3A) would develop into a fully-fledged democracy with an emerging civil society and an effective reform process. The country would become positively engaged in the network of international organisations in Europe and efforts would be made to deal with the legacy of ecological damage. Norway would contribute positively both through bilateral environmental agreements and through the work of the Barents Regional Council and other multilateral agencies. The relationship between Norway and Russia would be that of good neighbours between whom disagreements – such as that over the division of the Barents Sea – could be settled amicably.

The optimal development of the European Union (4A) is perhaps a matter of greater political choice – some would hope for a United States of Europe, others for a Europe des Patries. Perhaps the best outcome would be one where there was an agreed vision of the future by all the EU states, and one in which the institutions of the Union worked effectively to achieve that vision. It should at least be an outward looking Union that was prepared to bring in a number of the countries of East and Central Europe into a closer relationship, if not membership. At the same time it would have to build a fruitful relationship with Russia. In such a case, Norway might find itself more and more excluded from the decision-making centre. It might see a Union that could comfortably embrace the United Kingdom and the other Nordic states and welcomed in the likes of Poland, Hungary and the Czech Republic. This could be the incentive for a further Norwegian application for membership – this time preceded by a referendum.

Broader developments in the international system (5A) could see international organisations dealing with some of the global problems such as pollution, over-population and low living standards. Non-governmental organisations could be seen to be making a distinct contribution in a range of areas from human rights to disaster relief. In this case Norway would be in its element. Whether part of the EU or not, it would relish a worldwide missionary role, in the social policy as well as the spiritual realm.

An intermediary stage would be a move to a bipolar Cold War system with distrust between two major nuclear powers (1C). This would not be an exact return the Cold War divisions of the 1950s to 1980s, as Central and East Europe would not be under Soviet thrall, it would be unlikely that the Soviet Union would be completely re-established, and the level of armaments on both sides would be lower than that at the height of the New Cold War in the early 1980s. However, arms control agreements might be torn up and an arms race result, and Third World states could be pressured to choose sides. China could be a more significant actor than it was in the original Cold War and might threaten to throw its weight behind one side or the other side. Indeed a variation might be a Cold War between China and either the West or Russia (or, possibly, both). While such a reversal of the history can scarcely be seen with favourable eyes by small countries bordering a great power – such as Norway – it is at least a fairly familiar scenario and does not hold the horrors of the worst case (1Z).

In this case the United States (2C) may decide to stay in Europe and to maintain its military links with countries such as Norway. However, there is the danger that if such links had already been severed, it would be more difficult to re-establish them, leaving the Norwegians somewhat vulnerable.

Much would depend on the attitudes of Russia (3C) and the extent it reverted to a Soviet-style leadership. Revamping the military establishments on the Kola Peninsula and rebuilding the Northern Fleet could be attractive for a nationalist leadership and this would have negative consequences for Norway. Relations with Russia would again be those of a small country a potentially hostile large neighbour.

Such a change in Russia could persuade the European Union (4C) to develop its

Common Foreign and Security Policy and rapidly to include Central and East European states in a closer relationship with the Union. If some states – Belarus, Ukraine, Bulgaria, Rumania and possibly Slovakia – were left out in the cold to make their own arrangements with Russia, it would be in the interests of the Nordic states to ensure that the Baltic republics were on the West European 'inside' rather than the East European 'outside'. This could add to the incentives for Norway also to be on the inside of a larger, looser European Union.

Broader developments (5C) could lead to a policy of restraint and caution, should the Third World become a stage for Russo-American manoeuvring and should international organisations such as the United Nations become stymied by Great Power contests. This could leave little room for diplomatic activity by a small country such as Norway, which again might feel that its effort would be best concentrated in the EU.

The fourth general scenario (1Q) is one in which there is a continuation of the post-Cold War mid-1990s situation. This can be typified as being unstable and uncertain, but at least there would not be a descent into anarchy or a return to the bipolarity of the Cold War. International institutions would be important but states would pick and choose their use. There would be a general US hegemony within the institutions, though with the EU, Russia and Japan often maintaining a veto power.

The United States's policy towards Europe (2Q) would continue to be ambiguous. It would want to keep a presence in Europe but would insist on some payment in return from the European states. A rich country such as Norway could find the cost of keeping the option of American reinforcements would continue to increase.

Russia (3Q) may continue to participate in international fora and agreements such as the Barents Council and the CFE but would pursue a more rigid nationalist policy. This would mean that it would become more difficult to make agreements within such institutions and bilateral diplomacy would become a more favoured tool. This would not favour any small country on Russia's borders that had a number of outstanding problems to settle with Russia. Norway would seek to multilateralise these issues.

One way that this could be done is through EU membership (4Q). The EU would remain the uncertain instrument that it now is, but would offer enough collective action to prove its worth, even to sceptical members. Norway would no doubt continue to associate itself closely with a developing EU Common Foreign and Security Policy, and the time could come when non-membership has its costs and full membership – in a Union including Central European states and with a 'variable geometry' in policy areas – could even be acceptable to a majority of the Norwegian people. However, the factors that have been outlined in earlier chapters as keeping Norway and its people apart from the process of European integration as practised on the continent of Europe, could well again hold back Norway from membership.

Wider factors (5Q) could help to tip the balance in such a decision. For example, a decline in the price of petroleum over a period of time could weaken the attractiveness of life outside the EU as Norway became less rich and less of a special case. The spread of IT, satellite TV and other transnational means of communication could chip away at Norwegian culture and Norway's feeling of 'separateness' from much of the rest of Europe – though it should be remembered that the 'culture' transmitted by the new media is scarcely European.

12.5   Conclusions

The above illustrative examples show that there are circumstances where the change in Norway's security calculations would indeed encourage a further Norwegian application to the EU for membership. For the most part they represent changes in Norway's international environment that present the decision-makers – and the Norwegian public – with an increased threat from Russia and/or a European Union that has been adapted in such a way as to make it more acceptable for Norway. This is scarcely a resounding vote of confidence in the process of integration begun by Jean Monnet back in 1950. Norway was not intended to be part of that process and many Norwegians see little reason why that situation should change.

Notes

1   This refers to Article 5 of the modified Treaty of Brussels which provides the collective defence element of the WEU. The WEU Petersberg Declaration of June 1992 allowed for planning in the areas of crisis management, peacekeeping, humanitarian and rescue actions, and other similar tasks. These are also referred to as 'Petersberg tasks'.

2   New CFE regulations allowed Russia greater flexibility to redeploy treaty-limited equipment in the whole Northern Flank zone, thereby offering 'an increased challenge for Norway, Finland and the Baltic states' (Ellingsen, 1997, p. 3)

3   SFOR-related operations cost Norway about NOK1 billion for twelve months. Of the expenditure in 1996, about NOK300m came from cuts in materiel.

13

Prosperous at the Periphery?

13.1 Introduction

The issue of Norway's relationship with the process of European integration is one that has involved economic, commercial and security issues and has cut across the uncertain line between domestic and foreign policy. The previous chapter examined the immediate policy response to the 1994 referendum result of Norway in the security field and the consequences for Norway of some scenarios in that field. After a retrospective consideration of the 1994 result, this chapter will look at some of the political and economic consequences, both in the immediate and long term, of Norway's refusal to join the EU.

As in 1972–3, there were particular political and economic consequences to be addressed in the wake of the November 1994 vote. A policy that had been the cornerstone of all the government's policies was rejected by the electorate. This time the government did not resign but started to re-design its European policy to meet the new political situation. Unlike 1973, when negotiating a free trade agreement with the EC was a priority, Norway had the EEA agreement in place in 1994, though adjustments had to be made to meet the extension of EU membership to Austria, Finland and Sweden. The government has been helped in its ability to adapt by the political and economic situation within Norway after the referendum.

More long term, a number of alternatives can be considered. These include the situation where Norway may again apply for, and obtain, membership of the European Union; and the possible consequences of continued non-membership. The former would depend on the perception of Norwegians about the longer run success as a political and economic entity of their state as compared with the European Union. The latter would differ according to the relative conditions in which both the EU and Norway find themselves and would also depend on the effectiveness of alternatives to full EU membership.

13.2 The Result in Retrospect

Looking back on the referendum result, the Yes side should have had an easier task in 1994 than in 1972. The economic arguments against the EU had lost their force in that Norway already had accepted the four freedoms through the EEA agreement. After Finland and Sweden both voted for membership, Nordic unity could best be reached through Norway joining as well. The relationship to Eastern Europe was in 1994 an argument in favour of joining, as the EU itself had started opening up eastwards, unlike in 1972. Norway's policy of subsidising its own agriculture had become more restrictive, and the number of farmers had reduced. Half of the 1994 electorate had not had the right to vote in 1972. With the increasing internationalisation of the previous twenty years, with inter-rail, exchange students programmes and satellite television, young people in

1994 could be expected to be more open-minded and internationally oriented. This did not materialise in any positive conviction among young people about the EU. Indeed, it seems the contrary was true (Jenssen, Listhaug & Pettersen, 1995, p. 158).

On the other hand, selling an almost incomprehensible European Union, which demanded both Norwegian resources and money, was clearly more difficult in a prosperous oil-nation with declining unemployment, than selling the status quo, the task of the No side. It is clear that, as in 1972, the No side, by starting the campaign earlier, set the tone of the debate. Already in autumn 1988 the forerunner of 'Nei til EU', the 'Opplysningskampanjen om Norge og EF' (Information Campaign on Norway and the EC) had been established. No similar initiative was taken on the Yes side. The Prime Minister only announced her government's intention of applying for membership in April 1992, but the Yes campaign still had to wait another two years for the negotiation results before fully opening its campaign, and then the government's offensive did not start for another four months. The Maastricht Treaty, with its 'unifying' programme, did not help the Yes side and allowed the No campaigners to stress the dangers for Norwegian democracy of any Union.

However, despite the tactical campaign factors and the international events that went against the Yes campaign, the odds against a 'Yes' outcome always seemed high. A major survey of the referendum concluded that the indications were that 'the fight was already won for the no side' before the campaign (Jenssen & Valen, 1995, p. 205). In fact the pro-EU campaigners could congratulate themselves on a good result, if not a victory. As has been demonstrated in this book, the European option was not one that came easily to Norwegian politicians or their electorate. They preferred to look to the United Kingdom or the United States, and sometimes were even prepared to consider Nordic alternatives. Unlike Finland and Sweden, there was never a majority in the 1990s opinion polls in Norway in favour of EU membership. There were also enough members of the *Storting* prepared to fight a rearguard action that could have blocked membership, had the popular vote been just in favour. Perhaps the most surprising aspects of the referendum were that it took place at all – why should Norway want to join the EU? – and that the Yes vote was so high.

13.3   The Domestic Political Aftermath

Immediately after the referendum there was speculation about what course the government would choose, and whether there would be change both in the government and in the political leadership. Representatives of the by then dissolved 'Sosialdemokrater mot EU' (SME) publicly recommended Gro Harlem Brundtland to bring SME-people in from the cold. They claimed there would have to be a change of ministers, because some had lost credibility during the EU negotiations and campaign.

Speculations about a change of government and the possible resignation of Gro Harlem Brundtland immediately after the referendum were brushed aside by intense activity by the government. The most important thing was to secure the EEA agreement for Norway, and all resources were utilised to make it work as well as possible. Norway also had to bring forward a new EFTA agreement since Austria, Finland and Sweden no longer were members after 1 January 1995.

At a press conference the day after the referendum, Anne Enger Lahnstein made it clear that the Centre Party was prepared to become the Labour Party's main opponent and challenger in the 1997 general election, and that she herself would be the party's candidate for prime minister (*Aftenposten*, 30 November 1994, p. 3). The party's target was to become a broad popular party as an alternative to the Labour Party. To achieve this, it had fundamentally redefined its own position and policy. Its strategy was based on a political analysis of the different parties' policies, and a belief that the Labour Party had changed its policy.

According to its leader, the Centre Party was working along three main lines to fulfil its ambitions. First, it wanted to maintain the broad, popular alliance on the No side. Secondly, it intended to challenge the Labour Party on those issues where they knew there were tensions within that party. Thirdly, they wished to continue its tradition as a pragmatic party (*Dagens Næringsliv*, 3 December 1994).

At the same time, tension had been reported between the prime minister's office and the party leadership in the last phase of the EU campaign. Seemingly, Gro Harlem Brundtland's staff had wanted to press the EU issue harder, while the party and Thorbjørn Jagland (later to take over the post of prime minister) had held back out of fear of splitting the party as in 1972 (*Dagens Næringsliv*, 3 December 1994, p. 11). The cautious compromise between an effective campaign and the need to keep the party united swung more in favour of the latter. This was not surprising after the disastrous effect that the all-out campaign had on the Labour Party in 1972. In 1994, the Labour Party ran a campaign that came to life very late in the day, and the issue was not made a vote of confidence in the government, with party loyalty playing a less important role than in 1972 (Jenssen & Listhaug, 1995, p. 138). These factors helped to limit the damage inflicted on the Labour government of a 'no' vote.

At the Labour Party's national board meeting in December 1994 the party leader Thorbjørn Jagland referred to the Maastricht Treaty when he stressed the importance of having a policy of a small increase in prices, a low budget deficit, and control over the national debt. Such a policy would lead to lower interest rates, securing new investments and more employment (*Arbeiderbladet*, 13 December 1994, p. 12). These principles were unanimously agreed by the meeting, but with the reference to the Maastricht Treaty taken out. The unanimity of the meeting showed that the Labour Party again was unified after the EU battle.

The opinion polls after the referendum suggested that the Labour Party had not suffered the sort of electoral haemorrhage it experienced after the 1972 referendum. By March 1995 the party even appeared to have improved its rating in the polls by some 7% compared with the September 1993 election (Economist Intelligence Unit, 1995a, p. 9). The longer term effect was more mixed. The local election results in September 1995 showed the party some six points down on its 1993 general election share of the poll, though slightly up on their performance at the 1991 local elections, and Labour lost 2% of the share of the poll in the 1997 general election, enough for Mr Jagland to resign as prime minister (*Norway Now*, 1997, pp. 3, 6–7). However, the beneficiaries were not the anti-EU Centre Party or Socialist Left, both of which saw their share of the vote slide from 1991 and 1993 and again in 1997, but, in 1993, the pro-EU Conservatives and, in 1997 the Christian Democrats, and in both 1993 and 1997 the Progress Party, both of which had had an ambiguous attitude towards the EU question (Economist Intelligence Unit, 1995b, p. 7; *Norway Now*, 1997, p. 6–7). It seemed that, almost a year after the referendum, the EU question was no longer a major factor in deciding party votes. The post-1997 *Storting* had fewer anti-EU members than its predecessor. The referendum had perhaps helped in loosening voter loyalty to the parties and in making the electorate more volatile (Jenssen, 1995b, pp. 192–4).

A major difference from the aftermath of the 1972 referendum was that the Labour Party stayed in power in 1994, at least until the 1997 election. No ministers resigned or were sacked as a result of the referendum, neither did the SME break away from the party as had anti-EC Labour members in 1972. Indeed, the minority Labour administration entrenched its position throughout 1995 and 1996 under an increasingly popular Gro Harlem Brundtland, who retired as prime minister in October 1996 on a crest of popular esteem. This task was made easier by the failure of the opposition parties – especially the Centre Party – to capitalise on the defeat of a central part of the government's policy that the referendum represented. Anne Enger Lahnstein's attempt to utilise the vote by advancing her own claim to the prime minister's post was not well received. By 1996, the Centre Party was working with the Christian Democrats and Liberals in the *Storting*, but the group's relations with the Conservatives were as bad as during the referendum (Economist Intelligence Unit, 1996b, p. 8). Indeed, the Conservatives refused to join the centrist coalition formed after the 1997 election – consisting of the Christian Democrats, Centre Party and Liberals – not least because of the presence of the Centre Party.

13.4   Negotiating with the EU

Externally, the priority of the Brundtland government after the referendum was to patch up its relations with the EU. As mentioned, the EEA agreement continued to be the framework for the economic, trade and related sides of this relationship. However, the move of Austria, Finland and Sweden into the EU camp from 1 January 1995 left Norway with Iceland and Liechtenstein facing the expanded EU across the EEA table. EFTA shrank to Iceland, Liechtenstein, Norway and Switzerland.

As the EEA covered the four freedoms of movement of the EU's single market – those of goods, services, capital and labour – Norway's economic relations with the EU continued substantially as before. There were exceptions. The move of the three EFTA states to EU membership represented their transfer from one part of the EEA to another. Their trade relations with Norway were therefore, for the most part, unaffected. However, there were areas where the conditions for trade between Norway and three former-EFTA states once they had joined the EU differed from those between them as EFTA members. The most notable cases were those of processed agricultural goods and fish exports. Other points at issue between the EU and Norway involved the adoption of measures through the EEA. These will be examined to see how Norway fared in its post-referendum relations with the EU.

From 1 July 1995, a number of processed food products – such as chocolates, jam, sandwich spreads and pizza – that had been allowed tariff-free movement between EFTA countries, incurred EU tariffs when being exported from Norway to Sweden, Finland and Austria. A confusion arose as to the tariff status of these foodstuffs under protocol 2 of the EEA agreement and as to the quantities being imported by Norway and the duties on them. After eighteen months of discussion during which Norway had held up the implementation for Sweden of North Sea fisheries agreements, an agreement was struck concerning the free movement of the processed products.

Disputes over fish exports touched a larger slice of Norwegian exports. From 1 January 1995 EU duties were raised on Norwegian fish and fish products exported to Austria, Finland and Sweden. Norway wanted a return to the duty-free status that existed when the three states were in EFTA, as the tariffs added some NOK130 million to the NOK1.7 billion value of Norway's fish exports to those three states in 1994 (Economist Intelligence Unit, 1995a, p. 13). An agreement was reached in July 1995 on increased duty-free quotas on the export to the EU of fish such as mackerel, herring, shrimp and salmon. Norway was allowed to sell the same amount of fish to Austria, Finland and Sweden as before. However, it was significant that the agreement was held up for a week by the Swedes who claimed that Norwegian fish exports had increased beyond reasonable expectations. Grete Knudsen, the Norwegian trade minister involved in the negotiations, attacked Sweden for its attitude during the talks: '. . . I do not appreciate the way they have claimed to have won a fishing war with Norway. This is not the way to speak about a neighbour . . . At the moment, relations with Sweden are strained' (*Norway Daily*, 26 July 1995, p. 1). Though this was no doubt an exercise in protecting Swedish interests, it also made the point that EU membership had its advantages, and the need to display them sometimes outweighed Nordic solidarity.

Norwegian salmon exports are another fish problem between the EU and Norway. By early 1996 there was some evidence that the EU's minimum price regulations were being circumscribed and that Norwegian exports to the EU were increasing rapidly. Scottish salmon farmers demanded an EU quota on salmon imports that could have reduced the expected Norwegian total of 300,000 tons by around 90,000 tons, whereas the Norwegian fisheries minister aimed to cut his country's supply by introducing feed quotas on the industry. A similar restriction at the end of 1995 and start of 1996, after the EU had adopted its minimum price scheme, had reduced the supply of Norwegian salmon by 40,000 tons (*Norway Daily*, 18 December 1995, p. 1; Economist Intelligence Unit, 1996a, pp. 11–12). The issue was taken to the EU's Anti-Dumping Committee with a recommendation of import duties for Norwegian salmon being made by the Commission. In the end, the two sides reached a complex five-year agreement under which individual Norwegian salmon exporters will have to sign agreements with the EU Commission on minimum prices for exports to the EU. This agreement will exempt those exporters from anti-dumping action for five years. Furthermore, the Norwegian government agreed to limit the overall increase in its salmon exports to 12% in 1997 and 10% per annum between 1998 and 2002 (Economist Intelligence Unit, 1997). While this outcome could be seen as a success for the intense Norwegian diplomatic activity on behalf of its salmon producers, it also ties this part of Norwegian industry very closely to the EU and its regulatory system.

In another fisheries case, action by the EU drove Norway into an agreement with its North Atlantic neighbours. Norway had been in conflict with Iceland over the treatment of fish stocks in those parts of the North Atlantic – 'loopholes' – that are not within any state's fisheries zone. Norway considered its fishermen had first claim on spring-spawning herring caught in the 'doughnut hole' loophole between Norway, Iceland and the Faroe Islands (Godal, 1995c, pp. 13–14). In May 1996, Norway, Iceland, the Faroe Islands and Russia reached an agreement on the 1996 take which allowed Norway a 60% quota. This agreement was encouraged by the EU's decision to allow its own vessels to catch 150,000 tons of herring in the 'doughnut hole', three time their 1995 catch. The North Atlantic states felt that they should form a common front against the EU in any negotiations (Economist Intelligence Unit, 1996b, p. 10). One of the arguments for being part of the Common Fisheries Policy (CFP) was that Norway's negotiating position would be strengthened in dealing with third parties by the support of the other EU members. Norway had decided that, being on the outside of the CFP, one form of solidarity would have to be met with another.

A further issue negotiated with the EU states was that of the Schengen accord, which aimed at abolishing border controls between member states. The Nordic states had a well-established passport union that allowed free movement of persons within the area. Denmark, Finland and Sweden were not willing to join the Schengen agreement – which has been limited to EU states – unless the Nordic arrangement of some 38 years standing was preserved. This would have made Norway and Iceland part of Schengen, though neither were EU members. Most EU states considered that Schengen should be constituted solely of EU countries. A compromise that was advanced by Schengen's Belgian presidency during 1995 involved Norway and Iceland becoming associated with Schengen but without voting rights. In the end, Norway and the other Nordic states accepted observer status with the Schengen accord which allowed them to participate without undoing Nordic freedom of movement (Knudsen, 1996, p. 12). However, closer relations with Schengen were opposed by the Centre Party, which regarded it as a diminution of Norwegian sovereignty unless a formal and effective right of veto were obtained (Lahnstein, 1996, p. 13). The need to re-negotiate the Schengen agreement with the EU after the Treaty of Amsterdam of October 1997 incorporated it into the EU has proved to be a further point of division within Norwegian politics, with the Labour and Conservative parties pressing the new centrist coalition to start such negotiations despite the reluctance of the Centre Party members of the government.

An issue that arose within the EEA was that of the state monopoly on the import and retail of alcohol. This has been maintained in Norway for social reasons and has been supported by, among others, the churches, the Christian Democrats and the Centre Party. During the EEA negotiations, government ministers had informed the *Storting* that it was proceeding on the basis that the monopoly could be continued, but soon after ratification of the EEA agreement the EFTA Court of Justice – which deals with the legal aspects of the treaty in relation to the then EFTA states – ruled against the Finnish alcohol monopoly. In order to safeguard the retail monopoly, the Norwegian government decided, in February 1995, to follow the example of its Nordic colleagues and give up the state's import monopoly. This led to protests in the *Storting* by the Christian Democrats and the Socialist Left, but to little avail (*Norway Daily*, 14 February 1995, p. 1).

The EU's 'Oil directive' had been finessed as an issue between the Union and Norway during the membership negotiations (see section 5.5.1, above), whereby Norway accepted the EU's directive of 10 December 1993 but also obtained a protocol to the accession agreement that reaffirmed national control of petroleum resources. The directive dealt with the rules for fair competition in the search for, and production of, petroleum in the EU. With Norway's rejection of membership, the issue of the country's offshore petroleum resources came to be addressed by the EEA. In April 1995, Norway accepted that the directive should come into force on 1 July 1995 through the EEA (*Norway Daily*, 3 April 1995, p. 3), provided that the core element of the protocol were included in a joint declaration. This line was opposed by the Centre Party, the Socialist Left, and the Christian Democrats but the Labour government obtained enough support from the right-wing parties to pass legislation (Economist Intelligence Unit, 1995a, pp. 7–8).

In the above instances, Norway's success in dealing with the EU depended on a number of factors. The first was the relative salience of the issue for Norway and EU members. The issue where Norway clearly had a much stronger economic interest than the EU membership – offshore petroleum – led to a compromise that was acceptable both to the EU and the majority political opinion within Norway. An issue of equally high salience for Norway and a number of EU states – fishing – has been one of some contention between the two sides. The Norwegians have clearly felt that their negotiating strength would be assisted by a coalition with the other non-EU North Atlantic fishing states, and that seems to have been the case. Their position has been particularly enhanced on the occasions when they can rely on the support of the Nordic members of the EU, as in the case of the Schengen agreement, but Norway has had a tougher time when it has been opposed by a Nordic neighbour. This reality was recognised by the Norwegian Minister of Trade, Grete Knudsen, in a speech to the Nordic Council (Knudsen, 1996, p. 12). Likewise the intervention of the EFTA court within the EEA structure – as in the case of the alcohol monopoly – has substantially tilted the balance against the original Norwegian position. It should be recognised that in some cases such as the alcohol monopoly and agricultural tariffs, the requirements of outside bodies such as the EEA and the World Trade Organisation have conveniently obliged the Norwegian government to introduce measures with which it might not be unhappy but would not otherwise wish to make a political priority.

13.5　The Way Ahead

After its electorate refused membership of the EU, the Labour government decided that the best approach was to establish as close a relationship to the EU as possible. This meant using the EEA machinery, but also building channels in order to influence the EU decision-making process. In particular, links to the EU capitals, the Commission and the Nordic countries were favoured, with the chosen areas for action being those of energy, fisheries and shipping, where Norway's position was particularly powerful (Knudsen, 1996, p. 14). The development of a 'Europe of concentric circles', whereby certain EU members cooperated closely on some issues but other members held back, was felt by Labour ministers to hold certain possibilities for Norway. The EEA, association with Schengen, participation in the EU's INTEREG programme for regional cooperation seemed to place Norway in an outer ring outside EU cooperation (Knudsen, 1996, p. 12). The dialogue with the EU over Common Foreign and Security Policies, established after Norway had signed the treaty of accession, continued into 1995 (see section 12.2) and extra emphasis was placed on maintaining Nordic cooperation (Godal, 1995c, p. 5). The centrist government that came to power after the 1997 election has found it difficult to deviate from this pattern, though the anti-EU Centre Party is one of its members. This is because that party lost 21 of its 32 seats in the election and the Storting as a whole now has a strong majority in favour of such a pragmatic approach.

Though Norway was on the outside of the EU, it had to concern itself with the developments within the Union. The Intergovernmental Conference (IGC), which started in 1996 and led to the 1997 Treaty of Amsterdam, was carefully monitored, not least because it could have led to a reshaping of the EU for the next century. Norwegian official commentators were reluctant to be seen to interfere in the internal politics of the EU, but did point out that the results of the IGC would have consequences for Norway. A list of general principles that Norway hoped would be followed by the EU member states at the IGC were advanced, and comments made on specific points.

The State Secretary at the Foreign Ministry, Siri Bjerke, set out the government's preferences in September 1995. Broadly, the Norwegian government wanted strong and effective EU cooperation to meet the challenges of peace and security, employment and the environment, welfare and international criminality, and preference was expressed for a democratic, open Europe with a well-developed concept of subsidiarity rather than a centralised super-state exercising powers in an increasing number of areas (Bjerke, 1995, pp. 32–3). Heading the specific points where Norway wished for effective IGC agreement was employment. Norway had pressed the need for European action against unemployment through EU-EFTA meetings and gave active support to the Nordic initiative within the EU to have the Maastricht Treaty's concern for balanced budgets and economic stability matched by a concern with unemployment (Bjerke, 1996c, pp. 17–18). This line has found resonance in countries such as France and the United Kingdom, with their socialist and Labour governments.

Another important issue for Norway has been that of the environment. Here, it was felt that the IGC should require concern for the environment should be rooted in particular areas as agriculture, transport and manufacturing; and binding minimum requirements for the environment in the member states should be taken to a greater extent by qualified majority in the EU Council (Bjerke, 1996c, p. 19).

Other areas where Norway expressed an interest were those of cooperation in justice and home affairs, open government within the EU and the development of the Common Foreign and Security Policy. In each of these Norway was seen to have a locus standi because of its involvement in the EEA, Schengen or the WEU and NATO (Bjerke, 1996c, pp. 21–8).

Norwegian desires to see the IGC tackle certain issues in a particular way meant an acceptance that they would affect Norway but that Norway had no direct input into the Conference. For most part, the country relied on a commonality of interest with the Nordic EU members who had limited influence on the outcome of the discussions. There was in official Norwegian comment on the IGC a fairly sturdy recognition of the political realities of the Conference and thus a low level of expectation. In the end, the minimalist outcome in the form of the Treaty of Amsterdam presented few new problems for Norway, except the political fall-out created by the need to re-negotiate the Schengen agreement.

The Norwegian list reflects not just its concern as an EU non-member, but perhaps gives some indication as to how the EU should develop to become attractive to Norway. This begs the question as to whether Norway will apply again for EU membership, a topic that will now be examined.

13.6   European Options

Norway's long-term relationship with the EU has not been irrevocably determined by the November 1994 referendum. Membership was not on the Labour government's subsequent agenda (Godal, 1995c, p. 4), and the EU has to see the Treaty of Amsterdam ratified before considering the Central and East European Countries (CEECs) and

Cyprus as members. Given the complexity of the issues at stake, negotiations and ratifications for the next round of enlargement are unlikely to be completed before 2000. Not only will that produce new conditions for Norway's relationship with the EU, it will also be in the lifetime of the new *Storting* elected in 1997. Will this open up the opportunity for a further Norwegian attempt to join the EU? What are Norway's options in its relations with the EU for the period at the beginning of the next century?

The first option is for Norway *to stay as it is*, keeping its relationship with the EU on the present basis, suitably adjusted.

There are a number of advantages for this status quo. First, it should lead to the least domestic repercussions. This has its attractions for a number of Norwegian political parties, not least the Labour Party, which has now experienced two defeats for its European policy in referendums. Should the party be back in power, then risking a third could be seen as folly rather than boldness. However, as time goes by, the party may feel the opportunity for another try is auspicious and may feel that the 1994 defeat did it little harm. Furthermore, continuing the present EEA-based relationship with the EU may bring its own costs, as outlined in section 13.4 above.

A second advantage is that – despite any interim problems – the EEA agreement does seem to provide access to the EU's single market without Norway incurring many of the costs associated with membership. Though Norway has denied the wish to 'cherry-pick' by only taking the benefits without paying the costs (Knudsen, 1996, p. 14), the arrangement is one that excludes agriculture and fisheries (though not totally) and the difficulties associated with the Common Agricultural Policy (CAP) and Common Fisheries Policy (CFP).

Finally, the present arrangement suits Norway's economic profile (Ingebritsen & Larson, 1997, pp. 212–3). Norway's economy has thrived to a great extent because of its offshore oil and gas, which provided 16.8% of the country's gross domestic product in 1994 (Economist Intelligence Unit, 1995c, p. 20). In 1996 Norway was non-Russian Europe's largest oil producer and the world's fifth largest oil exporter. Though much of this oil and gas is exported to the EU, the fate of that industry is not decided in Brussels but on the world market and – as prices are marked in US dollars – in Washington DC. Norwegian shipping amounted to about 10% of the world tonnage in 1994 (Economist Intelligence Unit, 1995c, p. 26). Again the economic health of this sector depends on world markets, particularly on the demand for oil. Almost two-thirds of Norway's fish exports, which accounted for 7.7% of merchandise exports in 1994, go to the EU (Economist Intelligence Unit, 1995c, pp. 16–17), but Norway has the largest fisheries zone in Europe and many of the stocks outside the North Sea area are shared with non-EU countries. For these three industries that make up over half of the value of Norway's exports, the EEA agreement allows Norway national control (as in the case of fish stocks and the exploration policy for petroleum) and in two cases the market is more dependent on global factors than on EU decisions.

The disadvantages of maintaining Norway's present position partly lie in it not being tenable. The EU could itself start to change the balance of advantages by extending a number of policies to Norway through the EEA. Should these increasingly involve agriculture, shipping, energy and fishing, Norway could then be in the position of having to accept invidious decisions over which it had no say. This would be what was predicted of EU non-membership by those who wanted to go in; it is also what the opponents of the EEA said the Agreement would bring.

Secondly, Norway could find its ability to influence EU policy from outside even more circumscribed, should Central and East European states become members. They could demand a large slice of EU resources and time.

Thirdly, developments in the security field of the EU – the CFSP (see section 11.2) could lead to a reconsideration of the status quo, should Norway feel it was becoming marginalised.

A number of these factors are ones that the Norwegian government itself can affect. The centrality of Norwegian interests to EU consideration of particular policy will to some extent depend on the success of Norwegian diplomacy in using its various 'channels' to the EU. However, most will be outside Norway's control.

What of the option of *joining the EU?* The question here is best formulated as 'under what conditions can one expect Norway to join the EU?' The broad answer is that membership is more likely when the EU enterprise is seen to be more successful and attractive than the Norwegian state. There are two major problems with such an answer: as has been made clear above, the choice is not *either* Norway *or* the EU, as EEA membership provides a sort of half-way house. Secondly, how can success be measured? Is it by rates of unemployment, by economic growth or by other more ecological indicators? In truth, success – as well as attractiveness – is more likely to be subjective, though feelings about the EU and Norway may be based on empirical evidence such as economic statistics. What factors may change the balance of preference among the Norwegian voters? It has been the claim of this book that there is an enduring strength in the Norwegian wish to be apart from the integration process of continental Europe. However, as pointed out, that process had changed by 1994 so that it could include not only the United Kingdom but also three Nordic states. This was still not enough to convince a majority of the voting Norwegian public, though the result did prove closer than in 1972. What could change within the EU and Norway to shift the balance in favour of membership?

Within the EU, the organisation would have to become more Norwegian-friendly. The official Norwegian evaluation of the IGC (see above) gives some indication as to how this might be achieved. The EU could become less bureaucratic and more democratic, it could practise subsidiarity more overtly; it could reform the CAP and CFP to allow for more national variations; it could become more outward looking by admitting East and Central European candidates; and it could take a cautious approach to economic and monetary union. Broadly the EU could continue its move towards becoming a Union of concentric circles, a or a variable-geometry Europe, rather than a more centralised entity.

All these changes are possible and some are even likely, but it is doubtful whether all could be achieved or whether a number of weighty EU members might wish to make such changes.

For Norway to be less attractive outside EU membership, its present economic and political position would have to be weakened. Oil and gas prices would have to dip for a sustained period, with the Norwegian exchequer being emptied of its reserves. Cuts would have to be made in the welfare state with unemployment rising as a result. A further weakening of Norway's rural base with a decrease in the effective subsidising of agriculture would bite into some of the most activist anti-EU areas. Extended problems with Norway's non-EU neighbours over fishing, together with threats of being excluded from the EU's fish-products' market, could persuade some fishing communities that they could be better off within the CFP. A worsening of Norway's security position, with the

United States being less supportive than before, could help Norway to look to an EU that was developing its defence aspects.

Again, all of the above – and other changes that could adversely affect Norway – are possible, though all are unlikely to happen together and suddenly. It should also be noted that to encourage a successful application, Norway's position should be perceived as being in decline at the same time as the EU becomes more Norwegian-friendly. An application would be unlikely should the EU become more centralised and more strident and yet Norway's economic position improve. A move towards the EU is also unlikely from a Norway in economic and political trouble, should the EU also be seen to be in crisis. Should both entities be perceived as flourishing, a move to membership may not succeed if it is thought that Norway was doing better (however measured) than, say, its Nordic neighbours within the EU. Should the whole EU enterprise collapse, the question of membership will be removed for good, but Norwegian concerns will be about what takes the place of the Union. Something resembling the EEA would be acceptable, especially if ad hoc coalitions of states dealt with other issues such as security and border questions.

13.7 Conclusions

The Norwegian government has managed the immediate consequences of non-membership of the EU remarkably well, especially for a small country with limited diplomatic resources. It has emphasised its wish to be as close to the EU as a non-member can and has used multilateral agreements, such as those on the EEA, Schengen and the WEU, together with bilateral links, to that end. It has been helped by a relative political consensus at home and by the economic prosperity brought by the rapid exploitation of its oil resources. Should these peak at the start of the next century or should their value fall, life outside the EU may not seem so attractive. But that evaluation will depend on the perception of life within the EU, and here the progress of Sweden and Finland could provide indicators for the Norwegian electorate.

The retrospective view of the referendum campaign shows that the contest was conducted without inflicting the sort of wound on the Norwegian body-politic as in 1972. It seems that the Norwegian electorate approved of the referendum as a way of taking the EU-membership decision, and it seems unlikely that a similar future choice could be made without resort to a popular vote (Jenssen, 1996, pp. 194–202). Should Norway decide to try again, it is more likely that any government will *first* ask the electorate for its approval for such a move. A settlement could then be agreed which would be placed before the *Storting* after an election and membership would have to be agreed by a two-thirds majority of the *Storting*, according to paragraph 112 of the constitution. This would allow the electorate an indirect veto should they not be satisfied with the negotiated settlement. Otherwise, under paragraph 93 of the Norwegian Constitution, the agreement could be accepted by a three-quarters majority in the *Storting* after an advisory referendum. Either way, the Norwegian people will expect to have their say and will expect to be heard.

14

Conclusions

14.1 Introduction

This book has sought to examine Norway's involvement in European integration and Atlantic security. In particular, it has brought together the two policy areas in order to understand the way Norway has balanced its international commitments with its desire to remain itself and distance itself from some international activities. This chapter will summarise the main findings of the previous chapters and will then examine the elements that have shaped Norwegian European and Atlantic policy. Particular attention will be paid to the role of domestic factors in shaping key policies. Finally, the question will be asked whether Norway displays the characteristics of a typical small state.

14.2 Summary of Findings

Chapter 1, in introducing the plan of this book, listed a number of questions for each of the chapters. The responses to these queries will now be summarised before more general problems are addressed. The specific issues should help in providing answers to some of the wider puzzles associated with Norway, European integration and Atlantic security and with the ability of small states to act within the international system.

Chapter 2 set out the economic integration options open to Norway in the 15 years after the War. Of these four – Nordic, wider West European, continental West European and 'Outer Seven' – only the Nordic was one that Norway had played a major part in placing on the international agenda. To that extent, Norway had its 'menu for choice' set for it. In making that choice, two main considerations were important.

The first was the position of the United Kingdom, the country to which Norwegian politicians instinctively turned for leadership on such matters. After all, Britain was a maritime nation with wide trading interests, like Norway, and it was Norway's major trade partner and defence ally. The Second World War, when the Norwegian government was in exile in London, had confirmed Britain's position. British scepticism towards continental plans for closer European unity were easily shared by Norwegians who had their own dislike of 'union', with its resonance of the 1814 to 1905 link with Sweden. The British alternative of a wider trade arrangement, especially if it did not cover agriculture but could include a deal on fish, was welcome to Norway, and once that failed, the British alternative of EFTA was acceptable. The Nordic option was one that could be pursued, though not at the expense of losing wider free trade. Indeed, the creation of EFTA seemed to make the Nordic alternative redundant. Norway's promotion of Nordic trade arrangements anyhow suffered as negotiations progressed and the issue became more concrete.

It seems that the major reason for this reticence was the second main consideration, the position of Norway's own industry and commerce. This played an intrusive role in the Scandinavian customs union negotiations and also – in league with their Swedish and Danish colleagues – the Norwegian Federation of Industry actively promoted EFTA. On these matters, the hegemony of the Labour Party in Norway does not explain decisions taken – the government was prepared to listen to important groups in society that could otherwise be seen as their political opponents.

In the first round of applications and in their aftermath, from 1961 to 1977, a somewhat slothful Norway again followed the lead of the United Kingdom and, in this case, Denmark (Chapter 3). However, the decision to open negotiations with the EEC brought a reaction at home, not least because of the need for constitutional changes. Unlike EFTA, the EEC touched both on Norwegian sovereignty and agricultural (and, later, fishing) interests. As long as the issue was settled from outside of Norway – by de Gaulle's veto – it never had its full impact in Norway, but once it was clear that membership could be a reality, Norwegian society became mobilised. Norwegians quickly perceived the intrusive nature of the EEC, even at that stage. Brox's analysis of the 1972 referendum argued that the main explanation for the result was the Norwegians' fear that EC membership would threaten their way of life and the material conditions for their economic and social development (Brox, 1972, p. 772). According to Brox, the Yes-voters identified with the different industry branches while No voters identified with workers' class interests or with the countryside's cultural maintenance. Thus the primary producers and the rural areas voted strongly against membership (Brox, 1972, p. 782). In 1972 Norway was still a 'small town' country with strong relations and other ties between industrial workers and the self-employed, such as farmers and fishermen, thereby creating solidarity across sectors. An important question in Norway was 'what kind of society do we want?' and the answer was a preference for the status quo rather than opting for the unknown and, often, feared. This helped to undo any calculation the government may have had about the international position of Norway or the need to follow the United Kingdom.

The disappearance of the EC issue from the Norwegian political agenda (Chapter 4) can be mainly explained in terms of a reaction to the 1972 result and its aftermath. After 1972 a 'negative consensus' emerged not to raise the issue and this lasted for over fifteen years (Simonsen, 1989, p. 122). Neither the political parties nor the electorate wished a reprise. Nor was there the pressure from outside to re-consider membership. The EC had enough on its hands during the 1970s with adapting to the United Kingdom as a member. Though Greece, Spain and Portugal negotiated membership in the early 1980s, there was no consideration given to a more general expansion. Furthermore, the free trade agreement negotiated with the EC in 1973 dealt with the main cost of staying out by re-establishing free trade with the United Kingdom and Denmark and extending it to cover the EC as a whole. While this programme was being implemented, there was little to persuade Norwegian ministers that membership should be considered and there were domestic political incentives not to do so. During this period Norway was becoming an oil power and benefited from the increase in petroleum prices in 1973–4 and in 1979. The expansion offshore added to the Norwegian economy another industry based on a raw material. It was not one over which the Norwegians wished to cede control to the EC.

Why then did Norway start to reconsider its relations with the EC, starting in the mid-1980s? The impetus came from outside. With the implementation of the free trade agreement and the proposal for a Single European Market, there was the danger that

Norway could be sidelined from a major development in the European economy. The boom of the earlier years of the 1980s (the Yuppie time) foundered on the dramatic fall in oil prices in 1986 and the subsequent world stock market collapse. It had, however, opened up the Norwegian economy to international competition as never before. The development of European Political Cooperation by EC members had its attractions for Norway at a time when the United States was a difficult political partner. When, in January 1989, the President of the EC Commission suggested a new relationship between the EC and EFTA, there seemed little for Norway to lose. However, as negotiations for the European Economic Area advanced, scepticism grew among the political groups that had opposed EC membership that the EEA could be an extension of the EC but without the possibility of exercising control. This time the 'modernist' coalition of labour and industry – of the Norwegian Labour Party and the Conservatives – were able to persuade enough sceptics that the EEA could even be seen as an alternative to EC membership.

As shown in Chapter 4, the EEA debate became a trial run for the later membership embroilment. It was also a springboard for membership for some of the EFTA states. Austria led the pack by declaring its intention in 1989. The EC's agenda of not only creating a Single European Market but also Economic and Monetary Union, a coordinated foreign policy and, possibly, a defence function seemed to make the EC a centre of attraction to the newly-liberated Central and East European states. But the lead-up to the Maastricht Treaty with its expanded agenda for Community activity must have warned Norwegian politicians that the EC may have been about to change its name, but it was not about to change its spots. It was to become – even more so – the entity that the Norwegian people had rejected in 1972. Furthermore, the EEA debate in Norway only seemed to have benefited politically the anti-EC Centre Party.

Why then did the Labour government decide by April 1992 to submit an application for EC-EU membership, especially when they must have known that a sizeable section of their activists would be against such a move? It seems clear that the Swedish government's announcement of its intention to seek membership in summer 1991 brought forward Mrs Brundtland's plans. But why was membership on the Norwegian agenda at all? There are three possible sets of answers.

The first was that the Labour leadership believed there was no alternative. With Sweden and Finland joining Austria in making applications for full membership and Switzerland a possible candidate, it was likely that both EFTA and the EEA would fall into disuse. With Denmark inside and Sweden and Finland likely to follow, a Nordic alternative was ruled out, with the best way to promote Nordic cooperation being through EC/EU membership. Should the EU go to full Economic and Monetary Union and adopt a Common Foreign and Security Policy, then it was best for Norway to have some say in these as they would both affect the country substantially (Udgaard, 1995). This is a view of Norway as the reluctant European, having its menu written for it not only by the Maastricht meeting but by its EFTA colleagues.

The second explanation is that the leaders of the Labour Party supported the European project as represented in Maastricht and considered that Norway should be part of it. Certainly the Labour cabinet in 1992 was generally in favour of EC membership, with a leading opponent, Tove Strand Gerhardsen, being sacked as Minister of Labour and Public Administration in September 1992 for her outspoken views. However, formerly Euro-sceptic ministers – Jan Henry T. Olsen and Grete Knudsen – were appointed to key positions in the same reshuffle. It does seem from later statements by Mrs Brundtland and her trade minister, Bjørn Tore Godal, that they did have a vision of a wider EU that would be central to peace and prosperity in Europe. It seems out of character that Mrs Brundtland would embark on a European crusade knowing that she would be defeated by the electorate or that it would be to the detriment of her party. If true, this explanation of the application would be rooted in the leadership of the Labour Party rather than external factors. It would suggest that the Swedish move merely affected Norwegian timing. Clearly the membership option was open (Austria had already applied); the Labour leadership had decided to apply but was biding its time.

A third possibility was that the Labour leadership thought that the electorate was ready for membership. There are indications in the opinion polls that the Norwegian public was becoming more attracted by EC membership during the period from 1989 to 1991, and that when the Prime Minister made her statement in April 1992 there was a rising 'Yes' vote, an increasing number of 'don't knows' leaning towards the membership side and little between the two sides (Aardal & Jenssen, 1995, pp. 32–3).

The three explanations above are not all exclusive. The first two dispute whether the Labour leadership was pushed into an application because it saw little alternative or whether it wanted to jump at the new opportunity but wished to announce its intentions when it felt the electorate would be most receptive.

What happened after Mrs Brundtland had announced her intentions in April 1992? Unfortunately for her, external events took charge. The Danish 'No' to Maastricht in June 1992 was followed by a series of negative developments for the EC/EU. The Danish referendum proved to be a turning point for the Norwegian No side, one of which they took full advantage in the 1993 election (Aardal & Jenssen, 1995, pp. 32–3; see also Jenssen, Listhaug & Pettersen, 1995, p. 154).

The issues stressed by Norway during the membership negotiations (Chapter 5) were those that were the most important for particular key groups in Norway, the farmers, the fishermen, the regions and the oil industry. On the whole the deal agreed – with the exception of some aspects of the fisheries section – was the best on offer, but this was to have little positive effect on the chances of membership being accepted. A poor result with one or more ministers resigning would have had a negative outcome for the government, but, as it was, the farming and most of the fisheries organizations rejected the settlement.

The issues raised in the campaign (Chapter 6) were anyhow not those that took up so much negotiating time, but were more general. The most important reasons for membership were feelings about cooperation, membership and influence as well the security question, and, against joining, independence, increasing popular control and local democracy (Ringdal, 1995, p. 51). As in 1972, the No campaign started earlier than that of the Yes side and had more grass-roots support. The effect of the Finnish and Swedish referenda in drawing voters to the Yes side was weaker than expected (Bjørklund, 1996, p. 22), though once the government started campaigning in earnest, the difference between the two sides narrowed. The overall result of the campaign was to draw 'don't knows' to the Yes camp (Aardal & Jenssen, 1995, p. 35). Three main factors stacked the chances against a Yes vote, even before the post-negotiations campaign. The first were the cultural, economic and political divisions in Norway that left a sizeable part of the electorate well disposed to the anti-membership arguments. Though much had changed in the composition of the electorate since 1972, factors that could have helped the Yes side were more than balanced by changes that favoured the other camp. Opinion polls have shown that since the 1972 referendum, the Yes side scarcely ever managed to gain the support of more than a third of respondents, whereas the support for the No side was never lower than 40% and was even in the high 60s (Aardal & Jenssen, 1995, p. 33). Secondly, the collapse of the European Dream from 1992 to 1994 brought a scepticism about the EU throughout Western Europe, but it should be noted that, unlike in many other countries, this effect built on a solid base of existing hostility in Norway. Thirdly, the No campaign mobilised this scepticism in a four-year period before the Yes side could organise a response. In particular, the 1993 election campaign gave the No parties an opportunity – which they did not miss – to place their arguments before the voters more or less unchallenged. In retrospect, the most remarkable aspect of the result was that the Yes side came so close to victory.

The aftermath of the referendum was very different from that in 1972 (Chapter 13). The government seemed prepared for defeat and had not threatened to resign. Instead, the Labour Party seemed to benefit somewhat by its 'business as usual' approach. The necessary adjustments were made to the EEA agreement and ministers took a series of steps to come as close to the EU as non-membership allowed. A few important points were chosen on which Norway wished to relay its views to the EU as they began their Intergovernmental Conference in 1996. However, Norway was not a member and had to suffer some of the costs of remaining outside. These were kept down, especially where Norway had allies within the EU on an issue.

The search for security has been a constant issue in Norwegian politics since the Second World War. A second major theme of this book is the way that this theme has affected Norway's relations with the outside world, in particular with the Atlantic powers – the United Kingdom and the United States – with continental Western Europe and the other Nordic states.

Security and European integration are intimately linked. A number of West European states have undertaken close defence and security cooperation most prominently through NATO, but also through the WEU and the EU. It is often the unspoken tale of European integration. The Community process itself has, from the start, concerned itself with the security of its members. The Schuman Plan was aimed at banishing war between France and Germany, and the European Defence Community was meant to create a West European army. Though it failed, the idea did not disappear and has been revived within the WEU and the Common Foreign and Security Policy of the EU.

From a Norwegian perspective, this link between security and integration has not been an easy one to accept (Østerud, 1994). Norway's preferences in security policy did not, before the 1990s, give room to continental European plans.

In 1948–9, Norway faced a choice in security policy (Chapter 7). It could try to maintain its unaligned status, it could enter a Scandinavian defence union, or it could join the Western bloc. After a brief flirtation with its Nordic neighbours, it chose the West. This was not just because of allied persistence – there was by no means full enthusiasm in the ministries of the founding nations of the North Atlantic Treaty for Norwegian membership of the Atlantic Alliance – though the United States and the United Kingdom were content to have Norway by their side. Nor was it an emergency response to a direct Soviet threat. If that had been the case, Norway would not have sat down with Denmark and Sweden for nine months to discuss a Scandinavian defence union. Those discussions showed up the shortcomings of such an option not just to the Norwegian government but to activists in the Labour Party and the general public. Yet these negotiations shifted the basis for Norwegian security to one where a formal security agreement was the expected outcome. By 1949, the question had been moved from one of 'alliance or non-alliance' to one of 'alliance with whom?' It then became easier for those within the Labour Party who sought a Western link to gain acceptance for that option.

The then foreign minister's four reasons for not allowing allied bases on Norwegian soil reflected a mixture of external and domestic considerations. There was a concern for Finland, a desire not to provoke the Soviet Union, a wish not to alienate those in Norway who preferred neutrality, and the feared effect of bases on small communities (Lange, 1966, pp. 44–5). Added to this could be that the bases were not needed because Norway was unlikely to be attacked (Ørvik, 1986, p. 195) and that the allies had not asked for such bases (Riste, 1985b, p. 145). For whatever reason it was instituted, the base policy represented the start of a series of policies aimed at shielding Norway from the full intensity of alliance commitment.

During the Cold War period the dual policy of commitment and shielding was continued within NATO (Chapter 8). Norway became gradually more integrated into NATO, especially through its agreements with the United States and, to a lesser extent, the United Kingdom. Many of the approaches came from these two countries but, as with the base policy, securing the Northern Flank in NATO's early days was partly a Norwegian initiative. The existence of a Norwegian security policy consensus was the general rule from the end of the Second World War to the late seventies, and it was viewed as a vital contribution to the success of Norwegian security policy. However, it concealed disagreements and there were heated debates when policy choices were made. What emerged was the dual track policy of maintaining Western unity and encouraging negotiations with the USSR (Tamnes, 1991, p. 169). This was reflected in Norway's own receptive policy towards NATO that was matched by screening of some NATO activities involving itself. It also reflected disagreements within the ruling Labour Party, especially on the nuclear aspect of NATO. In retrospect, the policy that emerged seems a precursor not only to NATO's Harmel Report but also to the later methods adopted in the West's response to the post-Cold War Soviet Union.

During the period from 1963 to 1989, Norway – like other Alliance members – had to face major shifts in its security (Chapter 9). Broadly, Norway had to adjust to the requirements of the United States, but that was not the end of the story. The development continued of the Norwegian dual approach to security, in terms of commitment and screening. Both elements became intense during the period of the New Cold War as the United States became more active in Northern Waters (in response, partly, to the Soviet build-up there) and domestic opinion became more engaged in defence and security matters.

During the earlier period of NATO membership, Norway gave little consideration to plans for greater West European involvement in defence which were seen as possibly weakening Norway's Atlantic link (Tamnes, 1991, p. 168). In the period covered by Chapter 10, such ideas were more common. A greater involvement by West Germany in the Northern region was accepted, though this had originally been delayed because of fears of domestic opposition. In the general security policy field, Norway, realising that the US commitment to Europe was finite, associated itself with the foreign policy aspects of European Political Cooperation developed by the EC members. There was the concern that in any security arrangement Norway might be marginalised.

The major changes that took place in Central and Eastern Europe in late 1989 brought a new security menu for states such as Norway (Chapter 10). However, because of the implementation of certain arms control measures, Norway felt that some of the old threats were taking their time to subside in Northern Europe and – with the collapse of the Soviet Union, with which Norway had a frontier – new ones had arrived. The policy response by government spokesmen went beyond stressing the Atlantic Alliance to a more overt linkage of security with the question of EC/EU membership. The security aspects of the EC/EU were pressed by pro-membership campaigners during the referendum campaign (Chapter 11). However, the link between the EU and security was not seen by enough voters as a strong enough reason to accept EU membership. The electorate effectively removed one option – direct participation in the EU – from the Labour government's range of security policy options.

Part III takes up Norway's position after the referendum. On the security side (Chapter 12), the government seemed to have adapted fairly easily to the removal of a main policy plank. On the political and commercial policy side (Chapter 13), adaptation has also taken place, at a modest price. Norway's strong economy and political stability has allowed it to weather the referendum result. Both chapters examine the conditions under which Norway may join the EU and conclude that not only will the international situation have to be favourable, but Norwegian opinion will have to accept that membership can maintain peace and prosperity for Norway better than the country staying outside the EU.

14.3   General Conclusions

The Introduction set out a framework for understanding Norway, European integration and Atlantic security by using the concepts of opportunity and willingness (section 1.2). The intention was to examine the constraints at the international and domestic levels faced by Norwegian decision-makers (opportunity) and the perceptions and choices (willingness).

This study has demonstrated the importance to Norway of the international environment in providing its 'menu for choice' (Russett & Starr, 1992). A number of examples can be seen of this: the option of EU membership from 1989 to 1992 arose primarily because of the plans to strengthen the EC and create a European Union. Ironically, soon after Norway had made its choice – in 1992 – the international environment changed to make that choice less attractive (section 4.9). The security context in which Norway was placed from 1949 to 1989 changed several times as NATO strategy shifted from massive retaliation to flexible response to what appeared to be a more forward strategy in the 1980s. Since 1989 the end of the Cold War and the main Western adversary has altered the strategic context for Norwegian security policy (Chapter 10).

Opportunity also involves the ability of a state to be capable of certain actions. As pointed out in Chapter 1 (section 1.2), Norway's capability has grown considerably in the post-War period. The period between 1945 and 1961 saw a considerable social change and economic growth in both Norway and Europe generally. The difference between Norway at the end of the war and in 1961 was striking. The Second World War had seriously damaged the Norwegian economy, not least by denying it open access to foreign trade. By the 1960s Norway was again a trading nation, exporting wood and paper products, fish and ships. The following two decades saw another change, with Norway's main exports being ships by the mid-1970s and petroleum by the mid-1980s. The creation of Norway's oil and gas sector provided it with resources undreamt of by most states of its population size (Mjøset, 1989).

An important element in making a choice from options is that of perception by the decision-makers. As will be seen below, the locus of decision-making is important, as is the outlook of those in office. At this point, it is just worth pointing out that most Norwegian decision-makers saw themselves as being part of a Nordic-North Atlantic culture and, for a sizeable part of the post-War period, this affected their view of events in continental Europe. Arne Skaug, Norway's representative to the OEEC, wrote in 1950 that continental European politicians

> are by and large opposed to income equalisation and frequently opposed to public investments and control of investments... They are not really concerned with adhering to agreements about maintaining full employment. The Anglo-Scandinavian system is largely the opposite of the continental European. (cited in Pharo, 1993, p. 204)

Norwegian civil servants and politicians may have had a different view of the 'Continentals' (by then joined, somewhat reluctantly, by the British) by 1990, but the Social Democrats against the EU perhaps reflected a wider perception when, in 1994, they claimed that, in the EU, 'it is clear that the public sector income will be reduced, there will be a switch from public to private employment, and there will be a worse public welfare service.' (Gerhardsen et al., 1994, p. 15)

On a number of key issues, domestic Norwegian concerns have been critical in deciding Norwegian policy. The most obvious cases have been those of the 1972 and 1994 referenda, decisions that can be seen as the 'outcome of complex, underlying lines of domestic conflict' (Knudsen, 1990, p. 101). However, the original policy not to allow foreign bases on Norwegian territory (section 7.4) was to an important extent a response to domestic concerns, as were a number of the later Norwegian reservations about defence activities. Does this mean that Norway has had a domestically-driven foreign – and security – policy?

The answer is that Norway's European and Atlantic policies cannot be seen in terms of being driven or decided either at home or by outside powers. The concepts of opportunity and willingness allows for both influences and seek to examine the extent to which domestic concerns, say, may have affected the choice made from the options seen to be available.

An example of the importance of internal factors in Norwegian European and Atlantic policies can be seen in the dominant role taken in these decisions by the Labour Party from 1945 to 1961. As mentioned in Chapter 1 (section 1.2), there are weaknesses in interpreting foreign policy decisions during this period in terms purely of the hegemony of the Labour Party. The Scandinavian customs union talks saw the Labour government giving weight to the views of business groups. The decision to join the Atlantic Alliance was perhaps taken within the Labour Party's apparatus, though the cross-party consensus certainly eased the situation. Later defence-related decisions, such as that on nuclear weapons in 1957, reflected a range of concerns. The 1957 outcome can be seen as a result of a deliberate attempt by the prime minister, Einar Gerhardsen, to appease neutralist factions within the Labour Party and a move to 'semialignment' (Ørvik, 1986, p. 206). More properly, though the internal politics of the Labour Party had some influence, the policy was in line with a balanced view of NATO – less dependence on nuclear weapons, not more; matching deterrence and defence with détente – that was also the line of the Atlanticist foreign minister, Halvard Lange The latter part became the theme of NATO's Harmel formula (Tamnes, 1991, p. 169).

It can be claimed that the role of interest groups and the bureaucracy was one that grew in Norwegian foreign policy in the 1970s (Chapter 1, section 1.2). It was certainly the case that interest groups had a strong input to the Scandinavian customs union negotiations (section 2.2) and to the establishment of EFTA (section 2.3).There was also direct contact between economic interest groups and the ministries during the negotiations for EC membership in 1971 and in 1993–4. However, their influence tended to be in the realm of detail. The 'modernist' coalition of manufacturing industry, commerce and union leaders did not get its way. There were some organizations – such as the fishing and farming lobbies – that were opposed to the whole process, and in the end it was the *Storting* and the people that decided the policy outcome.

In all these decisions, however made, it should be remembered that they were taken within the framework set for them by international factors and the level of Norwegian resources available for policy implementation. Norway has been dependent on foreign trade and during the Cold War was a 'front line' state with a border with the Soviet Union.

However, the relevance of these factors has changed and they have to be perceived by decision-makers and the wider public.

A key area where perception has been vital is that of the EC. By the early 1970s decision-makers in the Labour Party, supported especially by the Conservatives, had come to view the Communities in more positive terms than those used by Skaug in 1950 (see above). However, Norwegian opinion was affected by other factors. The economic, cultural and political divisions in the country saw a sizeable part of the electorate accepting the view that the EC would adversely affect its style of life. By 1994, though some of the cleavages had changed, there was still a strong enough counter-culture (or cultures) that reckoned that the kind of society desired by its members was not that offered by the EC/EU, but could still be achieved within the Norwegian nation state. The anti-EC groups offered a combination of the nationalist and internationalist. They looked out to the sea and the Atlantic, rather than south to mainland Europe. If the EC supporters held up the prospect of being isolated and marginalised as a result of staying out of the EC, this had little sting for such groups who were often already distant from Oslo. However, they could compensate for their economically and socially weak position by a coalition with urban radicals who often had internationalist views, and by representation through important political parties (Knudsen, 1990, p. 114).

In summary, the balance between internal and external factors in deciding Norway's European and Atlantic policies can be described using Rosenau's four modes of adaptation (section 1.2).

Norway's European policy from 1945 to 1972 was generally acquiescent, meaning that it was mostly responsive to external factors. The United Kingdom was followed in most matters in the trade and political development of Europe, though Norwegian interests – such as fisheries – occasionally had to be protected. The exception was in the Nordic economic negotiations, where Norway made its own initiatives and seemed to have a general concept of what it wished to achieve. However, this wider view tended to dissipate when confronted by the interests of Norway's partners and the insistent demands of economic interest groups within Norway. Already in 1962 and again between 1970 and 1972, there were indications at home that the decision to seek membership of the EC was not going to be decided by the political elites and that the views of those groups would be bitterly challenged by sections of society that had previously only a limited experience with foreign affairs. A Nordic option was taken up a number of times but external events twice wiped it from the menu. Haakon Lie, the then powerful secretary of the Labour Party, considered that dropping the Scandinavian customs union option in 1958 was one of the major mistakes his party made, as the debates of 1962 and 1971–72 might have been avoided had there been a joint Scandinavian negotiation with the EC (Lie, 1975, p. 221).

The 1972 referendum was a classic example of an intransigent orientation in Norway's European policy. The calculations of the leading politicians, the business sector and the union leaders, and the negotiations of the diplomats and ministers were ripped up by a majority of voters who had decided what they wanted was not a ticket to Brussels, but Norway and the wider world. The period from 1973 until the mid-1980s saw something of a preservative orientation, with external and internal matters balanced in Norway's European policy, though, in reality, it was – to use a term not advanced by Rosenau – more a policy of quiescence. Little stimulus came from outside and common sense told most politicians – except the enthusiasts – not to raise the European issue at home.

The period from the mid-1980s until 1994 was more one of an active preservative orientation when the decision-makers tried to balance external factors against a rising domestic clamour. This again climaxed in another act of intransigence, the referendum of 28 November 1994. The Norwegian 'No' on that day demonstrated the electorate's rejection of arguments resting on the necessity of Norway to adapt to the outside world in a particular way. They either did not believe that there was a need to adapt (as with the security argument outlined in Chapter 11) or they considered that other methods would suffice (Chapter 6). Since then, Norwegian European policy has returned to its preservative stance, though increasingly it may be seen that there is a need to acquiesce in the EEA.

In the security field, there have also been distinct periods in the balance between the weight attached by decision-makers to external and internal matters.

From 1945 to 1948 Norwegian security policy was acquiescent, drifting along in the wake of liberation and the war-time experience. The key period from 1948 to 1949 was preservative, with consideration given to domestic political factors but with external elements – the Soviet's position, the Nordic aspect and the wish of the Western allies – being most important in setting the agenda and influencing decision-makers' choice. From 1950 to 1962 Norway tended to acquiesce to allied wishes in the general outline of its security policy. However, it did occasionally take initiates in drawing attention to the Alliance's northern region, and the Labour government sometimes showed intransigence, especially on nuclear matters and on the question of West Germany's position within NATO. The balance in Norway's security policy built up in this period was carried over into the 1963 to 1989 time-frame when the policy orientation was preservative, balancing internal and external demands. Generally, the latter were given preference, except on a few key issues – such as nuclear issues – when Labour Party and pressure group interests were accommodated. From 1989 onwards many of the domestic security concerns fell away and Norwegian policy had to adapt to a new external reality of a somewhat uncertain nature. Though acquiescent in general approach, Norwegian policy also took on a promotive tinge to it, responding less to particular external or domestic factors but advancing a particular liberal institutionalist 'world view'.

Perhaps Norway's European and Atlantic policies have been less 'domestically-driven' and more 'domestically-restrained'. On the whole, Norway has had to accept the short menu offered it, but occasionally the choice expected by allies and friends was overturned by domestic pressure. These may be explained by internal political battles, normally within the Labour Party, the influence of particular interest groups or by expressions of dissent on key policy issues by groups within Norwegian society. Furthermore, Norway's ability to make a choice has grown with its improved economic position, especially since it became an oil power. Particularly since the end of the Cold War, the international situation has allowed it a much wider choice of options in the security field and Norway has been willing to actively promote certain ideas about the running of international relations. Security policy was drawn into European policy even before the referendum campaign, but now, more than ever, the two overlap. While Norway maintains its Atlantic link as the keystone of its security policy, there is the recognition that, on many issues from the Baltic to former Yugoslavia, Norway has to coordinate with its Nordic neighbours and its European allies.

14.4   Norway: Small State with Big Ambitions?

How does Norway, and its actions as portrayed in European and Atlantic issues, measure up to the suppositions made about small states and identified in the literature by East (see Chapter 1)?

Does Norway exhibit a 'low level of participation in world affairs'? Compared with the United States, the answer must be 'yes'. It is difficult to decide on a measure for this variable and to interpret 'low level' in a meaningful way. Is a state considered 'small' because it shows, inter alia, this feature, or may a state, otherwise defined as small, still show a medium or high level of activity in world affairs? The latter seems more reasonable. Perhaps a common sense approach might be to examine the subjects regularly dealt with by the foreign ministry of the country involved to see whether it has a regional orientation or a wider scope. A brief survey of the Norwegian foreign ministry's press statements in early 1996 shows a heavy engagement in Middle East and former Yugoslav affairs, an involvement in United Nations conferences on human rights and social matters, agreements signed with African states and India, and concern about the peace process in Guatemala. In the Foreign Minister's address to station heads in 1995 much of his speech deals with Russia and maritime resources, but the Norwegian engagement in the Middle East is given special mention, and there is a promise to extend the Norwegian engagement in peace in Asia, Africa and Latin America (Godal, 1995, pp. 14–15). This does not seem, prima facie, to be a 'low level of participation' for a country of four million people.

Does Norway have a high level of activity in intergovernmental organizations? Again the references in foreign ministry documents seem to suggest a positive answer. Not only is there active participation in UN agencies, Norway has given continual support – in terms of money and manpower – for UN peacekeeping efforts and has taken a leadership role in a number of these. Within Europe, Norway is a member of all the main intergovernmental organizations, except the EU, and is particularly active in Baltic and Barents institutions (see section 12.3).

Does Norway give a high level of support for international legal norms? Again it is difficult to measure such support but Norway has shown enthusiasm for the World Court. It settled dispute with Denmark over East Greenland at the Permanent Court of International Justice and accepted a judgement not in its favour; and it has accepted mediation over a dispute with Iceland concerning maritime claims. Statements by foreign ministers have made special mention of the importance to small states of upholding legal norms (see Chapter 12).

Has Norway avoided the use of force as a 'technique of statecraft' (East, 1975, p. 160)? On the whole the Nordic area has been a 'zone of peace', and perhaps one of the reasons for this is that countries such as Norway have externalised some of their societal values, including that of the peaceful settlement of disputes (Archer, 1996). Since independence in 1905 (which was gained peacefully) Norway has only been at war during the Second World War, when it was invaded by Germany. Its only use of force since then has been in UN operations – for self defence purposes – and, at a low level, for fisheries protection.

Does Norway have a 'narrow functional and geographic range of concern'? As shown above, Norway's range of concern seems to be global, but an effort is made to concentrate resources in a few areas. The Foreign Minister, when addressing ministry station chiefs in 1995, picked out relations with the EU and Russia, involvement in NATO, the environment in the northern region, maritime resources and the Middle East. In its approach to the EU after the referendum, particular reference was made to three chosen areas – energy, fisheries and shipping – where Norway had special economic interests (section 13.5). In effect, Norway – like most states today – has to concentrate its foreign policy activity. What is surprising is that it is so wide and this is perhaps a result of the country's humanistic and moralistic traditions that tend to have a global reach.

Does then Norway exhibit another aspect of small states in certain situations, that of a willingness to engage in 'high risk, active and conflictual behavior' (Papadakis & Starr, 1987, p. 430)? The evidence of this book is that Norway has made every effort to avoid high risk policies, especially in the security domain. Indeed, it has gone for 'safety first'. It certainly has avoided conflictual behaviour, especially when there has been the danger of armed conflict. However, Norway has been active in world affairs. Perhaps the European Union was simply too small for such a country.

References

Aardal, Bernt, 1994, 'The 1994 *Storting* Election: Volatile Voters Opposing the European Union', *Scandinavian Political Studies*, vol. 17, no. 2.

Aardal, Bernt & Anders Todal Jenssen, 1995, 'Opinionsutviklingen 1972–1994', in Anders Todal Jenssen & Henry Valen (eds.), *Brussel midt imot. Folkeavstemningen om EU*, Oslo: Ad Notam Gyldendal, pp. 31–43.

Aardal, Bernt & Henry Valen, 1989, *Velgere, partier og politisk avstand*, Oslo: Statistisk sentralbyrå.

Aardal, Bernt & Henry Valen, 1995, *Konflikt og opinion*, Oslo: NKS-forlaget.

Aas, Even, 1995, 'Utviklingen innen handel og industri i Barentsregionen. Muligheter og visjoner', *UD Informasjon*, Oslo: Det Kgl. Utenriksdepartement.

af Malmborg, M, 1992, 'Sverige i Norden och Europa', in S. Tägil, (ed.), *Europa – historiens återkomst*, Hedemora: Gidlunds Bokförlag, pp. 455-90.

Aftenposten, 1992, 9 April.

Aftenposten, 1992, 9 November.

Aftenposten, 1993, 6 July.

Aftenposten, 1993, 18 October.

Aftenposten, 1993, 23 September, 'Baltikum vil kjøpe norske våpen'.

Aftenposten, 1994, 9 March.

Aftenposten, 1994, 16 March.

Aftenposten, 1994, 17 March.

Aftenposten, 1994, 27 March.

Aftenposten, 1994, 16 April.

Aftenposten, 1994, 20 June.

Aftenposten, 1994, 6 August.

Aftenposten, 1994, 9 August. Opinion.

Aftenposten, 1994, 23 September.

Aftenposten, 1994, 26 September.

Aftenposten, 1994, 15 October.

Aftenposten, 1994, 18 October.

Aftenposten, 1994, 24 October.

Aftenposten, 1994, 25 October.

Aftenposten, 1994, 30 November.

Aftenposten, 1995, 11 April, 'Bedrift konfiskert av russere'.

Agence Europe, 1993, no. 5946, 24 March, p. 7.

Agence Europe, 1993, no. 5947, 25 March.

Agence Europe, 1993, no. 5955, 5/6 April.

Agence Europe, 1993, no. 6006, 23 June.

Agence Europe, 1993, no. 6018, 9 July.

Agence international d'information pour la presse, 9–10 April 1994.

Allen, Hilary, 1979, *Norway and Europe in the 1970s*, Oslo: Universitetsforlaget.

Arbeiderbladet, 1994, 8 June.
Arbeiderbladet, 1994, 9 June.
Arbeiderbladet, 1994, 20 July.
Arbeiderbladet, 1994, 6 August.
Arbeiderbladet, 1994, 29 October.
Arbeiderbladet, 1994, 31 October.
Arbeiderbladet, 1994, 13 December.
Archer, Clive, 1971, 'Nordek: shadow or substance?', *Integration*, no. 2, pp. 108–16.
Archer, Clive, 1984, 'Deterrence and Reassurance in Northern Europe', *Centrepiece 6*, Aberdeen: Centre for Defence Studies, Winter.
Archer, Clive, 1989, '*Uncertain Trust: The British-Norwegian Defence Relationship*, Forsvarsstudier, no. 2, Oslo: Institutt for Forsvarsstudier.
Archer, Clive, 1994a 'Conflict Prevention in Europe. The Case of the Nordic States and Macedonia', *Cooperation and Conflict*, 29 (4), pp. 367–86.
Archer, Clive, 1994b, 'New Threat Perceptions: Danish and Norwegian Official Views', *European Security*, 3 (4), pp. 593–616.
Archer, Clive, 1994c, *Organizing Europe*, London: Edward Arnold.
Archer, Clive, 1995, 'Norway says "No" - again', *The World Today*, 51 (2), pp. 23–4.
Archer, Clive, 1996, 'The Nordic Area as a "Zone of Peace"', *Journal of Peace Research*, 33 (4), pp. 451–67.
Archer, Clive, 1997, 'Nordic Involvement in the Baltic States Security: Need, Motives and Success', *Working Papers 19*, Copenhagen: Copenhagen Peace Research Institute.
Archer, Clive & Fiona Butler 1996, *The European Union. Structure and Process*, London: Pinter, 2nd edn.
Arter, David, 1995, 'The EU Referendum in Finland on 16 October 1994: A Vote for the West not for Maastricht', *Journal of Common Market Studies*, 33 (3), pp. 361–387.
Asbeek-Brusse, W., 1991, *West European Tariff Plans 1947-1957. From Study Group to Common Market*, Ph.D. thesis, Florence: EUI.
Banks, Michael, 1985, 'The inter-paradigm debate', in Margot Light and A.J.R. Groom, *International Relations. A Handbook of Current Theory*, London: Pinter, pp. 7–26.
Barston, Ronald (ed.), 1973, *The Other Powers: Studies in the Foreign Policies of Small States*, London: Allen & Unwin.
Barth, Magne, & Nils Petter Gleditsch, 1982, 'COB-Programmet', *Internasjonal Politikk*, no. 3, pp. 463–501.
Berdal, Eivind, 1974, 'The Projection of Soviet Military Power in the North', *NATO's Fifteen Nations*, Feb-March, no. 139, Supplement.
Berdal, Mats, 1996, *The United States, Norway and the Cold War, 1954–1960*, Basingstoke: Macmillan.
Bergh, Trond, 1987a, *Arbeiderbevegelsens historie*, vol. 5, Storhetstid, Oslo: Tiden Norsk Forlag.
Bergh. Trond, 1987b, 'Norsk økonomisk politikk 1945–1965', in T. Bergh & H. Pharo, eds., *Vekst og velstand. Norsk politisk historie 1945-1965*, Oslo: Universitetsforlaget, 3rd edn, pp. 13–97.
Beukel, Erik, 1974, *Socialdemokratiet og stationeringsproblemet 1952-53. En sikkerhedspolitisk beslutning*, Odense.
Beukel, Erik, 1977, 'Norges basepolitikk – nogle overvejelser i Arbejderpartiets ledelse', *Internasjonal Politikk*, no. 3.
Bjerke, Siri, 1995 'EU's regjeringskonferense fra et norsk synspunkt', *UD Informasjon*, nr. 29, Oslo: Utenriksdepartementet.
Bjerke, Siri,1996a 'Towards cooperative security in a new Europe', *UD informasjon*, nr. 8, Oslo: Utenriksdepartementet.
Bjerke, Siri, 1996b, 'European Security - A Northern Perspective', *Paper presented to the Olof Palme International Center conference, 8 March 1996*, Stockholm, Olof Palme International Center, mimeo.
Bjerke, Siri, 1996c, 'EU-landenes regjeringskonferense. Innledning på Europabevegelsens Rådsmøte 8.juni 1996', *UD informasjon*, nr. 13, Oslo: Utenriksdepartementet.
Bjerve, Petter Jakob, 1965, *Norges økonomi etter krigen*, Oslo: Statistisk Sentralbyrå.
Bjørklund, Tor, 1981, *Mot strømmen. Kampen mot EF 1961-1972*, Oslo: Universitetsforlaget.
Bjørklund, Tor, 1994, 'En reprise fra 1972?', *Dagbladet*, 30 November.
Bjørklund, Tor, 1996, 'The Three Nordic 1994 Referenda Concerning Membership in the EU', *Cooperation and Conflict*, 31 (1), pp. 11–36.
Bjørklund, Tor & Sparre S. Nilson, 1981, 'Høyre mellom by og land. Noen regionale og historiske trekk', in Tor Bjørklund & B. Hagtvedt (eds.), *Høyrebølgen – epokeskifte i norsk politikk? Høyres velgerframgang og Arbeiderpartiets 80-årsdilemmaer i sosial, økonomisk og politisk belysning*, Oslo: Aschehoug.
Blidberg, Kersti, 1987, *Just good friends – Nordic Social Democracy and Security Policy 1945–50*, Oslo: Institutt for Forsvarsstudier, Forsvarsstudier 5.

Brofoss, Erik, 1948, Minutes from a meeting at Sømarka, 3 May 1948, Box 150.

Brofoss, Erik, 1958, Letter from the President of the Federation, N. Aars-Nicolaysen, to the Industry minister, G. Sjaastad, 20 October 1958, *Private Archives*, Box 151.

Brox, Ottar, 1972, 'Hva hendte i Norge 25. sept. 1972?', *Internasjonal Politikk*, nr. 4B – Supplement, pp. 771–82.

Brundtland, Arne Olav, 1985 'Norwegian Security Policy: Defense and Nonprovocation in a changing context', in Gregory Flynn (ed.), *NATO's Northern Allies*, Totowa: New Jersey: Rowman & Allanheld for the Atlantic Institute of International Affairs, pp. 171–223.

Brundtland, Arne Olav, 1986 'Atomvåpenfri sone i nordisk område. Observasjoner om et sikkerhetspolitisk debatt-tema i parlamentarisk sammenheng', in *Norsk Utenrikspolitisk Årbok 1985*, Oslo: NUPI, pp. 43–60.

Brundtland, Gro Harlem, 1994a, *Norge-EU. Om forhandlingsresultatet*, Pressehefte, 16 mars 1994: Oslo: Utenriksdepartementet.

Brundtland, Gro Harlem, 1994b, *Statsminister Gro Harlem Brundtland. Måløy, 15 august 1994*, Oslo: Statsministerens kontor, mimeo.

Brundtland, Gro Harlem, 1994c, 'Statsminister Gro Harlem Brundtlands redegjørelse for Stortinget om resultatet av forhandlingene med den Europeiske union om vilkårene for Norsk medlemskap 17 mars 1994', *UD Informasjon*, nr. 8, Oslo: Utenriksdepartementet.

Brundtland, Gro Harlem, 1996, 'Prime Minister Gro Harlem Brundtland. Address at the University of Vilnius. 19 March 1996', *UD informasjon*, nr. 8, Oslo: Utenriksdepartementet.

Bull-Hansen, Fredrik, 1993, 'Forsvarets fremtid - fra invasjonsforsvar til hva?', *Norsk Militært Tidsskrift*, no. 3, pp.10–19.

Bush, George, 1991,'The World after the Persian Gulf', *US Department of State Dispatch*, 11 March, pp.161–3;

Camps, Miriam, 1964, *Britain and the European Community 1955-1963*, London: Oxford University Press.

Central Bureau of Statistics, 1972, *Folkeavstemningen om EF/The advisory referendum on Norway's accession to the EC*, Oslo: Statistisk sentralbyrå.

Central Bureau of Statistics, 1977, *Stortingsvalget 1977*, Oslo: Statistisk Sentralbyrå.

Central Bureau of Statistics, 1995, Folkeavstemningen 1994 om norsk medlemskap i EU, *Norges offisielle statistikk*, C235, Oslo: Statistisk sentralbyrå.

Churchill, Robin, 1988, 'The Soviet Union and Jurisdictional Disputes in Northern Waters', in Clive Archer (ed.), *The Soviet Union and Northern Waters*, London: Routledge, pp. 44–61.

Churchill, Robin & Geir Ulfstein, 1992, *Marine Management in Disputed Areas. The Case of the Barents Sea*, London and New York: Routledge.

Claude, Inis, 1968, 'International Organization: the process and the institutions', in D. Sills (ed.), *International Encyclopedia of the Social Sciences*, vol. 8, New York: Macmillan and Free Press.

Cole, Paul, 1990, *Neutralité du Jour. The conduct of Swedish security policy since 1945*, Ph.D. thesis, University of Michigan.

Council of Ministers, 1993, 'The Challenge of Enlargement. Commission Opinion on Norway's application for Membership', *Bulletin of the European Communities. Supplement 2/93*, Brussels: European Communities' Commission.

Dagbladet, 1972, 22 September.

Dagbladet, 1989, 21 September.

Dagbladet, 1991, 4 September.

Dagbladet, 1993, 27 October.

Dagbladet, 1994, 9 June.

Dagbladet, 1994, 23 July.

Dagbladet, 1994, 31 October.

Dagbladet, 1994, 30 November.

Dagens Næringsliv, 1989, 7 October.

Dagens Næringsliv, 1993, 25 June, Interview, Janne H. Matlary

Dagens Næringsliv, 1993, 24 September.

Dagens Næringsliv, 1993, 27 September.

Dagens Næringsliv, 1993, 28 September.

Dagens Næringsliv, 1993, 19 October.

Dagens Næringsliv, 1993, 25 October.

Dagens Næringsliv, 1993, 28 October.

Dagens Næringsliv, 1994, 9 February.

Dagens Næringsliv, 1994, 21 October.

Dagens Næringsliv, 1994, 31 October.

Dagens Næringsliv, 1994, 3 December.

Dale J., 1979, *Nordøk 1968-1970. En nordisk mellomakt. Norsk bakgrunn* (thesis in history), Oslo: University of Oslo.

Dalhaug, A. B., 1989, 'Norsk forsvarspolitikk. Fremtidsperspektiv og langtidsmelding' in *Norsk Utenrikspolitisk Årbok 1988*, Oslo: NUPI, pp. 39–52.

Den norske Atlanterhavskomité, 1991, *Årsberetning for den norske Atlanterhavskomité*, Oslo: DNAK.

Deutsch, Karl, et al., 1957, *Political Community and the North Atlantic Area*, Princeton: Princeton University Press.

East, Maurice, 1975, 'Size and foreign policy behavior: a test of two models', in C.W. Kegley, Jr. et al. (eds.), *International Events and the Comparative Analysis of Foreign Policy*, Columbia, SC: University of South Carolina Press, pp. 159–78.

Economist Intelligence Unit, 1993a, *Country Report: Norway*, 1st quarter, London: Economist Intelligence Unit.

Economist Intelligence Unit, 1993b, *Country Report: Norway*, 2nd quarter, London: Economist Intelligence Unit.

Economist Intelligence Unit, 1993c, *Country Report: Norway*, 4th quarter, London: Economist Intelligence Unit.

Economist Intelligence Unit, 1994, *Country Report: Norway*, 3rd quarter, London: Economist Intelligence Unit.

Economist Intelligence Unit, 1995a, *Country Report Norway*, 2nd quarter, London: Economist Intelligence Unit.

Economist Intelligence Unit, 1995b, *Country Report Norway*, 3rd quarter, London: The Economist Intelligence Unit.

Economist Intelligence Unit, 1995c, *Country Profile Norway 1995-96*, London: Economist Intelligence Unit.

Economist Intelligence Unit, 1995d, *Country Report Norway*, 4th quarter, London: Economist Intelligence Unit

Economist Intelligence Unit, 1996a, *Country Report Norway*, 2nd quarter, London: Economist Intelligence Unit.

Economist Intelligence Unit, 1996b, *Country Report Norway*, 3rd quarter, London: Economist Intelligence Unit.

Economist Intelligence Unit, 1997, *Country Report Norway*, 3rd quarter, London: Economist Intelligence Unit.

EFTA Bulletin, 1989, Declaration from Oslo Summit, Meeting of the EFTA heads of governments in Oslo, 14–15 March

Eide, Espen Barth, 1996, 'Adjustment strategy of a non-member: Norwegian Foreign and Security Policy in the Shadow of the European Union', *Cooperation and Conflict*, 31 (1), pp. 69–104.

Eide, Vigleik, 1988, 'Forsvarets status og stilling sett i lys av Langtidsmeldingen', Lecture by Chief of Defence Vigleik Eide, 15 October, mimeo.

Ellingsen, Ellmann (ed.), 1988, *The Military Balance in Northern Europe 1987–1988*, Oslo: The Norwegian Atlantic Committee.

Ellingsen, Ellmann (ed.), 1991, *The Military Balance in Northern Europe 1990–1991*, Oslo: The Norwegian Atlantic Committee.

Ellingsen, Ellmann (ed.), 1992, *The Military Balance in Northern Europe 1991–1992*, Oslo: The Norwegian Atlantic Committee.

Ellingsen, Ellmann (ed.), 1994, *Militærbalansen 1994-1995*, Oslo: Brassey's & The Norwegian Atlantic Committee.

Ellingsen, Ellmann (ed.), 1996, *The Military Balance in Northern Europe 1995–1996*, Oslo: The Norwegian Atlantic Committee.

Ellingsen, Ellmann (ed.), 1997, *The Military Balance in Northern Europe 1996–1997*, Oslo: The Norwegian Atlantic Committee.

Eriksen, Knut Einar, 1972, *DNA og NATO*, Oslo: Gyldendal.

Eriksen, Knut Einar, 1977, 'Norge i det vestlige samarbeidet', in Trond Bergh and Helge Pharo (eds.), *Vekst og velstand. Norsk politisk historie 1945–1965*, Oslo: Universitetsforlaget, pp.167–281.

Eriksen, Knut Einar, 1987, 'Norge i det vestlige samarbeidet', in Trond Bergh & Helge Pharo (eds.), *Vekst og velstand. Norsk politisk historie 1945–1965*, Oslo: Universitetsforlaget, 3rd edn.

Eriksen, Knud Einar & Helge Pharo, 1991, 'De fire sirklene i norsk utenrikspolitikk 1949–61', in C. Due-Nielsen, J. P. Noack and N. Petersen (eds.), *Danmark, Norden og NATO 1948-1962*, Copenhagen: Jurist- og Økonomforbundets forlag, pp. 193–220.

Eriksen, Knut Einar & Helge Pharo, 1993, 'Norway and the early Cold War: Conditional Atlantic cooperation', *IFS Info*, no. 5.

Eriksen, Knut Einar & Magne Skodvin, 1981, 'Storbritannia, NATO og et skandinavisk forbund', *Internasjonal Politikk*, no. 3.

Erlander, Tage , 1992, 'Speech by the Prime Minister at the Congress of the Swedish Steel and Metalworkers' Union; 22nd August', *Documents on Swedish Foreign Policy*, Stockholm: Ministry for Foreign Affairs, pp. 120–2.

Evensen, Jens, 1983, 'Refleksjoner omkring atomvåpen og atonvåpenfrie soner i Europa', in Torstein Eckhoff and Stein Owe (eds.), *Nordisk atomvåpenfri sone*, Oslo: Aschehoug, pp. 21–52.

Financial Times, 1993, 7 July.

Financial Times, 1993, 2 September.

Financial Times, 1993, 12 October.

Folkebevegelsen mot norsk medlemskap i Fellesmarkedet, 1972, *Folkebevegelsens melding om Norges forhold til De Europeiske Fellesskap (EF) (Motmelding til Regjeringens Stortingsmelding nr. 50), 1971-72*, Oslo: Folkebevegelsen mot norsk medlemskap i Fellesmarkedet.

Førland, Tor Egil, 1988a, '1949 som "vendepunkt": Er NATO-medlemskapet bare kulisse?', *Internasjonal Politikk*, no. 6, pp. 69–85.

Førland, Tor Egil, 1988b, *"Vi sier intet" – Norge i COCOM 1948–53*, Oslo: Pax.

Forsvarsdepartementet, 1987, *Hovedretningslinjer for Forsvarets virksomhet i tiden 1989–1993*, Oslo.

Forsvarsdepartementet, 1992, *Forsvarsbudsjettet '93*, Oslo: Ministry of Defence.

Forsvarsdepartementet, 1994, *FD faktablad*, no. 3, Oslo: Presse- og informasjonsseksjonen.

Forsvarsdepartementet, 1995, 'Sikkerhetspolitiske rammebetingelser for Norsk forsvars- og sikkerhetspolitikk', *FD faktablad*, no. 03/1995, Oslo: Forsvarsdepartementet.

Forsvarskommisjonen av 1974 , 1978, (Defence Commission of 1974), Oslo: Norges Offentlige Utredninger.

Forsvarskommisjonen av 1990, 1992, (Defence Commission of 1990), Oslo: Norges Offentlige Utredninger, 12.

Frydenlund, Knut, 1966, *Norsk utenrikspolitikk i etterkrigstidens internasjonale samarbeid*, Oslo: Tidens ekko, Norsk Utenrikspolitisk Institutt.

Frydenlund, Knut, 1982, *Lille land - hva nå?*, Oslo: Universitetsforlaget.

Gerhardsen, Tove Strand, Wegard Harsvik, Finn Erik Thoresen & Steinar Strøm (eds.), 1994, *Sosialdemokratisk alternativ*, Oslo: Sosialdemokrater mot EU.

Ginsberg, R. H., 1989, *Foreign Policy Actions of the European Community*, Boulder, CO: Lynne Rienner.

Gleditsch, Nils Petter, 1972, 'Generaler og fotfolk i utakt. EF-avgjørelsen i de tre skandinaviske land', *Internasjonal Politikk*, 4B - Supplement, pp. 795–805.

Gleditsch, Nils Petter, 1978, 'Basepolitikkens begrensninger', in Nils Petter Gleditsch, Ingvar Bottnen, Sverre Lodgaard & Owen Wilkes, *Norge i atomstrategien*, Oslo: Pax.

Gleditsch, Nils Petter & Sverre Lodgaard, 1978, 'Base- og atompolitikk', *Paxleksikon*, vol. 1, Oslo: Pax.

Godal, Bjørn Tore, 1995a, 'Foreign Minister Bjorn Tøre Godal's address to the Oslo Military Society, 2 October 1995', *UD informasjon*, Oslo: Utenriksdepartementet.

Godal, Bjørn Tore, 1995b, *Foreign Minister Bjorn Tøre Godal's statement on foreign policy to the Storting, Thursday 19 January 1995*, Oslo: Ministry of Foreign Affairs.

Godal, Bjørn Tore, 1995c, 'Moment til Utenriksminister Bjørn Tøre Godals redegjørelse for stasjonssjefmøtet 22.8.95', *UD Informasjon*, Oslo: Utenriksdepartementet.

Granell, Francisco, 1995, 'The European Union's Enlargement Negotiations with Austria, Finland, Norway and Sweden', *Journal of Common Market Studies*, 33 (1), pp. 117–141.

Griffiths, Richard T. & F.B. Lynch 1984, 'The Fritalux/Finebel Negotiations 1949/50', *EUI Working Paper*, no. 84/117.

Griffiths, Richard T., 1991a, 'British attitudes towards European integration', EFTA History II, *EFTA Bulletin*, no. 2, pp. 17–22.

Griffiths, Richard T., 1991b, 'The failure of the European free trade area', EFTA History III, *EFTA Bulletin*, no. 3–4, pp. 15–20.

Griffiths, Richard T., 1992, 'The importance of fish for the creation of EFTA', EFTA History IV, *EFTA Bulletin*, no. 1, pp. 34–40.

Grønmo, S., 1975, 'Skillelinjer i partipolitikken 1969–1973: Noen virkninger av EF-striden', *Tidsskrift for samfunnsforskning*, vol. 16, no. 2, pp. 119–53.

Hanisch, Ted J. & E. Lange, 1986, *Veien til velstand. Industriens utvikling i Norge gjennom 50 år*, Oslo: Universitetsforlaget.

Hanisch, Ted J. & G. Nerheim, 1992, 'Oljen i norsk økonomi', *Norsk Olje Historie. Fra vantro til overmot*, Oslo: Leseselskapet, vol. 1, chapter 7.

Hansen, S. O., 1990, *Det norske EFTA-sporet i 1950-åra - en studie av Norges Europa-politikk, med særlig vekt på perioden 1956-1960*, (thesis in history), Oslo: University of Oslo.

Harbo, H., 1993, 'Oljedirektivet - kamp om symboler', *Aftenposten*, 18 October.

Helgesen, Jan-Petter, 1994, 'Flyforsterkninger fortsatt til Sola', *Stavanger Aftenblad*, 30 March, p. 6.

Hellevik, Ottar & Nils Petter Gleditsch, 1973, 'The Common Market Decision in Norway: A Clash between Direct and Indirect Democracy', *Scandinavian Political Studies*, no. 8.

Heradstveit, Daniel, 1975, 'The red/green alliance in Norwegian politics: a strange partnership', in Nils Ørvik (ed.), *Norway's NO to Europe*, Pittsburgh, PA: International Studies Association, Occasional Paper no. 5, pp. 7–19.

Hermansen, Hans Petter, 1980, *Fra krigstilstand til allianse. Norge, Vest-Tyskland og sikkerhetspolitikken 1947-1955*, Oslo: Universitetsforlaget.

Hernes, Gudmund, 1975, *Makt og avmakt. En begrepsanalyse. Et utgangspunkt for kartlegging av de faktiske maktforhold I det norske samfunn*, Oslo: Universitetsforlaget.

Hetland, Tom, 1985, 'Atomrasling og avspenning, Sovjet og norsk tryggingspolitikk 1953-1958', in Rolf Tamnes (ed.), *Forsvarsstudier 1985*, Oslo: Tano.

Hoel, Alf Håkon, 1994 'The Barents Sea: Fisheries Resources for Europe and Russia', in Olav Schram Stokke and Ola Tunander (eds.), *The Barents Region. Cooperation in Arctic Europe*, London: FNI/PRIO/SAGE, 1994, pp. 116–117.

Høivik, Tord, Ottar Hellevik & Nils Petter Gleditsch, 1971, 'Folkeopinion og EEC', *Samtiden*, no. 4.

Holst, Johan Jørgen, 1966, 'Norsk sikkerhetspolitikk i strategisk perspektiv', *Internasjonal Politikk*, no. 5, pp. 463–90.

Holst, Johan Jørgen, 1967a, *Norsk sikkerhetspolitikk I strategisk perspektiv. Bind I*, Oslo: NUPI.

Holst , Johan Jørgen, 1967b, *Norsk sikkerhetspolitikk I strategisk perspektiv. Bind II*, Oslo: NUPI.

Holst, Johan Jørgen, 1984, 'Europapolitikk: Forutsetninger og målsettinger', *NUPI-notat no. 297*, Oslo: NUPI, April 1984.

Holst, Johan Jørgen, 1985a, 'Ensidige bindinger i norsk sikkerhetspolitikk', in Johan Jørgen Holst & Daniel Heradstveit (eds.), *Norsk Utenrikspolitikk*, Oslo: TANO.

Holst, Johan Jørgen (ed.), 1985b, *Norwegian Foreign Policy in the 1980s*, Oslo: Norwegian University Press.

Holst, Johan Jørgen, 1985c, 'Norsk havretts-og nordpolitikk', in Johan Jørgen Holst & Daniel Heradstveit (eds.), *Norsk Utenrikspolitikk*, Oslo: TANO.

Holst, Johan Jørgen, 1989 'Norway and Strategic Developments on NATO's Northern Flank', in Jan Olsen (ed.), *The Air Situation in the North, Year 2000 and Beyond*, Oslo: The Norwegian Atlantic Committee.

Holst, Johan Jørgen, 1991a, 'The New Europe: A View from the North', *Lecture to the Fundacion Jose y Gasset, Madrid, October 29, 1991*, mimeo.

Holst, Johan Jørgen, 1991b, 'The Post-Cold War Security Landscape: Arms Control Rewritten', *Keynote address to SIPRI's 25th Anniversary Conference, Saltsjöbaden, Sweden, November 13, 1991*, mimeo.

Holst, Johan Jørgen, 1994, 'The Barents Region: Institutions, Cooperation and Prospects', in Olav Schram Stokke & Ola Tunander (eds.), *The Barents Region. Cooperation in Arctic Europe*, London: FNI/PRIO/SAGE, pp. 11–24.

Holst, Johan Jørgen & Daniel Heradstveit (eds.), 1985, *Norsk Utenrikspolitikk*, Oslo: TANO.

Huitfeldt, Tønne, 1985 'Options and Constraints in the Planning of Reinforcements: A Norwegian Perspective', in Johan Jørgen Holst, Kenneth Hunt and Anders Sjaastad, *Deterrence and Defense in the North*, Oslo: Norwegian University Press.

Huitfeldt, Tønne, 1987, 'NATO and the Northern Flank', in Rolf Tamnes (ed.), *Forsvarsstudier (Defence studies) VI*, Oslo: Tano.

Iden, Mark, 1986, 'Turning point 1975. US Policy and Northern Flank Security', *FHFS notat*, no. 1.

Ihlen, Joakim, 1957, *Næringsliv og politikk*, Oslo: Gyldendal.

Ingebritsen, Christine & Susan Larson, 1997, 'Interest and Identity: Finland, Norway and European Union', *Cooperation and Conflict*, 32 (2), pp. 207–22.

Innst. S. nr. 165, 1961–62, *Innstilling fra den utvidede utenriks- og konstitusjonskomité om Norges forhold til Det Europeiske Økonomiske Fellesskap (EEC)* (Stortingsmelding 15 og 67).

Innst. S. nr. 244, 1987–88, *Innstilling fra utenriks- og konstitusjonskomitéen om Norge, EF og europeisk samarbeid* (Stortingsmelding 61 (1986–87) og 63, kap.3.2 (1986–87)).

Innst. S. nr. 15, 1992–93, *Innstilling fra utenriks- og konstitusjonskomiteen for godkjenning av en avtale i form av en brevveksling mellom Norge og Det europeiske økonomiske fellesskap om utvikling av det bilaterale fiskerisamarbeidet* (St. prp. nr. 102 for 1991–92).

Innst. S. nr. 92, 1992–93, *Stortingets behandling av St. prp. nr. 8 1992–1993*.

International Institute for Strategic Studies, 1993, *The Military Balance 1993–1994*, London: Brassey's.

International Institute for Strategic Studies, 1994, *Strategic Survey 1994–1995*, London: Brassey's.

Jagland, Thorbjørn, 1994, *En ny hverdag – den politiske situasjonen etter folkeavstemningen*, Speech at the Labour Party's 'landsstyremøte' 11–12 December 1994, p. 8. A-INFO, 34/94.

Jensen, L. Dalgas, 1989, 'Denmark and the Marshall Plan, 1947–48: the Decision to Participate', *Scandinavian Journal of History*, vol. 14, no. 1.

Jenssen, Anders Todal, 1995a, 'Ouverturen', in Anders Todal Jenssen & Henry Valen (eds.), *Brussel midt imot. Folkeavstemningen om EU*, Oslo: Ad Notam Gyldendal, pp. 13–29.

Jenssen, Anders Todal, 1995b, 'Etterspill', in Anders Todal Jenssen & Henry Valen (eds.), *Brussel midt imot. Folkeavstemningen om EU*, Oslo: Ad Notam Gyldendal, pp.187–207.

Jenssen, Anders Todal & Ola Listhaug, 1995, 'I kampens hete: Mistillit, fiendskap og intoleranse', in Anders Todal

Jenssen & Henry Valen (eds.), *Brussel midt imot. Folkeavstemningen om EU*, Oslo: Ad Notam Gyldendal, pp.117–140.

Jenssen, Anders Todal, Ola Listhaug & Per Arnt Pettersen, 1995, 'Betydningen av gamle og nye skiller', in Anders Todal Jenssen & Henry Valen (eds.), *Brussel midt imot. Folkeavstemningen om EU*, Oslo: Ad Notam Gyldendal, pp. 143–163.

Jenssen, Anders Todal & Henry Valen (eds.), 1995, *Brussel midt imot. Folkeavstemningen om EU*, Oslo: Ad Notam Gyldendal

Joenniemi, Pertti & Ole Wæver, 1992, *Regionalization around the Baltic Rim: Notions on Baltic Sea Politics*, Stockholm: the Nordic Council.

Jølstad, A., 1995, 'Det tyske problem. Norsk sikkerhetspolitisk samarbeid med Vest-Tyskland 1955–1965', *Forsvarsstudier*, no. 5.

Kissinger, Henry, 1991, 'What kind of New World Order?', *Washington Post*, 3 December.

Knudsen, Grete, 1996, 'Norge i Europa', *UD informasjon*, nr. 10, Oslo: Utenriksdepartementet.

Knudsen, Olav, 1990, 'Norway: Domestically Driven Foreign Policy', *The Annals of the American Academy of Political and Social Science*, vol. 512, November, pp. 101–115.

Knutsen, Torbjørn, 1995, 'Norsk utenrikspolitikk som forskningsfelt', in Torbjørn Knutsen, Gunnar Sørbø & Svein Gjerdåker (eds.), *Norges utenrikspolitikk*, Oslo: Cappelen Akademisk Forlag, pp. 16–39.

Kosmo, Jørgen, 1995, 'Norges forsvar. Hvor står vi – hvor går vi', address to Oslo Militære Samfund, 9 January, mimeo.

Kosmo, Jørgen, 1996, 'Long-term challenges for Norwegian defense', Oslo, mimeo.

Kozyrev, Andrei, 1994, 'Cooperation in the Barents Euro-Arctic Region: Promising Beginning', in Olav Schram Stokke & Ola Tunander (eds.), *The Barents Region. Ccoperation in Arctic Europe*, London: FNI/PRIO/SAGE, pp. 25–30.

Lahnstein, Anne Enger, 1993, *EF og Grunnloven*, Oslo: Senterpartiets Hovedorganisasjon.

Lahnstein, Anne Enger, 1996, Stortingets debatt 8.2.1996 vedrørende Utriksministerens utenrikspolitiske redegjørelse i Stortinget 30.1.1996, *UD informasjon*, 13 februar nr. 5, Oslo: Utenriksdepartementet.

Lange, Halvard, 1966, *Norges vei til NATO*, Oslo: Pax.

Laursen, J., n.d., 'Mellem Fællesmarkedet og frihandelszonen. Dansk markedspolitik, 1956–58', unpublished paper, mimeo.

Leonardsen, D., 1984, 'Det nordiske alternativ – idé eller ideologi? En diskusjon av de nordiske økonomiske samarbeidsbestrebelser i etterkrigstida', Lillehammer: *Oppland distriktshøyskoles skriftserie*, nr. 48.

Lie, Haakon, 1975, . . . *slik jeg ser det*, Oslo: Tiden Norsk Forlag.

Lindstøl, A., 1978, *'De 13'. 'Protesten mot atomvåpen' – et utenomparlamentarisk initiativunder atomdebatten i Norge våren 1961* (thesis in history), Oslo: Oslo University.

Lodgaard, Sverre, 1982, 'Atomvåpenfri sone i Norden?', in *Norsk Utenrikspolitisk Årbok 1981*, Oslo: NUPI.

Lundestad, Geir, 1980, *America, Scandinavia and the Cold War 1945–1949*, Oslo: Universitetsforlaget.

Lundestad, Geir, 1992, 'The Evolution of the Norwegian Security Policy: Alliance with the West and Reassurance with the East', *Scandinavian Journal of History*, vol. 17, no. 3.

Lyng, John, 1976, *Mellom øst og vest*, Oslo: Cappelen.

Martens, H., 1979, *Danmarks ja, Norges nej. EF-folkeavstemningerne i 1972*, Copenhagen and Århus: Munksgaard, Dansk Udenrigspolitisk Instituts Skrifter 6.

Matlary, Janne H., 1993, '"And Never the Twain Shall Meet" Reflections on Norway, Europe, and Integration', in Teija Tiilikainen & Ib Damgaard Petersen (eds.), *The Nordic Countries and the EC*, Copenhagen: Copenhagen Political Studies Press.

McNamara, Robert, 1962, *Remarks by Secretary McNamara. NATO Ministerial Meeting, 5 May 1962. Restricted Session*, mimeo.

Melby, Svein, 1986, 'NATO kommunikéer, SDI og Norge', *Internasjonal Politikk*, no. 6, pp. 7–18.

Melchior, Arne, 1991, 'EØS – en gjøk i EFTA-redet? Norge og forhandlingene om the Europeisk Økonomisk Samarbeidsområde', *Norsk Utenrikspolitisk Årbok 1990*, Oslo: NUPI, pp. 11–42.

Meyer, Johan Kristian, 1989, *NATOs kritikere, Den sikkerhetspolitiske opposisjon, 1949-61*, Oslo: Institutt for Forsvarsstudier, no. 3.

Milward, Alan S., 1984, *The Reconstruction of Western Europe 1945–51*, London: Methuen.

Ministry of Defence, n.d., *Norwegian Defence Main Guidelines, 1994–98*, Oslo: Norwegian Ministry of Defence.

Ministry of Defence, 1991a, 'The Defence Budget – 1', *Fact Sheet*, nr. 04/91, Oslo: Ministry of Defence, October.

Ministry of Defence,1991b, 'The Defence Budget 1992 – key information', *Press Release*, nr. 076/91, Oslo: Ministry of Defence.

Ministry of Defence, 1991c, 'The Defence Budget 1992 – 2', *Fact Sheet*, nr. 05/91, Oslo: Ministry of Defence, October 1991, p. 3.

Ministry of Defence, 1993a, *Main Guidelines for the Activities and Development of Norway's Defence for the Period 1994–1998. St.meld. nr.16 for 1992-1993*, Oslo: Ministry of Defence.

Ministry of Defence, 1993b, *Security Factors Determining the Activities of Norway's Armed Forces*, (translation of the Introductory Chapter on security policy in the Ministry of Defence's budget proposal to the parliament for 1994), Oslo: Ministry of Defence.

Ministry of Defence, 1994, *Security factors determining the activities of Norway's armed forces*, (translation of Introduction to St. prp. nr.1, 1993-4), Oslo: Ministry of Defence.

Ministry of Defence, 1995a, 'Adaptation of Norway's Self-Imposed Restraints', *Fact sheet*, nr. 02/95, Oslo: Ministry of Defence.

Ministry of Defence, 1995b, 'Security Policy Framework', Oslo: Press Release.

Mitrany, David, 1975, *The Functional Theory of Politics*, London: Martin Robertson.

Mjøset, Lars, 1989, 'Norway's Full Employment Oil Economy – Flexible Adjustment or Paralysing Rigidities?', *Scandinavian Political Studies*, 12 (4).

Molvig, Finn, 1994, 'Norsk forsvarspolitikk I 1970- og 1980-årene', *IFS Info*, No 4 – 1994, Oslo: Institutt for forsvarsstudier.

Moses, Jonathon & Bent Sofus Tranøy, 1995, 'Norge I den nye verdensøkonomien', in Torbjørn Knutsen, Gunnar Sørbø & Svein Gjerdåker (eds.), *Norges utenrikspolitik*, Oslo: Cappelen, pp. 106–23.

Mouritzen, Hans, 1996, 'Introduction', in Hans Mouritzen, Ole Wæver and Håkan Wiberg, *European Integration and National Adaptations. A Theoretical Inquiry*, Commack, NY: Nova Science Publishers, pp. 3–5.

Næringslivets Hovedorganisasjon, 1993, *Europadokument*, February, Oslo: NHO.

Narum, H., 1972, *Hvordan Nordisk Råd ble til*, (thesis in history). Oslo: University of Oslo.

Nei til EF, 1993, *Vedtekter for Nei til EF vedtatt på landsmøtet 19.-21. november 1993. Kap. 1. Sentrale ledd, §1 Formål*, Oslo: Nei til EF.

Nei til EU, 1994a, *Organisasjonshåndboka*, Oslo: Nei til EU.

Nei til EU, 1994b, *Norge og EU. Virkninger av medlemskap i Den europeisk union*, Oslo: Nei til EU.

Nordisk Kontakt, 1992a, no. 10.

Nordisk Kontakt, 1992b, no. 12.

Nordisk Kontakt, 1993, no. 1.

Nordlys, 1994, 15 April.

Nordlys, 1994, 22 July.

Nordlys, 1994, 16 November, editorial.

Norge og Europa, 1983, Oslo: Høyre.

Norinform, 1993, 18 May, Oslo: The Royal Ministry of Foreign Affairs.

Norinform, 1993, 31 August, Oslo: The Royal Ministry of Foreign Affairs.

Norway Daily, no. 6, 1994, 10 January, Oslo: The Royal Ministry of Foreign Affairs.

Norway Daily, no. 7, 1994, 11 January, Oslo: The Royal Ministry of Foreign Affairs.

Norway Daily, no. 29, 1994, 10 February, Oslo: The Royal Ministry of Foreign Affairs.

Norway Daily, 14 February 1995, Oslo: The Royal Ministry of Foreign Affairs.

Norway Daily, 3 April 1995, Oslo: The Royal Ministry of Foreign Affairs.

Norway Daily, 26 July 1995, Oslo: The Royal Ministry of Foreign Affairs.

Norway Daily, 18 December 1995, Oslo: The Royal Ministry of Foreign Affairs.

Norway Daily, 16 July 1997, Oslo: The Royal Ministry of Foreign Affairs.

Norway Now, no. 6, 1994, medio April, Oslo: Nytt Fra Norge.

Norway Now, no. 18, 1997, ultimo Septemberl, Oslo: Nytt Fra Norge.

Nuttall, Simon, 1992, *European Political Co-operation*, Oxford: Blackwells.

Nyhamar, J. 1990, *Nye utfordringer 1965-1990. Arbeiderbevegelsens historie, vol. 6*, Oslo: Tiden, 1990.

Official Journal of the EC, 1988-9, Debate of the European Parliament No 3-373, 1988–89. Report of Proceedings from 16 to 20 January 1989, *Official Journal EC*, no. 2/373.

Øidne, G., 1958, 'Litt om motsetninga mellom Austlandet og Vestlandet', *Syn og Segn*, vol. 63, no. 3.

Olsen, Jan Henry T., 1993, 'Med gode og rimelige krav', *Dagbladet*, 17 July.

Ørvik, Nils, 1972, 'Fears and Expectations', in Nils Ørvik (ed.), *Fears and Expectations. Norwegian attitudes towards European integration*, Oslo: Universitetsforlaget.

Ørvik, Nils, 1986, 'Norway. Deterrence versus Nonprovocation', in Nils Ørvik (ed.), *Semialignment and Western Security*, London: Croom Helm, pp. 186–247.

Østerud, Øyvind, 1994, 'EU som sikkerhetsgaranti?', *Alternativ Framtid*, no. 3, pp. 91–96.

Papadakis, Maria & Harvey Starr 1987, 'Opportunity, Willingness, and Small States: The Relationship Between Environment and Foreign Policy', in Charles Hermann, Charles Kegley, Jr and James Rosenau (eds.), *New Directions in the Study of Foreign Policy*, London: Allen & Unwin, pp. 409–32.

Pharo, Helge, 1976, 'Bridgebuilding and Reconstruction. Norway faces the Marshall Plan', *Scandinavian Journal of History*, vol. 1, pp. 125–153.

Pharo, Helge, 1986, 'The Third Force, Atlanticism and Norwegian attitudes towards European Integration', *EUI Working Paper*, no. 86/255.

Pharo, Helge, 1988a, 'Norge, EF og europeisk samarbeid', *Internasjonal Politikk*, no. 6, pp. 41–67.

Pharo, Helge, 1988b, 'Norwegian Social Democrats and European Integration in the 1950s', *EUI Colloquium Paper*.

Pharo, Helge, 1991, 'Norge, Norden og europeisk integrasjon som etterkrigshistorisk forskningsfelt', *LOS-senter Notat*, 91/26.

Pharo, Helge, 1993, 'The Norwegian Labour Party', in Richard Griffiths (ed.), *Socialist Parties and the Question of Europe in the 1950s*, New York: E.J. Brill.

Putnam, Robert, 1988, 'Diplomacy and domestic politics: the logic of two-level games', *International Organization*, 42 (3), pp. 427–60.

Ramberg, T., 1972, 'Sovereignty and Cooperation', in Nils Ørvik (ed.), *Fears and Expectations. Norwegian attitudes towards European integration*, Oslo: Universitetsforlaget.

Rapoport, Jacques (ed.), 1971, *Small States and Territories*, New York: Arno/UNITAR.

Regjeringens informasjonsutvalg for Europasaker, 1990, *EFTA-EF forhandlingene. Kartlegging og forberedelser*, (Annex 16), Oslo: Regjeringsutvalget for EF-saker.

Regjeringens informasjonsutvalg for Europasaker, 1994, *Informasjon om EØS-avtalen*, pp. 16–17, Oslo: Regjeringens informasjonsutvalg for Europasaker.

Reid, George L., 1974, *The Impact of Very Small Size on the International Behavior of Microstates*, Beverly Hills, CA: Sage.

Ries, Tomas, 1988, 'Soviet Military Strategy and Northern Waters', in Clive Archer (ed.), *The Soviet Union and Northern Waters*, London & New York: Routledge.

Riksarkivet, 1956, *Cabinet Conference, 11 December*, Oslo: Norwegian National Archives.

Ringdal, Kristen, 1995, 'Velgernes argumenter', in Anders Todal Jenssen & Henry Valen (eds.), *Brussel midt imot. Folkeavstemningen om EU*, Oslo: Ad Notam Gyldendal, pp. 45–64.

Riste, Olav, 1982, 'Functional Ties – A Semi Alliance? Military Cooperation in North West Europe 1944–47', in Olav Riste (ed.), *Forsvarsstudier-Defence Studies I. Årbok for FHFS/FH 1981*, Oslo: TANO.

Riste, Olav, 1984, 'Frå integritetstraktat til atompolitikk: Det stormaktsgaranterte Norge 1905-1983', in Rolf Tamnes (ed.), *Forsvarsstudier-Defence Studies III. Årbok for FHFS/FH 1983–84*, Oslo: TANO.

Riste, Olav, 1985a, 'Historical Determinants of Norwegian Foreign Policy', in Johan Jørgen Holst (ed.), *Norwegian Foreign Policy in the 1980s*, Oslo: Norwegian University Press, pp. 12–24.

Riste, Olav, 1985b, 'Was 1949 a turning point? Norway and the Western Powers 1947–50' in Olav Riste (ed.), *Western Security: The Formative Years*, Oslo: Universitetsforlaget, pp. 128–49.

Røhne, N. A., 1989, 'De første skritt inn i Europa. Norsk Europa-politikk fra 1950' *Forsvarsstudier*, 5/89, Inst. for Forsvarsstudier.

Rokkan, Stein, 1966, 'Norway: numerical democracy and corporate pluralism', in Robert Dahl (ed.), *Political Oppositions in Western Democracies*, New Haven, CT: Yale University Press, pp. 70–115.

Rokkan, Stein, 1967, 'Geography, religion and social class. Crosscutting cleavages in Norwegian politics', in Seymour Martin Lipset & Stein Rokkan (eds.), *Party systems and voter alignments*, New York: The Free Press.

Rokkan, Stein, 1970, *Citizens, Elections, Parties. Approaches to the Comparative Study of the Process of Development*, Oslo: Universitetsforlaget.

Rokkan, Stein & Henry Valen, 1964, 'Regional contrasts in Norwegian politics', in Erik Allardt & Y. Littunen (eds.), *Cleavages, Ideologies and Party Systems*, Helsinki: Westermarck Society.

Rosenau, James, 1970, *The Adaptation of National Societies: A Theory of Political System Behavior and Transformation*, New York.

Russett, Bruce & Harvey Starr 1992, *World Politics: the menu for choice*, New York: W.H. Freeman & Co, 4th edn.

Sæter, Martin, 1985, 'Norge utenfor EF: Broer til Europa', in Johan Jorgen Holst & Daniel Heradstveit (eds.), *Norsk utenrikspolitikk*, Oslo: TANO.

Sæter, Martin & Olav Knudsen, 1991, 'Norway' in H. Wallace (ed.) *The Wider Western Europe. Reshaping the EC/EFTA Relationship*, London: Pinter.

Scrivener, David, 1989, *Gorbachev's Murmansk Speech: The Soviet Initiative and Western Response*, Oslo: The Norwegian Atlantic Committee.

Secretariat of the Presidium, 1991, *Nordic Council, Extraordinary session in Mariehamn, 13 November 1991*.

Summary of Business and Recommendations, Stockholm: Nordic Council, Secretariat of the Presidium.

Seip, Jens Arup, 1963, 'Fra embetsmannsstat til ettpartistat', in Jens Arup Seip, *Fra embetsmannsstat til ettpartistat og andre essays*, Oslo: Universitetsforlaget.

Simenson, Brant, 1989, 'The Norwegian Security Policy Consensus – Rhetoric or Reality?', *NUPI rapport nr. 132*, Oslo: NUPI.

Skodvin, Magne, 1971, *Norden eller NATO? Utenriksdepartementet of alliansespørsmålet 1947–1949*, Oslo: Universitetsforlaget.

Skogan, John Kristen, 1980, 'Virkemidler, begrensninger og forutsetninger i norsk sikkerhetspolitikk', *NUPI-notat*, no. 192, Oslo: NUPI.

Skogan, John Kristen, 1985 'Norsk sikkerhetspolitikk i brytningen mellom allianse og nøytralitet', in Johan Jørgen Holst and Daniel Heradstveit (eds.), *Norsk Utenrikspolitikk*, Oslo: TANO. pp. 33–57.

Skogan, John Kristen, 1986, *Sovjetunionens Nordflåte 1968–85*, Oslo: NUPI, NUPI Rapport, nr. 105.

Sloan, Stanley, 1991, 'The US Role in a New World Order: Prospects for George Bush's Global Vision', *Congressional Reference Service Report*, March 28.

Sogner, Ingrid, 1992, *Norges holdning til nordisk økonomisk samarbeid 1947–1959*, (thesis in history), Oslo: University of Oslo.

Sogner, Ingrid, 1993, 'The European Idea: The Scandinavian Answer. Norwegian Attitudes towards a closer Scandinavian Economic Cooperation 1947–1959', *Scandinavian Journal of History*, vol. 18, no. 4, pp. 307–27.

Sogner, Ingrid & Clive Archer 1995, 'Norway and Europe: 1972 and Now', *Journal of Common Market Studies*, 33 (3), pp. 389–410.

Sollie, Finn, 1988, 'The Soviet Union in Northern Waters – Implications for Resources and Security', in Clive Archer (ed.), *The Soviet Union and Northern Waters*, London: Routledge, pp. 13–43.

SOU (Statens Offentliga Utredningar), 1994, *Om kriget kommer . . . - Förberedelser för mottagande av militärt bistånd 1949-1969 (Betänkande av Neutralitetspolitikkommissionen, 1994:11)*, Stockholm: Statsrådsberedningen.

St. prp. 100, 1991–92, *Protokoll 9 om handel med fisk og andre produkter fra havet, Artikkel 2*, Oslo.

St. prp. 8, 1992–93, *Om Landbruk i utvikling*, Oslo.

Statusrapport, 1990. *Lysebu Declaration, October 1989, European Chapter, point 3 and 5*.

Staveley, Admiral Sir William, 1986, 'Overview of British Defence: Policy and the Relevance of the Northern Flank', *Britain and the Security of NATO's Northern Flank*, London, 7–8 May 1986, conference paper, mimeo.

Steen, Anton, 1989, 'Velferdsstat, korporatisme og selvregulering', in Klaus Nielsen & Ove Pedersen (eds.), *Forhandlingsøkonomi I Norden*, Oslo: Tano.

Stenersen, Ø, 1977, 'Venstrekreftene i norsk politikk', in Trond Bergh and Helge Pharo (eds.) *Vekst og Velstand. Norskpolitisk historie 1945-1965*, Oslo: Universitetsforlaget, pp. 379–381.

Stokke, Olav Schram & Ola Tunander 1994a, 'Introduction', in Olav Schram Stokke & Ola Tunander (eds.), *The Barents Region. Cooperation in Arctic Europe*, London: FNI/PRIO/SAGE, pp. 1–3.

Stokke, Olav Schram & Ola Tunander (eds.), 1994b, *The Barents Region. Cooperation in Arctic Europe*, London: FNI/PRIO/SAGE.

Stoltenberg, Thorvald, 1992, 'Opening Address', in Valter Angell (ed.), *Norway Facing a Changing Europe. Perspectives and Options*, Oslo: FNI, IFS, PRIO & NUPI.

Stoltenberg, Thorvald, 1994, 'Foreword', in Olav Schram Stokke & Ola Tunander (eds.), *The Barents Region. Cooperation in Arctic Europe*, London: FNI/PRIO/SAGE, pp. ix–xi.

Stortingsforhandlinger, 1961–62, vol. 7b.

Stortingsforhandlinger, 24 and 24 June 1970.

Stortingsforhandlinger, 1992-3a, nr. 4, 15.-16. October.

Stortingsforhandlinger, 1992-3b, nr. 74.

Stortingsmelding 87, 1954.

Stortingsmelding 15, 1961–62, *Om Det Europeiske Økonomiske Fellesskap og de europeiske markedsproblemer*.

Stortingsmelding 67, 1961–62, *Om Det Europeiske Økonomiske Fellesskap og de europeiske samarbeidsbestrebelser*.

Stortingsmelding 86, 1966–67, *Om Norges Forhold til de Europeiske Fellesskap*.

Stortingsmelding 92, 1969–70, *Om Norges Forhold til de Nordiske og Europeiske Markedsdannelser*, Oslo.

Stortingsmelding 50, 1971–72, *Om Norges Tilslutning til De Europeiske Felleskap*, Oslo.

Stortingsmelding 9, 1973–74, *Hovedretningslinjer for Forsvarets virksomhet i tiden 1974–78*, Oslo.

Stortingsmelding 25, 1973–74 *Petroleumsvirksomhetens plass i det norske samfunn*.

Stortingsmelding 94, 1978–79, *Forsvarskommisjonens utredning og hovedretningslinjer for Forsvarets virksomhet i tiden 1979-83*, Oslo.

Stortingsmelding 79, 1981, *Langtidsprogrammet, 1982–1985* [Long Term Programme], Oslo: 1981.

Stortingsmelding 61, 1986–87, *Norge, EF og europeisk samarbeid.*
Stortingsmelding 54, 1987–88, *Hovedretningslinjer for Forsvarets virksomhet i tiden 1989–93 .*
Stortingsmelding 11, 1989–90, *Om utviklingstrekk i det internasjonale samfunn og virkinger for norsk utenrikspolitikk.*
Stortingsmelding 40, 1993–94, *Om medlemskap i den europeiske union,* Oslo: Ministry of Foreign Affairs.
Stortingstidende, 1955
Stortingstidende, 1966–67, vol. 7c, pp. 4557–4558.
Stortingstidende, 1978–9, vol. 7c, pp. 2172–4
Stortingstidende, 1985–86, pp. 1269–1276. Foreign Minister Svenn Stray's speech in the Storting, 9 December 1985.
Stortingstidende, 1985–86, p. 3063. Foreign Minister Knut Frydenlund's speech in the Storting, June 1986.
Stortingstidende, 1987–88, vol. 7c, 7 June 1988
Stortingstidende, 1989–90, Debate 1 December 1989.
Stortingstidende, 1991a, vol. 7c, 20 June 1991.
Stortingstidende, 1991b, vol. 7c, 14 October 1991.
Stortingstidende, 1992/3.
Stråth, Bo, 1978, *Nordic Industry and Nordic Economic Cooperation - The Nordic Industrial Federations and the Nordic Customs Union negotiations 1947–1959,* Stockholm: Almqvist & Wiksell.
Tamnes, Rolf, 1983, 'Den norske holdningen til en nordisk atomvåpenfri sone 1958-1983', in Rolf Tamnes (ed.), *Forsvarsstudier 1982,* Oslo: Tanum-Norli.
Tamnes, Rolf, 1986a, 'Ettpartistat, småstat og særinteresser. Tre skoler i norsk sikkerhetspolitikk', *Nytt Norsk Tidsskrift,* 3 (3), pp. 42–64.
Tamnes, Rolf, 1986b, 'Fra SAC til MAB. Nordområdene i amerikansk strategi 1945–1985', *FHFS notat,* no. 1.
Tamnes, Rolf, 1987, 'Integration and Screening. The Two Faces of Norwegian Alliance Policy 1945–86', in R. Rolf Tamnes (ed.), *Forsvarsstudier – Defence Studies VI. Årbok for FHFS/FH 1987,* Oslo: TANO.
Tamnes, Rolf, 1989, 'Handlefrihet og lojalitet', in Trond Bergh and Helge Ø. Pharo (eds.), *Historiker og veileder. Festskrift til Jakob Sverdrup,* Oslo: Tiden Norsk Forlag.
Tamnes, Rolf, 1991, *The United States and the Cold War in the High North,* Oslo: Ad Notam.
Thomas, M., 1993, 'The effects of the new EC system', *Euroil,* August, pp. 20–1.
Thowsen, Atle, 1995,'Business goes to war: The Norwegian merchant navy in Allied war transport', in Patrick Salmon (ed.), *Britain and Norway in the Second World War,* London: HMSO, pp. 51–66.
Treaty on European Union, 1992, Brussels: Commission of the European Communities.
UD, dossier 44 3/4, vol. 19. The Federation's comment on the report from the Nordic Economic Cooperation Committee, 27 February 1958.
UD, dossier 44 3/4, vol. 5. Various documents.
UD, dossier 44 3/4, vol. 6. Note to the Foreign Minister by O. Sollie, 29 September 1950.
UD, dossier 44 3/4, vol. 15a. Protocol from the 9th meeting in the NECC, 29–30 August 1956.
UD, dossier 44 3/4, vol. 15b. Note by D. Juel, 1 October 1956.
UD, dossier 44 3/4, vol. 21. Message from the Danish Prime Minister H. C. Hansen to Prime Minister Gerhardsen, 28 January 1959.
UD, dossier 44 3/4, vol. 4a. Letter from the Norwegian Federation of Industries to the Ministry of Foreign Affairs, 15 December 1949.
Udenrigsministeriets gråbog, 1969, *Dansk sikkerhedspolitik gennem tyve år,* Copenhagen: Vinten.
Udgaard, Nils Morten, 1973, *Great Power Politics and Norwegian Foreign Policy. A Study of Norway's Foreign Relations, November 1940–February 1948,* Oslo: Universitetsforlaget.
Udgaard, Nils Morten, 1995, 'En politisk kastrert stat i Europa', *Aftenposten,* 28 March.
UD-informasjon, 13 June 1991.
UD-informasjon, 20 August 1991, no. 23.
UD-informasjon, 21 August 1991, no. 24.
UD Informasjon, 1996, 'Stortings debatt 8.2.1996 vedrørende Utriksministerens utenrikspolitiske redegjørelse i Stortinget 30.1.1996', Oslo: Utenriksdepartementet.
Ulfstein, Geir, 1995, *The Svalbard Treaty. From Terra Nullius to Norwegian Sovereignty,* Oslo: Scandinavian University Press.
US Naval Institute Proceedings, 1986, *US Naval Institute Proceedings January 1986. Maritime Strategy Supplement.*
Utenriksdepartementets arkiv, 1948.
Utenriksdepartementet, 1991, *Kjernevåpenfri sone i nordisk område Rapport fra den nordiske embetsmannsgruppe for undersøkelse av forutsetningene for en kjernevåpenfri sone i nordisk område,* Aktuelle utenriksspørsmål, Oslo: Utenriksdepartementet.

Utenriksdepartementet, 1991–2 *Avtale om Det europeisk økonomiske samarbeidsområde, særskilt vedlegg til St. prp. nr. 100 (1991–92)* Oslo: Utenriksdepartementet.

Værnø, Grete, 1993, *Lille Norden – hva nå? Splittelse og samling i EFs kraftfelt*, Oslo: Cappelen/Europa-programmet.

Valen, Henry, 1973, 'Norway: 'No' to EEC', *Scandinavian Political Studies*, no. 8, pp. 214–226.

Valen, Henry & Stein Rokkan, 1970, 'The election to the Norwegian Storting in September 1969', *Scandinavian Political Studies*, vol. 5, pp. 287–300.

Valen, Henry & Stein Rokkan, 1974, 'Norway: Conflict Structure and Mass Politics in a European Periphery', in Richard Rose (ed.), *Comparative Electoral Behavior*, New York: The Free Press.

van Tol, Robert, 1988 'A Naval Force Comparison in Northern and Atlantic Waters', in Clive Archer (ed.), *The Soviet Union and Northern Waters*, London: Routledge, pp. 134–163.

Vaughan, R., 1979, *Twentieth-Century Europe. Paths to Unity*, London: Croom Helm.

Vefald, O, 1972, 'The 1967 EEC Debate', in Nils Ørvik (ed.), *Fears and Expectations: Norwegian Attitudes Towards European Integration*, Oslo: Universitetsforlaget.

Verdens Gang, 19 January 1948.

Villaume, Paul, 1989, 'Neither Appeasement nor Servility: Denmark and the Atlantic Alliance 1949–1955', *Scandinavian Journal of History*, 14 (2), pp. 155–179.

Villaume, Paul 1995, 'Danmark, NATO og den kolde krig. En studie i dansk sikkerhedspolitik 1949-61', *Vandkunsten*, 11/12, April.

Wæver, Ole, 1992, *Introduktion til Studiet af International Politik*, Copenhagen: Forlaget Politiske Studer.

Warner, Edward L., III, 1989, 'New thinking and old realities in Soviet defence policy', *Survival*, Jan./Feb., pp. 13–34.

Weinland, Robert, 1986, 'The Soviet naval buildup in the High North: a reassessment', in Sverre Jervell & Kåre Nyblom (eds.), *The Military Buildup in the High North, America and Nordic Perspectives*, London & Boston:University Press of America.

Wicken, Olav, 1988, 'Stille propell i storpolitisk storm, KV/Toshiba-saken og dens bakgrunn', *Forsvarsstudier*, No. 1, Oslo: Norwegian Institute for Defence Studies.

Widfeldt, Anders, 1996, 'Sweden and the European Union', in Lee Miles (ed.), *The European Union and the Nordic Countries*, London: Routledge, pp. 101–16.

Wilkes, Owen, Nils Petter Gleditsch & Ingvar Botnen, 1987, *Loran C and Omega. A Study of the Military Importance of Radio Navigation Aids*, Oslo: Norwegian University Press.

Index

Unless otherwise noted, entries refer to Norway.

The following abbreviations have been used in this index:

COB   Collocated Operating Bases
EC   European Community
EEA   European Economic Agreement
EEC   European Economic Community
EFTA   European Free Trade Association
EU   European Union
IGC   Intergovernmental Conference
NATO North Atlantic Treaty Organization
WEU   Western European Union